Traditional
KOREAN MUSIC

Traditional
KOREAN MUSIC

Edited by
the Korean National Commission for
UNESCO

The Si-sa-yong-o-sa Publishers, Inc., Korea
Pace International Research, Inc., U.S.A.

Published simultaneously in KOREA and the UNITED STATES

KOREA EDITION
First printing 1983
The Si-sa-yong-o-sa Publishers, Inc.
5-3 Kwanchol-dong, Chongno-ku
Seoul 110, Korea

U.S. EDITION
First printing 1983
Pace International Research, Inc.
Tide Avenue, Falcon Cove
P.O. Box 51, Arch Cape
Oregon 97102, U.S.A.

ISBN: 0-89209-016-2

This series is a co-publication by The Si-sa-yong-o-sa Publishers, Inc.
and The International Communication Foundation.

Foreword

The Korean people are artistic, expressing their inner-most being in pottery, painting, poetry, drama, music and dance. To most foreigners familiar with Chinese and Japanese art, Korean art comes as a profound revelation and a delightful experience. Korean art differs from the strong, bold aspects of continental Chinese art and from the dazzling colours of Japanese art. Its basic characteristic is simplicity, reinforced by the atmosphere of quiet and serenity which it creates.

Following the publication of *Modern Korean Short Stories*, the Korean National Commission for UNESCO embarked upon a new project, dedicated to seeking real character of Korean culture. This new series deals with various aspects of Korean culture—language, thought, fine arts, music, dance, theatre and cinema, etc. It concentrates on baring the roots of the Korean cultural tradition and demonstrating the process of its transformation. It is hoped in this way to reveal the framework of traditional thought which is fundamental to any understanding of Korea's past and present.

Profound thanks are due to the writers of the individual articles and to the generous sponsorship of the Si-sa-yong-o-sa Publishers, Inc., who once again have turned a dream into a reality. This series, edited by the Korean National Commission for UNESCO, is published by the Si-sa-yong-o-sa Publishers, Inc., in commemoration of the thirtieth anniversary of the Korean National Commission for UNESCO.

Bong Shik Park
Secretary-General
The Korean National Commission
for UNESCO

Contents

Traditional
KOREAN MUSIC

Introduction to Korean Music

YI HYE-GU

Korean music here means the traditional music of today, no matter whether it is indigeneous or derived from Chinese music, excluding new works by Korean composers either in Western or Korean style. The traditional music comprises the following types of music. The characteristic of each type of music will be given in brief, followed by some of the problems remaining to be solved.

Confucian Shrine Music

Confucian Shrine Music which derived from Lin Yü's *Ta-cheng yüeh-p'u* in 1430 A.D. (The copy of the original and its derivative are included in the *Annals of King Sejong*) is performed twice a year; in February and August in the lunar calendar. The ancient sacrificial music uses two orchestras, one on the terrace (*tŭng'ga*) and the other on the ground (*hŏn'ga*), which are never met with in music other than A-ak. The two orchestras employ bronze-bell chimes (*p'yŏnjong*), stone chimes (*p'yŏn'gyŏng*), a square box with a hammer running through the cover (*ch'uk*), and a wooden tiger scraped with a split bamboo stick (*ŏ*), which are only used for A-ak. Those Chinese musical instruments which are used in the sacrificial music can not be employed for Korean music, for the intonation of Chinese music, which is determined by the fifth cycle like the Pythagorean scale, is different from that of

1

Korean music.

The Chinese text of Confucian Shrine Music consists of eight lines of four syllables. Each syllable is set to one note, and the duration of each note is one and the same, while Korean music has irregular rhythm. One line of the text in Chinese is punctuated by three strokes of the drum. Chinese *A-ak* begins and ends with the central tone, while Korean music ends with the central tone, but does not always begin with it.

The problems are: Confucian Shrine Music is performed only twice a year and consequently lacks devotees so that musical instruments such as the single bronze-bell (*tŭkchong*) and the single stone chime (*tŭkkyŏng*) are already in disuse. The text of the songs not being sung any more, the seven-stringed zither (*kŭm*) and the twenty-five-stringed zither (*sŭl*) which are indispensable to the accompaniment, just appear in the orchestra, but do not sound. Of the four modes, *kung*, *sang*, *kak* and *u*, which are used for the welcoming of the spirits (*yŏngsin*) in *Ta-ch'eng yüeh-p'u*, only the *kung* mode has been employed in Korea.

Royal Ancestor Shrine Music

As the Royal Ancestor Shrine as well as the Confucian Shrine are Chinese institutions, the music was also Chinese *A-ak* until 1464 A.D., when it was replaced by Korean music, *Pot'aep'yŏng* and *Chŏngdaeŏp*, each of which is a series of eleven songs. The new music is included in the *Annals of King Sejo*, and its later version in *Sog-ak wŏnbo* vol.6. As the text of the songs was written in Chinese, however, Korean music set to the text accordingly adopted the style of Chinese music. Korean Royal Ancestor Shrine music adopted the system of two orchestras just as in Confucian Shrine music, and borrowed such Chinese musical instruments of *A-ak* as the bronze-bell chimes, the stone chimes, the starter of the music (*ch'uk*) and the stopper of the music (*ŏ*), and played those foreign instruments together with the Korean cross flute (*taegŭm*), which can follow the intonation of Chinese music. The original Korean music was changed so as to begin and end with the central tone, *hwangjong*, as Chinese A-*ak* does. However, the three outstanding features of Royal Ancestor Shrine music which distinguish it from that of Confucian Shrine music are as follows: (i) The scale of Korean music which in general consists of five tones, differs from that of Chinese A-*ak* which has seven tones. (ii) Korean music is in sol mode (*p'yŏngjo*) or in la mode (*kyemyŏnjo*), while Chinese A-*ak* in Korea is in fa mode (*kungjo*). (iii) The duration of each note of Royal Ancestor Shrine music is unequal and the rhythm of it is irregular, while that of Confucian Shrine music is equal.

The problem is that out of twenty-two pieces of Royal Ancestor Shrine music only five pieces are identified as being derived from Korean songs of the Koryŏ dynasty, the rest remain unidentified. A comparison of the original Korean songs and the modified songs with Chinese text helps to understand the characteristics of Korean and Chinese music.

Tang-ak

Tang-ak, literally translated, is music of the T'ang dynasty, but when Chinese *tz'u* music of the Sung dynasty replaced the music of the T'ang dynasty in Korea, it meant Chinese music in the broad sense, excepting sacrificial music, Chinese A-*ak*, and it was used as the antithesis of *Hyang-ak* (Korean music).

Tz'u, the Chinese irregular verse form, includes two kinds of verse, *man* and *ling*. Both of them consist of two stanzas of four lines, but *man* has a longer line of from seven to fifteen syllables, while *ling* has a shorter line of from five to seven syllables. Of the two kinds of *tz'u* only *ling* was handed down in Korea, *man* being lost during the sixteenth century. Only two pieces of *Tang-ak* survive; *Loyang-ch'un* and *Pu-hsu-tzu*, the music of which is contained in *Sog-ak wŏnbo* vol. 4 and 5 respectively.

According to the old music, *Sog-ak wŏnbo*, which used the mensural notation, one line of *ling*, no matter whether it consists of five, or six, or seven syllables, is set regularly to eight lines of Korean notation (equivalent to eight measures) as follows:

Sha ch'ung wei hsiao / huang ying yü— /
Hueh— lu— / shao ts'an chu— /
Chin wei luo mu / tu ch'un han— /
Tso yeh li— / san ching yü— /

(Gauze windows glimmer and the yellow nightingale twitters,
In the fireplace some fire lingers still,
Silk curtains and tapestries protect me from spring chill,
Late last night it rained.)

In every fourth and eighth line of the Korean notation the clapper (*pak*) comes in, which is marked with "/". The notes of every seventh line of *Sog-ak wŏnbo* are prolonged to the eighth line. The prolongation of tone is marked with "—". Thus the above verse, *Loyang-ch'un* with those two marks illustrates that the irregular length of the verse is set regularly to eight lines of Korean notation.

Tz'u music is no longer sung with the orchestra as before, but is played by the orchestra alone. And the orchestra itself underwent changes; the iron slabs (*panghyang*) which were used in *Tang-ak* were replaced by the bronze-bell chimes and stone chimes of Chinese *A-ak*, *Tang pip'a* and the mouth organ (*saeng*) was in disuse, and the Korean cross flute (*taegŭm*) was added to the Chinese cross flute *(tangjŏk)*, making the Chinese and Korean orchestras undistinguishable.

Later the regular length of the phrase of *tz'u* music was made irregular as in *Loyang-ch'un*, and the syllabic style of Chinese music was turned into the melismatic style of Korean music with added embellishments as in *Pu-hsu-tzu*, the style of

Tang-ak being Koreanized.

However, the old Korean mensural notation of *Pu-hsu-tzu* and *Loyang-ch'un* will throw light on the rhythmic interpretation of *tz'u* music in *Pai-shih Tao-jen Ko-chü* of the Sung dynasty where only the pitch is notated and the duration signs are absent.

Hyang-ak

Hyang-ak, translated literally, means indigenous music and it is the antithesis of *Tang-ak*. However, *Hyang-ak* as well as *Tang-ak* is limited to court music, just as *Komagaku* (Japanese for Korean music) and *Tōgaku* (Japanese for T'ang music) constitute Japanese court music, *ga-gaku*.

Indigenous music as well as Chinese music involves two styles of music; *hyŏn-ak* which is music mainly for strings and which originally accompanied songs and *kwan-ak* which is music mainly for wind instruments and accompanied the dance and was also used for processions. Now *kwan-ak* is played more often than *hyŏn-ak*.

Korean music for strings (e.g. *Hyŏn-ak Yŏngsan Hoesang*) in which the six-stringed zither (*kŏmun'go*) is the leading instrument, is complete without digestion. The comparison of *Yŏngsan hoesang* of today with that of *Taeak hubo* will show that they are equally complete. On the other hand, the music for wind instruments (e.g. *Kwan-ak Yŏngsan hoesang*) in which the cylindrical oboe (*p'iri*) is the leading instrument is mostly an abbreviation and modification of the music for stringed instruments.

Korean music mainly for wind instruments is performed with the cylindrical oboes which play the principal melody as mentioned before, the cross flutes which embroider the melody, the two-stringed fiddles *(haegŭm)* and the hourglass drum. The characteristic feature of its style is the so-called *yŏnŭm* which comes in between the end of a musical phrase and the beginning of the following one. Such linking of the musical phrases is to be found neither in Korean music for stringed instruments, nor in Chinese music. This bridging-over part is played by the cross flutes and the two-stringed fiddles, making the cylindrical oboes and the drum rest for the while. Such style of performance gives the impression of two groups of players on the one hand, and makes the phraseology clear on the other hand. The *yŏnŭm* occurs in *Yŏngsan hoesang* of wind instruments (or *P'yojŏng-manbang-ji-gok*), Chŏngŭp (or *Sujech'ŏn*) and *haeryong* (or Soilhwa-ji-gok).

The problems are: very little information is available on why the music for wind instruments is a selection from the music for stringed instruments and what the function of *yŏnŭm* is.

Ch'wit'a, Military Music

Ch'wit'a, meaning "blowing and striking," signifies military band music. It was performed by two bands: a louder one to precede and a softer one to follow an important person such as a king. Conical oboes (*t'aep'yŏng-so*) which only play the melody, brass trumpets (*nabal*) and shell trumpets (*nagak*) sounding a single note like a drone, not continually, but intermittently, cymbal, gong and drum were used in the front band, while the rear band had cylindrical oboes, cross flutes, two-stringed fiddles, hourglass drum and round drum. The main repertory of the front band is *tae-ch'wit'a* (or *Muryong-ji-gok*), and that of the rear band is *ch'wit'a* (or *Manp'a chŏng-sik-ji-gok*).

The rhythmic pattern within twelve beats is characteristic of military band music, and it is as follows: one and two and three and *four, five, six,* and and and.

This drum pattern of Korean military music resembles the rhythm of drums in Western marches, one and two and/*three, four, five,* and, in that both of them are divided into two parts, with the latter part beginning with three successive beats of the drum. The Korean drum pattern differs from that of Western music in that the former has two-six beats and the latter has two-four beats. A six beats' pattern is most common in Korean music.

There is no way of identifying the origin of Korean military music (*Muryong-ji-gok*), which is in the pentatonic scale, because the old musical notation is lacking.

Chŏng-ak, Chamber Music

Chamber music is a respectable form of recreation for gentlemen, not performed by hired musicians. Its main repertory, *Yŏngsan hoesang,* was originally a Buddhist chant with the short text "*Yŏngsan hoesang pulbosal*" which means "great Buddha preaching on *Yŏngsan* Mountain." The Buddhist music with its text is notated in *Taeak hubo* of the fifteenth century.

Later, the song, dropping its text, became independent instrumental music. Instrumental music was covered with added embellishment and then it was divided into four parts (*chang*) based on the identical final phrase (musical rhyme). Instead of being repeated *Yŏngsan hoesang* proper (Ponyŏngsan) was followed by its variation (*Chung-yŏngsan*), the pitch level of which was raised from *e flat* to *a flat*. Variation 1 was again followed by variation 2 (*Chan-yŏngsan*) which was faster than the preceding music. And again variation 2 was followed by variation 3 (*Karak tŏri*) which was simplified from and faster than the preceding music. Lastly, to these four were added eight other popular pieces of music, thus making the chamber music a kind of suite. The course of evolution mentioned above can be traced by a chronological study of the music of *Yŏngsan hoesang.*

The existing five pieces that follow variation 3 are not identical to the corresponding music of the old music book

Yuye-ji. The relationship of the old and the new has to be closely studied.

Samhyŏn, Dance Music

Dance music, in contrast to chamber music, is performed by professional musicians. The wind instruments used are the same as those in Korean court music though smaller in number. The most popular repertory of dance music is the series *Yŏmbul, T'aryŏng, Kut-kŏri. Yŏmbul,* a grave and slow movement in six beats in which mostly two slow steps are danced; *T'aryŏng,* a gay rhythmical piece in 12/8 time in which mostly four lively steps are danced; and *Kut-kŏri,* a rippling and comparatively fast movement in 6/8 time in which mostly two flowing steps are danced.

The first two pieces of dance music are similar to chamber music only in the terminology and the meter, but they are different from the latter in the style and the melody. Chamber music is written down in notation and fixed. On the other hand dance music has not its old music and takes its course freely sometimes with a short phrase recurring, and sometimes apparently being varied or developed according to the occasion. Each performer of the dance music, without any notation and rehearsal, plays his own music on the spot, resulting in heterophony.

There has been no transcription of dance music which is spontaneous and impulsive and it is laboursome to transcribe the ensemble music. But to study how the short phrases are weaved and how the heterophony is produced requires the transcription of dance music.

Sanjo, Solo Music for String or Wind Instrument

Sanjo is characteristic of music of the southern region. It is an instrumental version of *p'ansori*, a dramatic song of the southern region. The instrumental version of dramatic song is strongly emotional with the conspicuous alternation of tension and relaxation. The instrumental solo music is cast into three movements. The first slow movement (*chinyangjo*) mostly consists of phrases of four measures, each measure equivalent to six half notes. The second movement (*chung-mori*) mostly has four-measure phrases of triple time. The third fast movement (*chajin-mori*) has mostly two-measure phrases in 12/8 time, ending with the fastest movement (*tan-mori*) in 4/4 time which is very rare in Korean music. Within this framework the soloist freely expresses the various emotional content.

The slow movement where the long melody undulates with microtonal shading, opens with the melody in the so-called *u* mode which gives the effect of stateliness and ends with the melody in the *kyemyŏn* mode which is sorrowful. The moderate movement is enlivened by music in the light *kangsan* style. In the fast exciting movement the twelve-stringed zither, *kayagŭm*, weaves complex rhythm such as hemiola and other devices, while the hourglass drum keeps the fundamental rhythmic pattern. Hence the interlocked rhythm is comparable to the dissonance in arousing mental disturbance. Because of its emotional content and virtuosity, *sanjo* is today most widely appreciated.

Sanjo was taught by rote until around 1950 A.D. when it was transcribed for the first time. Analysis of *sanjo* sentence by sentence is needed to understand its structure.

Kagok, Lyric Song

The Korean lyric consists of five lines instead of four as in Chinese poems, the length of the lines being irregular as follows:

1. Tongch'ang i— / palgat nŭnya—
2. Nogojil i— / ujijinda—
3. So ch'inŭn ahae nom ŭn— / sang'gi ani irŏtnŭnya.
4. Chae nŏmŏ—
5. Sarae kin patŭl— / ŏnje kalyŏ— / hanŭni.

(East window / is light with sunshine?
Skylarks / are singing
The cow-feeding boy / is still not awake?
Over the hill
Billows of the field / when is he to plough?)

In general, the slow music has the following three features.
(i) The first syllable of a word is set to a note of short duration
something like Scotch snap that may permit the word to be
clearly understood. This is called *ŏ tan*, which means the word
should be short. Such instances are marked by underlines. (ii)
On the other hand, the last syllable of a word or the
postposition is sung to a long sustained note. That is called
song ch'ang, which means "the voice should be long." Such
instances are marked by—. There is also a Chinese saying "ko
yung yen," which means that "the song is the word long
sustained." In case of *kagok*, the end of a word is not sung to a
long sustained note as in *sijo*, but to a long melismatic passage.
(iii) Another feature of the slow music is its abrupt ending
which is marked with a period. The abrupt ending makes the
close of the music clear against the several long sustained notes
set to the last syllables of the words.

Kagok repertory is divided into two groups based on the
form of the text. The first group of *kagok* consists mainly of
Ch'o-sudaeyŏp, I-sudaeyŏp and *Sam-sudaeyŏp*, the verse form
of which is, as given above, the basic one. The second group
consists of *Nong, Nak* and *P'yŏn*, the verse form of which is
similar to the basic form in the number of lines, but which is
different from the basic form in that one of the five lines
contains more syllables.

Basically the five lines of the asymmetrical text are set to music as follows:

Section 1. 11 beats/21 beats (5.11.5)
Section 2. 11 beats/16 beats (5.11)
Section 3. 16 beats (5.11)/21 beats (5. 11. 5)
Interlude 16 beats (11.5)
Section 4. 27 beats (11. 5.11)
Section 5. 16 beats (5.11)/16 beats (5.11)/16 beats (5.11)
Postlude 53 beats (5.11.5.11.5.11.5)

In fast *kagok* like *P'yŏn-lak* and *P'yŏn*, the unit of 11 and 5 beats is reduced to 7 and 3 beats respectively, resulting in the long melisma cut short.

Kagok repertory is also divided into two groups, based on the mode used. *Kagok* uses two modes, *u* mode and *kyemyŏn* mode which are as follows:

u mode : e flat (the central tone), f, a flat, b flat, c
kyemyŏn mode: e flat (the central tone), a flat, b flat

To convert *Ch'o-sudaeyŏp* in *u* mode into *kyemyŏn* mode, *f* and *a flat* of the *u* mode are replaced by *a flat* and *b flat* respectively.

Kagok repertory is again divided into two groups; one for the male voice and the other for female voice. The latter is smaller in number; it lacks *Ch'o-sudaeyŏp*, *Sam-sudaeyŏp*, *Soyong*, *Ŏllong*, *Ŏllak* and *P'yŏn-lak* which are robust and not tender in character.

Although there are forty-one songs in *kagok*, and many ways of classifying them as mentioned before, all but one seem to be variations of one song, for chronological study of *kagok* music (strictly speaking, *sagdaeyŏp*) reveals that as time goes back, the number decreases to three or two.

Kasa, Narrative Song

While *kagok*, the lyric song, has a short text, *kasa* has an extensive one. The representative form of *kasa* is as follows:

Ch'unmyŏn ŭl / nŭjŭt kkae-yŏ
Chuk-ch'ang ŭl / pan-kae hŏni
Chŏng-hwa nŭn / chak-chak hŏnde
Kanŭn nabi / mŏmunŭn tŭd, etc.

(Rising late / from sweet sleep,
When I / opened the bamboo window
The beds of flowers / blazed,
The passing butterfly / was charmed in the air, etc.)

As the text from *Ch'unmyŏn-gok* (Spring Indolence) shows, mostly eight or seven syllables make one-line, and two of them make a stanza.

Eight syllables of the text are set either to two-six beats, as in *Ch'unmyŏn-gok*, or to two-five beats, as in *Sangsa pyŏlgok* (Longing for the Parted Love). This four syllables of the text to six beats of the music, in contrast to three syllables of the text to eleven beats of the music of the lyric song, indicates that the words of the narrative song are more clearly understandable.

Except *Ŏbu-sa* (Song of the Fisherman) which alone is strophic, the stanza of the other *kasa* are set to different music, some to two recurring stanzas such as A, A, B, A, A, B, A, A, (*Hwanggye-sa*, Song of the painted cock), some to very different music such as A, A', B, C, D, A, E, C (*Ch'unmyŏn-gok*). Such a variety of music is necessary for the long text of *kasa* in order to avoid monotony.

The narrative song is accompanied by a cross flute (*taegŭm*) and an hourglass drum, and sometimes only by the latter. This striking difference from the lyric song accompaniment by the small orchestra illustrates that the chief interest lies in the text rather than in the music.

Kasa with its slow rhythm, its use of falsetto, and its quiet style has its own beauty. However, there is very little old music of *kasa* notated, and some of the long texts were cut short, so that there is no way of finding the important concluding form.

Sijo, Another Short Lyric Song

The text of *sijo* which is borrowed from *kagok* is divided into three lines instead of the original five as follows:

Tongch'ang i / palgat nŭnya / nogojil i / ujijinda
So ch'inŭn / ahi nom ŭn / sang'gi ani / irŏtnŭnya
Chae nŏmŏ / sarae kin patŭl / ŏnje kalyŏ hanŭni.

Though *sijo* is as slow as *kagok*, the long trail of melismas attached to "Tongch'ang i", "nogojil i", and especially "chae nŏmŏ" are cut away and are replaced by a single sustained tone which makes the rhythm almost insensible. *Sijo* accompanied by the hourglass drum, and sometimes without any accompaniment at all, employs only three notes, *e flat, a flat* and *b flat*. These facts suggest that it was cultivated by gentlemen amateurs.

However, the subtle gradation of intensity attracts attention. Its decrescendo is like when one lifts a heavy object upon one's head, or when the wind sweeps through the forest, and the vibrato that follows the decrescendo is like the rustling of the leaves as the straining boughs are returning to this original position after the wind has passed. Slow *sijo* with simple melody and without any pulsating rhythm, but with only subtle dynamic shading is a unique music.

P'ansori, Dramatic Song

P'ansori is a vocal form in which a professional singer,

accompanied by a drummer, relates a long dramatic tale with song, speech and action before the audience and makes them weep and laugh. As *p'ansori* is not notated, the singer begins with the phrase in the basic rhythmic pattern so that the drummer may easily follow him, and then the music is carried on in its natural development. To appreciate the development of *p'ansori*, therefore, it is important to pay attention to the beginning of every song.

The existing repertory of *p'ansori* comprises five, of which *Ch'unhyang-ga* (Story of Ch'unhyang) and *Simch'ŏng-ga* (Story of Simch'ŏng) are most popular. Within the range of two octaves (A to *a'*) the central tone changes from *d* to *g*, or from *g* to *c'*, or vice versa. The so-called modes of *u* and *kyemyŏn* and several styles of melody are used in *p'ansori* as well as in *sanjo*. Movements such as *chinyangjo*, *chung-mori* and *chajin-mori* are used in *p'ansori* as well as in *sanjo* (see *sanjo*). All these serve as palette for the singer to create the required effect. For example, *Paksŏk-t'i* (Hill of *Paksŏk*) from the Story of Ch'unhyang, with slow movement, *chinyangjo*, and the lofty *u* mode combined, depicts a quiet scene and the contemplative feeling aroused by it. *Ch'unhyang's* lament (*Ibyŏl-ga*) expresses a strong feeling of sadness through the union of the *chung-mori* movement and the *kyemyŏn* mode. "Inspector's attack" (*Ŏsa ch'ulto*) from the Story of Ch'un-hyang depicts the scene of disturbance with a fast movement, *chajin-mori*, in complex rhythm, four triple meter changing into three duple meter, or the last note of a rhythmic pattern running over the following pattern, or after accelerando a high tone being drawn down long accompanied by the continuously pattering drum as if the fastest movement were no more describable with song.

The long-continued song is relieved by speech which describes comic scenes. Speech in *p'ansori* is invaluable for the singer, for it gives him time to take breath. It is welcome for the audience as well, for it permits them to laugh and relax.

The function of the drum in *p'ansori* is different from that in court music and chamber music in that the drummer does not merely beat the time with a recurring rhythmic pattern, but adds embellishment by shouting "nice" to induce the performer to sing, or reserves the stroke of the drum while the singer is singing to make the words understandable. With all its rich variety of devices *p'ansori* unfolds the long dramatic song vividly. However, *p'ansori* has been taught orally and it has left no music. Since transcriptions of *p'ansori* have come out recently, it is desirable to make an attempt to list the melodic pattern, if any, from the transcriptions.

Chapka, Popular Song

Chapka from the central region comprises a standing song (*ip-ch'ang*), a chorus performed in the open area, and a sitting song (*chwa-ch'ang*), solo or duet sung indoors. The standing song is performed by a troupe which consists of a leader who sings the short lead melody with his hourglass drum hung from his neck, and three or four chorus members join in the solo song each with their own hand drum. The standing song's repertory proper, which is known as *San-t'aryŏng*, are Nollyang, *Ap* (preceding) *san-t'aryŏng*, *Twit* (succeeding) *san-t'aryŏng*, and *Chajin* (fast) *san-t'aryŏng*. The cheerful and virile *san-t'aryŏng* begins with the solo song opening with the high note *d'* (a fifth higher than the central tone) or *e'* drawn long and sustained by the thumping rhythm of the drum, and closing with pulsating rhythm, and it ends with the chorus, the end of which is drawn long in the central tone, as if waiting for the solo to begin. Nollyang is a puzzle; the meaning of its title is vague, its text mixed with nonsense syllables has neither continuity nor any form, and the music shows very little repetition of phrase.

Sitting songs are performed by one or two persons (usually by women) accompanied by the hourglass drum. The songs with long texts are also called "long *chapka*" (*kin chapka*). Of

the twelve repertories half of them borrowed their text from
p'ansori (see above). For example, *So-Ch'unhyang-ga* consists
of sixty three measures in 18/8 time which are divided into
eleven musical sentences of irregular length. The subject
matter, the long text, the large dimension of music and recurring phrases of repeated notes suggests that the sitting song
belongs to narrative song.

Both standing and sitting songs were taught by rote and
recently they were transcribed. The descriptive analysis of the
transcription is being waited for.

Folk Song

In contrast to the folk songs of China and Japan, those of
Korea are almost all in triple meter, and triplets instead of
dotted rhythms are also characteristic. Korean folk songs
clearly reflect the idiom of the local region in which they are
sung, so there are many versions of songs as popular as
*Arirang: Seoul Arirang, Chindo Arirang, Milyang Arirang,
Kangwŏn-do Arirang, Chŏngsŏn Arirang* present the regional
differences of style. *Arirang* is the nonsense syllables of the
refrain.

All these five *Arirangs* mentioned above consist of solo and
chorus parts both of which have eight measures either in 3/4 or
in 9/8 time. Solo part differs from the chorus in the first two
measures, for the solo singer begins his song with a note an
octave higher than the opening note of the chorus. In general
the solo singer begins his song a fifth or an octave higher than
the central tone, and rarely with the central tone or a fourth
lower than it. So Korean many folk songs are in fixed stanzaic
form, owing to the improvisation of the solo singer.

If the singers have to sing more songs, they borrow words
from other songs which makes it hard to distinguish the
original text of the folk songs from the borrowed one. And if
the borrowed words happen to be shorter or longer than the

original text, the singer has to diminish or extend the original melodic phrase to fit the borrowed text. Borrowing of text from other folk songs makes it harder to have them in fixed stanzaic form.

Recently many folk songs have been recorded by scholars and radio station staffs interested in them, but the transcription of the recorded music is not yet published. Comprehensive studies in folk songs in relation to its music have not been attempted.

Nong-ak, Farmers' Music

Nong-ak is not limited to farmers, but also is performed by professional musical bands. *Nong-ak* held in an open area as popular entertainment (*p'an'gut*) is a variety of music, dance, acrobatics and singing. The entertainment begins with group dance and formation, followed by individual performances. The individual performances by the small gong, the hourglass drum and the hand drum comprise music, dance and acrobatics.

The band consists of: (i) the small gong (*kkwaenggari*), the player of which is the leader of the band. He makes signs to the band to make a circle formation or two opposing rows that change their relative positions, or to let an individual come out into the centre to perform music, dance and acrobatics, striking his small gong. To change the rhythmic pattern, he beats out an accelerando in order to capture the attention of the band, then he beats out the new rhythmic pattern which is followed by the band. (ii) The large gong (*ching*) from a chord held by the hand reinforces strong beats. The deep-toned gong sounds one, or two, or three beats within one rhythmic pattern, so it is useful in identifying the rhythmic pattern. (iii) The hourglass drum (*changgo*) is hung from the neck and beaten by two sticks held in each hand. The player of this hourglass drum shows his virtuosity by playing with both sticks beating only one side (right side) of the drum. (iv) A barrel-shaped drum (*puk*), hung from the right shoulder and held by the left hand. It reinforces strong beats, like the large gong. (v) Several hand drums (*sogo*), the rims of which are held by the hands. The chief roles of the hand drum players are rather group dance formation and acrobatics.

While *sanjo* has a fixed movement order, *nong-ak* constantly weaves back and forth between various rhythmic patterns. In the exuberant music the original form of a rhythmic pattern in 12/8 time, only appears at the beginning of a section, and then it develops freely, sometime introducing hemiola (6/4 time) and sometime heterometer. The loudness is reinforced with such heterometer to enhance the excitement.

Recently a few transcriptions of *nong-ak* were published. However, to study the rhythmic structure of *nong-ak* which is so flexible and variable, many more transcriptions are needed, and the constant and the variants of rhythmic phrase should be picked out from the transcriptions to help the description of the rhythmic structure.

BIBLIOGRAPHY

BOOKS

Chang, Sa-hun. *Han'guk Akki Taegwan* (Korean Musical Instruments). Seoul: Munhwajae Kwalliguk, 1969. Although written in Korean, the book has an English summary.

Kaufmann, Walter. *Musical Notations of the Orient.* Bloomington: Indiana University Press, 1967. P. 49.
Text includes yulja-bo (Chinese Lü notation), kongch'ŏk-bo (Chinese letter notation), chŏnggan-bo (Korean mensural notation), oŭm yak-bo (Korean abbreviated letter notation), yuk-bo (Korean solmization notation), ku-ŭm (Korean solmization), and yŏnŭm-p'yo (Korean neumatic notation).

Keh, Chung-sik. *Die Koreanische Musik.* Strassburg: Heitz & Co., 1935., P.77. The text is organized in the following order 1) Historical survey of Korean culture 2) Philosophy of Music 3) Essence of Korean music

4) Form and method of playing instruments 5) Transcriptions of 17 gramophone records.

Korea, Republic of. National Classical Institute, Ministry of Culture and Information. *A History of Korean Music.* Seoul, n.d.

The text is a brief by Yi Hye-gu and is divided by a brief introduction to Korean Traditional Music and Korean dance and a long explanation is given to the description and the characteristic of the musical instruments.

Korea, Republic of. National Academy of Arts. *Survey of Korean Arts: Traditional Music.* Seoul, 1973.

The text is divided into two parts: Part I; 1) History of Korean music 2) Musical education in past and present 3) Korean musical instruments 4) Notational systems 5) Theory. Part II; 1) Court orchestral music 2) "String music" 3) "Wind ensemble" 4) Koch'wi and ch'wit'a 5) Ritual music 6) Art songs 7) Sanjo 8) P'ansori 9) Chapka 10) Folk songs and 11) Nong-ak.

———. *Survey of Korean Arts: Folk Arts.* Seoul, 1974. pp. 273–315.

Chapter III is about Folk Music and is divided into introduction, sanjo, nongak, p'ansori and folk song.

Yi, Hye-gu. *Han'guk Ūmak Sōsōl* (Topics in Korean Music). Seoul: Seoul National University Press, 1975. p. 510.

Although the text is written in Korean each of the 19 articles has an English summary, and especially the whole text of the ''Musical Paintings in a Fourth-century Korean Tomb,'' is translated by Robert C. Provine, Jr.

———. *Han'guk Ūmak Nonch'ong* (Essays on Korean Music). Seoul: Sōmmun-dang, 1975. p. 426.

The text is written in Korean originally there is *a very good English summary.* It is a collection of 15 articles, including A Short History of Korean Music, Les caracteristiques de la musique Coréene, the preface to the Aak-po in the Annals of King Sejong, Music in the Confucian Shrines of Korea, with comparison to the current situation in China, Chronology of Pak Yōn's pitch pipes and the Kwansūp Togam translated by Robert C. Provine, Jr.

Rockwell, Coralie. *Kagok, a Traditional Korean Vocal Form.* Providence, Rhode Island: Asian Music Publications, 1972. p. 302.

The text is divided as follows: 1) History and introduction to kagok 2) The instruments in the kagok ensemble 3) Male and female vocal technique and ornamentation 4) the ''jo'' of kagok 5) The relationship of mode and text in the kagok form 6) Melodic titles in model variation 7) ibid.

Song, Pang-song. *An Annotated Bibliography of Korean Music.* Providence,

Rhode Island: Asian Music Publications, Brown University, 1971. p. 250.

Provine, Robert C. Jr. *Drum Rhythm in Korean Farmers' Music.* Seoul, 1975. P. 53.

ARTICLES

Courant, Maurice. "La Musique en Corée," *Encyclopedie de la Musique et Dictionaire du Conservatoire,* edited by Albert Lavignac. Paris: Charles Delagrave, 1913–31. Vol. I, pp. 211–41.

Deuchler, Martina and Yi Hye-gu. "Koreanische Musik," *Die Musik in Cheschlichte und Gegenwart.* Cassel; Barenreter Verlag, forthcoming.

Han, Man-yŏng, "Religious Origins of Korean Music," *Korea Journal.* Vol. 15, No. 7 (July, 1975), pp. 17–22.

Yi, Hye-gu. "The Yukcha-paegi," *Asian Music,* Vol. II, No. 2 (New York, 1971), pp. 18–30.
      A critical examination of Dr. Kye Chong-sik's transcription of Yukcha-paegi in his book, *Die Koreanische Musik,* 1935.

_____ . "Musical Paintings in A Fourth-Century Korean Tomb," *Korea Journal.* Vol. 14, No. 3 (March, 1974), pp. 4–14.

Yi, Pyŏng-wŏn. "Korean Music and Dance," *Grove Dictionary of Music and Musicians.* London: MacMillan, forthcoming.

_____ . "A Short History of Pŏmp'ae: Korean Buddhist Ritual Chant," *Journal of Korean Studies.* Seattle: University of Washington, Vol. I, No. 2 (1971), pp. 109–121.

Provine, Robert C. Jr., "The Treatise on Ceremonial Music (1430) in the Annals of the Korean King Sejong," *Ethnomusicology* (Ann Arbor, Michigan). Vol. XVIII, No. 1 (Jan., 1974), pp. 1–29.

_____ . "Sejong and the Preservation of Chinese Ritual Melodies," *Korea Journal,* Vol. XIV, No. 2 (Feb., 1974), pp. 24–39.

_____ . "Brief Introduction to traditional Korean Folk Music," *Journnal,* Vol. 15, No. 2 (Jan., 1975), pp. 29–31.

Rockwell, Coralie J. "Trends and Developments in Korean Traditional Music Today," *Korea Journal,* Vol. 11, No. 3 (March, 1974), pp. 15–20.

_____ . "The Traditional Music of Korea," *Korea Frontier* No. 10: pp. 10–13, 27, and 33.

Song, Bang-song, "Supplement to an Annotated Bibliography of Korean Music," *Korea Journal.* Vol. 14, No. 12 (Dec., 1974), pp. 59–72; Vol. 15, No. 1 (Jan., 1975), pp. 59–72; No. 2 (Feb., 1975), pp. 58–68, No. 3 (March, 1975), pp. 64–70 and No. 4 (April, 1975), pp. 69–76.

_____ . "The Korean Pip'a and Its Notation," *Ethnomusicology* (Ann Arbor, Mich.) Vol. XVII, No. 3 (Sept., 1973), pp. 460–493.

_____. "Korean Kwangdae Musicians and Their Musical Traditions," *Korea Journal*, Vol. 14, No. 9 (Sept., 1974), pp. 12–18.

_____. "Book Review: Kagok, A Traditional Korean Vocal Form," *Ethnomusicology*, Vol. XVIII, No. 2 (May, 1974), pp. 315–321. A critical review of Kagok, A Traditional Korean Vocal Form (Providence: Asian Music Publication, 1972), by Mrs. Coralie Rockwell.

_____. "P'ansori in Korea's Epic Vocal Art and Instrumental Music," *Asian Music* (New York, 1974). Vol. V, No. 2, pp. 66–71. A critical review of a disc, P'ansori: Korea's epic vocal art and instrumental Music (12″ 33 1/3 rpm disc. Stereo 1972, Nonesuch Record H—72049 (Explorer Series).

_____. "The Etymology of the Korean Six-stringed Zither, Kōmun'go: A Critical Review," *Korea Journal*, Vol., 15, No. 10 (October, 1975), pp. 18–23.

Sōng, Kyōng-nin. "Korean Music," *Arts of Asia* (Hong Kong, Sept.-Oct., 1972), Vol. 2, No. 5, pp. 52–57.

_____. "Korean Dance," *Arts of Asia* (Hong Kong, Nov.-Dec., 1973), Vol. 3, No. 6, pp. 39–45.

Sur, Donald. "Korea," *Harvard Dictionary of Music*, by W. Apel. 2nd ed. Cambridge, Mass.: Harvard University Press, 1969, pp. 456–459.

UNPUBLISHED DISSERTATIONS

Yi, Pyōng-wōn. "Hossori and Chissori of Pōmp'ae—An Analysis of Two Major Style of Korean Buddhist Ritual Chant," M. A. dissertation in ethnomusicology, University of Washington, p. 1971, p. 111.

_____. "An Analytical Study of Sacred Buddhist Chant of Korea," Unpublished Ph. D. dissertation in Ethnomusicology, University of Washington, 1974, p. 206.

Suh, In jun. "Traditional Korean Stringed Instrument," Unpublished M. M. thesis, Indiana University, 1972. I. Introduction, II. Bowed Instruments: Ajaeng and Hae-gūm, III. Plucked Instruments: Kōmun'go, Kaya-gūm, Taejeng, Kūm, Sil, Hyang-bip'a, Tang-bip'a, Wōl-gūm Konghu. IV. Strucked Instruments: Yang-gūm, and V. Conclusion.

Tianen, Walter, "Melodic Movement in Yōngsan Hoesang," Unpublished M. A. thesis in ethnomusicology. University of Washington, 1971. I. Brief Survey of Korean Music (Ritual music, Tangak and Hyangak). II. The Kōmun'go, Tanso, and Changgo. III. The Kōmun'go Melody. IV. The Tanso Melody.

DISCOGRAPHY

Disques Vogue. *Musique Buddhique de Corée.* One 12″ 33 1/3 rpm disc, LVLX-253, Collection Musée de l'Homme, 1964.

Side One: Kō-ryŏngsan, Side Two: Samguiui-rye, Panya Simgyŏng, Hwach'ŏng and Ch'ŏnsu-bara.

Explorer Series. *P'ansori: Korea's Epic Vocal Art and Instrumental Music,* One 12″ 33 1/3 rpm disc, Nonesuch Record H-72049, Stereo, 1972.

Folkways Records and Service Corp. *Folk and Classical Music of Korea.* One 12″ 33 1/3 rpm disc, Ethnic Folkways Library, FE-4424, 1951.

Ch'angbu T'aryŏng, Tan'ga, Norae-garak, Chajin Nongbu-ga kyemyŏn, ujo, Changch'un Pulno, Manpa-sik and Chongmyo-ak.

_____. *Korea: Vocal and Instrumental Music.* One 12″ 33 1/3 rpm disc, Ethnic Folkways Library FE-4325.

A-ak, Arirang, Toraji T'aryŏng, Tan'ga, Ch'anggŭk-cho, T'aryŏng, Nong-ak and kayagŭm sanjo.

_____. *Music of the World's People.* Vol. IV. Two 12″ 33 1/3 rpm discs, Ethnic Folkways Library FE-4507, 1958.

Lyrichord Discs Inc. *Korean Social and Folk Music.* One 12″ 33 1/3 rpm disc. Lyrichord LLST-7211.

Sice One: Kōmun'go sanjo, ajaeng sanjo, hojŏk sanjo, Saet'aryŏng, Side Two: P'ansori Ch'unhyang-ga, sōdo minyo, and Kyŏnggi minyo.

_____. *Korean Court Music.* One 12″ 33 1/3 rpm disc, Lyrichord LLST-7206, 1969.

Side One: Munmyo Ung'anji-ak, Nagyang-ch'un, Su-jech'ŏn, Kōmun'go tasŭrŭm, Side Two: Kagok, Sijo, Ch'wit'a, Kilgunak, P'yŏn-gyŏng and P'yŏn-jong.

UNESCO Collection Musical Sources. *Korean Music, Art Music from the Far East.* VIII-1, Philips 6586 011, 1973.

Religious Origins of Korean Music

HAN MAN-YŎNG

According to the *Akhak kwebŏm* (Standards of Musical Science, 1493), Chinese musical theory related strictly to social elements. The 'kung,' 'sang,' 'kag,' 'pyŏnch'i,' 'chi'i,' 'u' and 'pyŏn'gung' of the heptatonic scale were comparable to the king, king's cabinet, common people (*ch'i*), problems of state and objects (*u*). Pyŏnch'i and pyŏn'gung, the additional tones, were compared to hot flavored sauce in soup (lit. "spicy ornaments"). According to this theory no tones were permitted to rise above the kung tone (king tone) even though it was regarded as the basic tone of all modes. Also according to this theory, all music must begin and end with kung, meaning that the king is the complete and all powerful ruler of the state. Therefore, society ruled by a king was strictly reflected in early Yi dynasty music.

In Western music, the twelve tone music reflects the revolution of the republic against the monarchy. Since the 'king' (tonic) and 'queen,' 'prince and princesses' (the dominant or subdominant) are driven out, every tone and harmony is independent. This is similar to the idea that every citizen has the right to be president, since every tone is equal and every tone can be the 'tonic' of a mode. In my opinion, this shows how music reflects the society of which it is an integral part.

In this paper, Korean music will be considered only from before the end of the Yi dynasty (early twentieth century). Just as Korean politics has always been associated with the monarchy and music has been closely related to politics, so

23

religion as another integral part of society has also been bound up with music.

Shaman Music and Rituals

The main religions which have ruled the minds of the Korean people and Korean society in a significant way are Shamanism, Buddhism, Confucianism, and in the twentieth century, Christianity.

Shaman music has different characteristics depending on the region from which it comes, and it has largely the same style as the folk songs of that region. Modes and *changdan* (rhythmic patterns) are usually identical, and quite often whole folk songs are inserted into the ritual shaman music and vice versa. Sometimes shaman music has been changed into complete folk songs, for example *ch'angbu t'aryŏng* and *norae karak* of the Seoul area.

Similarly *p'ansori*, the long dramatic narrative song genre of the southwestern region of Korea, is almost identical to the folk song style of that area. Mostly based upon the folk-song style of the Chŏlla area, *p'ansori* has also, however, adopted the *kyŏngjo*[1] of Seoul folk-song style, *menarijo*[2] of the eastern area of Korea, *tonggangsanjae minyo* style of northwest Korea, and *ujo*[3] which was adapted from the *sijo* and *kagok* répertoires. The basic *jo* or mode of *p'ansori* is, in actual fact, *kyemyŏnjo*, which, like a white sheet, has painted on it various additional colors which enhance and vary the many moods of the *p'ansori* style.

Just as *p'ansori* adapted the gentle style of *sijo* and *kagok* so the music of the shaman ritual contains certain elements of Confucianism and Buddhism. For example, one can see, in the *pyŏlsin kut* (village *kut*) of Kangnŭng city on the northeastern seaboard of Korea, a *kut** for Sejon, a disciple of Buddha, and at the end, a Confucian rite in which local officials wear

---

* *kut* : shamanistic ceremony.

Confucian robes and read the 'chemun' or memorial address to Confucius.

The fact that *nongak* (farmers band) instruments such as *kkwaenggari, ching, puk* and *changgo* are used in shaman rites, and that *nongak* and *kut* were originally synonymous words, shows a close link between the two forms of music and ceremony. *Nongak* was also known as *p'ungmul, turae, p'ungjang* or *kut*, and was used for various folk plays and village exorcisms. According to its various usages, *nongak* is respectively called *mae kut, chisin kut, sulmaegi kut, homissisi kut* and *turae kut (p'ungjang kut)*. Shaman music and *nongak* are therefore of "the same flesh."

Mae kut is performed on the eve of the lunar new year for the exorcism of evil spirits from houses and villages. This *kut* is also held to pray for happiness and blessing in the coming year.

Chisin kut, or *madangbalkki kut* (Treading down the Earth Spirits) is executed early in the new year, or for other specific reasons, by travelling *nongak* performers known as *kŏllipp'ae*, who go into the rooms of every village house and play *nongak* and sing incantations. *Sulmaegi kut* or *homissisi kut* are executed after the farmers have finished the third weeding of the rice fields. One day is set aside for the ritual, and at a specified time all the villagers gather together for *nongak*, wine and music. *Turae kut* or *p'ungjang kut*, is *nongak* that is performed in the fields while the farmers are weeding.

Looking at *nongak* as a whole, therefore, we can see that it is done to encourage the farmers as they work, and to drive away evil spirits.

The typical mountain songs known as *chapka* and *ipch'ang* that are performed by *sadangp'ae*, or professional singers, dancers and acrobats, are more like *minyo* (pure folk songs) and shaman music because the singers have always had low social status.[4] Instrumental music such as *sinawi* and *sanjo* are also of the same character as *minyo* of the southwestern region of Korea and the *p'ansori* based on the *kyemyŏnjo* style of the same area.

All of these forms — shaman music, *minyo, p'ansori, nongak, chapka* and *sanjo* — are known as "folk music." What, then, are the essential characteristics of folk music that originated from shaman music?

According to the Music Section[5] of *Samguk sagi* (History of the Three Kingdoms), U Rŭk of Silla took the *kayagŭm* made by King Kasil of Kaya and composed twelve compositions. His three disciples called the music "flamboyant and crude" (繁且淫), and accordingly rearranged the twelve works into five "sorrowful but not too grievous, and pleasant but not too rapturous" compositions. The original twelve *kayagŭm* pieces may have actually been contemporary folk songs of various areas in the Silla kingdom, while the five "graceful" pieces were most probably a kind of classical art music.

The label "flamboyant and crude" as applied to U Rŭk's music meant that the melody was exaggerated and direct in expression, melismatic in style, and in a fast tempo with many "chattering" melodic ornaments. Such folk music has always been typical among the common people, and reflects their way of life and its various characteristics.

Historically speaking, shaman music is the oldest of all music in Korea. Music of the period before the Three Kingdoms was inseparable from religion, politics, entertainment and art. Such clans as Puyŏ, Koguryŏ, Ye, Mahan, Pyŏnhan and so on, drank and caroused after harvesting and seed planting were finished, and also after completing the ritual ceremony to heaven.[6] In the Puyŏ clan area the ritual to heaven was known as *Yŏnggo*; in Koguryŏ, *Tongmaeng*; and in the Ye clan area it was called *Much'ŏn*. The ritual dance involved some ten, twenty or thirty people, and the songs that accompanied the dancing might well have been in the nature of solo and response. Such shaman music is closely akin to *pyŏlsin kut* (kut for spirits of the dead) or *todang kut* (village exorcism) where the performers play *kkwaenggari, puk* and *ching* while they dance and make a very noisy scene.

During the Silla dynasty there was also music played for the *hwarang* spirits, which was performed only by the highest-ranking shamans, *Sŏnp'ung* and *Kuksŏn*. These rituals were passed on the Koryŏ dynasty *p'algwanhoe* shaman ceremony which was held for the spirits of the mountains, rivers and sea ("dragon king *kut*"). This *kut* is performed by *Sŏllang*, *Kuksŏn* and *Sŏnga* shamans, also of the highest rank.[7]

In the first year of the reign of King T'aejo of Koryŏ, the palace courtiers said: "The previous kingdom (Silla) used to hold *p'algwanhoe* as a blessing for the people every November, so let us follow that practice." The king followed their suggestion, and the *p'algwanhoe* ceremony continued to flourish together with various plays and games which were accompanied by drums and gongs. Later in the Koryŏ dynasty the *p'algwanhoe* was stopped because the courtiers of the palace thought it was too noisy.[8] However, such court exorcisms as the *ch'ŏyongmu* dance, which is a type of shaman rite, continued on into the Yi dynasty.

Buddhism and Its Music

Buddhism was imported into the Three Kingdoms in the fourth century A.D., but documents on Buddhist music did not appear until the eighth and ninth centuries.[9]

During the early ninth century the monk Chingam went to T'ang China to learn T'ang Buddhist chant. After returning to Korea he taught the Chinese-style chant to many disciples at Ssangye Temple in Hadong, South Chŏlla Province. The *Samguk yusa*, however, relates that Buddhist chants were already being performed in the eighth century in Korea, which indicates that Buddhist chant existed before its later documentation by a Japanese monk. Silla Buddhist chant is well documented in the books of a Japanese monk,[10] who stated that there was one Silla Temple called Chŏksanwŏn, in Tungju on the Shantung peninsula in China, where T'ang,

Silla and Japanese-style Buddhist chants were all taught.[11]

That Silla-style Buddhist chant existed at that time indicates that Buddhism was already Koreanized. This Silla Buddhist chant is still sung today as the *hossori* chant of contemporary Buddhist ceremonies, and the modes of this chant are identical to those of *minyo* of the eastern part of Korea, originally Silla territory. From this it would seem that the people of Silla adopted the music of the foreign religion into their own folk music. Such a "Koreanization" of a T'ang chant into Silla style occurred over a long period of time, as did the same evolution of Chinese T'ang court music into the Koryŏ dynasty court répertoire.

Japanese-style Buddhist chant was probably imported from central Asia, and is closely related to present-day *chissori* chant of Korea and the chants of Tibet and Mongolia.[12]

The main characteristic of the Buddhist chant is a long sustained sound followed by multiple melodic ornamentations (*changin kulgok* 長引屈曲). Such a singing style might be compared to the sound of the Buddhist bell and its slow reverberations. *Yŏngsan hoesang*, literally "Great Buddha preaching on Yŏngsan mountain," is pure Buddhist music in instrumental form, while *kagok* (long lyric song) has many melodic patterns similar to those found in Buddhist chants. *Hyangak* court music pieces such as *yŏmillak* or *ch'wit'a* (court military music) have also come under the influence of the neumatic melodic style of chant.

Buddhism as a religion was adopted by the *yangban* (nobility) when it was first imported to Korea, and because the *yangban* fostered and appreciated the performances of *chŏngak* (literally "correct music" — a kind of "chamber music" genre existing outside court circles), certain Buddhist elements were bound to occur in the music. It also shows that *chŏngak* reflected the thinking and way of life of the intelligentsia. However, that such folk music styles as *hwach'ŏng* and *hoesimgok* exist in Buddhist chant even today shows that Shamanism and Buddhism have merged to some extent. One can, in fact, see inside the Buddhist Temple compounds of *Sansin-dang* or "Mountain Spirit House" and *Ch'ilsŏng-gak* or "Heavenly spirits' house," both of which are directly related to Shamanism and are outside Buddhism itself. Since the Koryŏ dynasty accepted Buddhism as the national religion, Buddhist chant naturally flourished at that time and greatly influenced folk music. *Hyangak* court music pieces, too, such as *Tongdong, Sŏgyŏng pyŏlgok, Chahadong, Hallim pyŏlgok, P'ungipsong, Chŏnggwajŏng, Samogok, Ssanghwajŏm, Chŏngsŏkka, Ch'ŏngsan pyŏlgok, Kasiri, Yugugok, Sangjoga, Yasimsa, Manjonch'un, Chŏngŭp, Isanggok, Ponghwangŭm* and *Pukch'on*—all of the Koryŏ dynasty—were composed in the style of Buddhist chant (with its long sustained tones), although the texts are secular. These musical compositions may be compared with Koryŏ celadon pottery and its splendid but magnificently mournful sheen.

For the Confucianists of the Yi dynasty though, these Koryŏ pieces were crude, somewhat "earthy" in character, and related to love songs, so the texts were changed and the music made more syllabic, like Confucian music.[13] Despite these changes, many of the *hyangak* court banquet pieces retained the neumatic style of Buddhist chant and so did the later *chŏngak* répertoire that evolved separately from court patronage. This seems to prove that, despite attempts by the king and his Confucian advisors to maintain Confucianism as the official religion, Buddhism, which was deeply rooted among the people, continued to flourish.

Confucianism and Its Music

In 1116 A.D. the Emperor Hŭijong of the Sung dynasty in China sent court ritual music books, instruments, and instructions for execution to King Yejong of Koryŏ. This was the first importation of Chinese Confucian music into Korea. Essentially this music reflected the idea of peace and symmetry in its style as one music book stated:[14]

Music stems from the center of the emotions, and behavior stems from outside heart. When music comes from the center of the emotions, it is serene. Behavior that comes from outside the center of the heart results in variable and unreliable behavior. Great music should, therefore, be simple and great ceremony must be simple. When music reaches its height, no resentment can be fostered in men's hearts. Similarly, when ceremony reaches its extremity righteousness must prevail. Ruling with humility is surely reflected in this music and related behavior.

Music has relevance to the king's reign and to courteous behavior. Among the emotions of joy, anger, sorrow and pleasure, the last is most suitable for expression in music. Such music must not be fast in tempo, but slow. It must not have an elaborate style, but a simple style. This graceful, peaceful and "symmetrical" music which is still performed twice a year in the Confucian Temple, is known as *a-ak*, literally "graceful music."

According to the documentation of Han, T'ang, Sung and Ch'ing, King Sejong's music master Pak Yŏn wrote the Korean versions of *a-ak* and at the same time remodelled the Chinese Chou dynasty (1122-771 B.C.) methods of music execution and instrumentation.

Characteristics of this music are a syllabic style with each tone having equal duration, no ornamentation is found, and four musical tones are sung to one syllable. The overall form, too, is symmetrical. Such music was played for all the royal court ceremonies during the Yi dynasty when Confucianism flourished.

'Chŏngdaeyŏp' and 'Pot'aep'yŏng' of the Royal Ancestral Shrine Music répertoire were composed by King Sejong, who used both *hyangak* and Chinese *Koch'ui* (military "striking and blowing music") as the basis for this particular *a-ak* style. It was not originally *a-ak*, therefore, in the strict Chinese sense, but by the middle of the Yi dynasty it was transformed into the *a-ak* syllabic style. This music thus retains graceful and symmetrical qualities.

Sujech'ŏn is a *hyangak* composition in a slow tempo and smooth rhythm, but as each tone has almost equal duration, and the beginning of each tone has an accent marked by the *changgo* (although the text is deleted) it appears to be very close in style to Chinese syllabic *a-ak*. (Sujech'ŏn is thought to have originally been more melismatic, but it gradually changed into the Chinese style.) My belief is that because this music was used for the procession of the King or princes, it became more dignified and graceful in the Confucian style.

Another example of a change toward the Confucian style is found in the composition *Ssanghwajŏm* which was originally a Koryŏ dynasty composition with a Korean text in neumatic style, as follows:

> To the *ssanghwajŏm* rice cake shop I went to buy *ssanghwa-ttŏk* (rice cakes placed on twin flowers)
> An Arabian man grasps my arm.
> If a scandal is spread then it is because you, little *kwangdae* (little dancer-musician in training).
> It is because you, little *kwangdae*, have spread the rumor.

This composition was, however, later changed into syllabic style with a noble text in Chinese characters. Each note became an equal duration in the style of Chinese music based upon the concept of courtesy in music. (This change occurred during the reign of King Sŏngjong in the early Yi dynasty 1470-1494.)

On the other hand, such Chinese "popular" classical music as *pohŏja* and *nagyangch'un*, originally in syllabic style, underwent Koreanization and changed to neumismatic style.[15]

Christianity and Its Music

Western music which was brought to Korea at the beginning of the twentieth century was initially Christian music. Western music has been ruled in my opinion largely by

Christianity and has not absorbed other religions very much. One could say, therefore, that the history of Western music is not one of changes in religion, but of changes in individuals and their creativity.

Many Korean musicians today study Western music through Christian hymn books, and in this respect one could say that this has constituted a strong influence on contemporary Korean music.

Such music was first brought to Korea through Japan, and upon arrival in Korea it was fostered and sheltered only by the intelligentsia. Korean Christian culture as a whole was protected by the intelligentsia, who accepted the new Western harmony and tempered scale. This gave them a new conception of Korean music, and also a new conception of the individual as an important medium of expression. In this way, then, Western music composed by Koreans was the start of a completely new and individual style of composition.

When we look at our music from its religious origins, at the same time remembering that this comprises the whole of Korean society we find that there are influences of Shamanism, Buddhism imported during the Three Kingdoms period, Confucianism which flourished from the latter part of the Koryŏ dynasty, and Christianity which was imported at the beginning of the twentieth century. The ancient religious practices are still surviving and flourishing in the middle of modern Western technology, and despite modern progress one can find shaman *kuts*, and Buddhist temples in the mountains holding their ceremonies, and the domination of Confucian thought and morality.

Shamanist music which is characterized by a flamboyant and "earthy" style, is closely related to the folk beliefs of the people and has greatly influenced *minyo*, *p'ansori*, *nongak* and *sanjo*. It has also influenced *chŏngak* to produce such variants as *nong, nak* and *pyŏng* in the *kagok* répertoire, *Yŏkkŭm* and *Hwimori chapka* in the *sijo* répertoire, *sijo* and *Chosaga, Yangyangga, Maehwaga,* and *Suyangsan'ga* in the *kasa* réper- toire. In Buddhist chant, *hossori* and *hwach'ong* are entirely in folk music style.

Buddhist chant, which is characterized by a neumatic style and long sustained melodies with ornamental endings, is closely related to the present day *chŏngak* which was original- ly banquet music of the Yi dynasty, or even the *hyangak* réper- toire distinct from *a-ak* and *tangak.* Not only *Yŏngsan hoesang, kagok* and *kasa* are based on Buddhist chant, but also such Chinese music as *Nagyangch'un* and *Pohŏja.*

Confucian music, characterized by its syllabic style and "great, peaceful elegance", was adapted for the royal ceremonies and rituals at the beginning of the Yi dynasty, but with the decline of the dynasty most of the royal ceremonies were discarded, and only the Confucian temple music remains today. The concept of Confucianism has, however, transform- ed *hyangak* pieces such as *Chŏngdaeyŏp, Pot'aepy'ŏng, Su- jech'ŏn.*

Western music was originally first represented in Korea by Christian music, and through it the tempered scale and harmony were introduced.

This style of music has traveled in one direction only—that is, from Europe to this country—and as yet our Korean modern music has not exerted a counter influence on western music.

NOTES

1. Yi Po-hyŏng, "Study of *P'ansori Kyŏngjo,*" *Songang-dang,* Vol. 1, 1971.
2. Han Man-yŏng, "The Mode of Eastern Korean Folk Song," *Yesul- nonmunjip* (Journal of the National Academy of Arts), 1973.
3. ——, "*P'ansori ŭi Ujo*" (Ujo in *p'ansori*), *Hanguk ŭmak Yŏn'gu*

34   *Religious Origins of Korean Music*

(Studies in Korean Music), Vol. II, 1972.

4. ____, "Study on the Mountain Songs of Korea," *Ŭmdae Hakbo* (Journal of the College of Music, Seoul National University), Vol. V, 1970.

5. King Kasil of the Kaya kingdom saw the instrument of T'ang and re-arranged it because, he said, "every country has its own language and dialects, so how can music be the same?" The king let U Rŭk of Sŏngyŏlhyŏn town compose twelve pieces of music for the instrument. Afterwards, U Rŭk took the instrument and surrendered it to King Chinhŭng of Silla, since the Kaya kingdom had been annexed by Silla invasion. The king took him in and let him live at Kukwŏn, nowadays Ch'ungju in North Ch'ungch'ŏng Province. He then sent Pŏp-chi and Kego (officially known as Taenam-a) and Mandŏk (official title, Taesa) to learn the music. The three men had already learned the eleven musical pieces, and had decided that they were too coarse, so five rearranged pieces were devised from the original ones. When U Rŭk discovered this he was very angry, but after he heard the five pieces he wept for joy and admired them, saying: "They are pleasant but not too rapturous, and sorrowful but not too grievous." So it can be said that this music was "correct and proper" in the sense of *chŏngak*. U Rŭk made his three disciples play the music at the king's court, and when the king heard the music he was greatly pleased.

6. Chin-su, *Sankuo chi,* Weishu Tungich'uan 3rd century A.D.

7. *History of Koryŏ,* Vol. 69, Chapter 32.

8. *History of Koryŏ,* the first reign year of Sŏngjong in November.

9. In the epitaph of the monk Chingam at Sanggye Temple, it is written that Chingam went to China (T'ang) in 804 A.D. and learned Bud-dhist chant there, returning to Korea in 830. Also King Kyŏngdŏk, in the 19th year of his reign (760 A.D.) saw two suns appear in the sky, and called for Buddhist chant to banish one of them but the man fail-ed to do so. The same king also met a Buddhist monk who could sing nothing but folk songs, and one song in particular was called *Tosol ka.* (From the *Samguk yusa,* Vol. 5)

10. Yen-in, *Shigakku Tai-shi,* "Journey to T'ang China to learn Buddhism." (Yen-in went to T'ang in 838 and returned to Japan in 847 A.D.)

11. Yi Hye-gu, "Buddhist Chant of Silla," *Studies in Korean Music,* 1957.

12. Hahn Man-young, "*Chissori and Hossori* in Buddhist Chants." *Festschrift for Dr. Yi, Hye-gu,* 1969.

13. Yi Hye-gu, "*Ssangwhajŏm,*" *Topics in Korean Music,* 1967.

14. *Ak-ki,* Music Notation Book.

15. Yi Hye-gu, "Transformation of Chinese Music in Korea and Japan," *Topics in Korean Music,* 1967.

Difference between
Hyang-ak and *Tang-ak*

YI HYE-GU

The differences between *Hyang-ak* and *Tang-ak* will be studied with respect to the musical structure, disregarding the subjective elements of these two types of music. Korean music will be illustrated with several short songs from the old music of the 16th century, *Siyong hyangakpo*, 時用鄕樂譜, and Tang music with *Nagyang ch'un* (Spring of Nagyang) which was introduced to Korea during the 12th century, so that the date of these examples may be as close as possible. The reason why *Pohŏja*, 步虛子, one of the two extant pieces of Chinese music, is not used as exemplifying T'ang music is that this originally Chinese music is labeled *Hyang-ak*, Korean music, in the *Taeak hubo* 大樂後譜, a collection of songs of the 15th century, and actually the music shows a Koreanized style, that is, a style of many notes to one syllable, while *Nagyang ch'un* retains the Chinese style, one or a few notes to one syllable.

Tang-ak, Chinese Music

The text of *Nagyang ch'un* (Chinese: *Loyang ch'un*) 洛陽春 consists of two four-line verses, that is, even-numbered lines, the lengths of which are irregular, having variously five, six, or seven syllables as follows:

紗窓未暁　　黃鶯語
蕙　爐　　　燒殘炷
錦帷羅幕　　度春寒
昨夜裏　　　三更雨

繡簾閑倚　　吹輕絮
歛眉山　　　無緒
把花拭涙　　向歸鴻
問來處　　　逢郎不

This text might be rendered in English as follows:

Spring in Loyang

Gauze windows glimmer and the yellow nightingale twitters.

In the fireplace some fire lingers still.

Silk curtain and tapestry hold me warm from spring's cold.

Late last night it rained.

Leaning on the screen, I see light-winged seeds afloat in the air.

I knit my eyebrows, my heart disturbed.

Flowers in hand, drying tears, I ask the returning wild geese:

Have you seen my love on your way?

(a) *Nagyang ch'un*, the text of which consists of two verses as shown above, has naturally two musical sentences, or musical cadences. Each musical sentence consists of four musical phrases, that is, even-numbered musical phrases. Usually, however, only the first musical phrase of the second sentence (see music example 2) which is different from the opening phrase of the first musical sentence (see example 1), is written in the music notation, the remaining three musical phrases of the second sentence which are a repetition of those of the first sentence not being written but indicated with the characters "*hwanip*" 還入 which means "repetition." The rendering of *Nagyang ch'un,* following the incomplete musical notation, ends at the first musical phrase of the second musical sentence, not heeding the letter indication of the repetition of its remaining three musical phrases. Thus the music notation and the rendition of *Nagyang ch'un* give the impression that the Chinese music consists of five musical phrases, that is, odd-numbered phrases. However, originally and properly the musical structure of *Nagyang ch'un* consists of two equal musical sentences of even-numbered phrases.

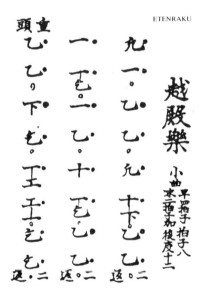

ETENRAKU

(b) While the text of *Nagyang ch'un* has irregular length of lines (see the verse shown above), the music has regular length of musical phrases. One musical phrase is incorporated in eight columns of 16 squares of the Korean traditional notation (see music example 1). Incidentally the eight columns of Korean traditional notation are equivalent to the eight dots of the Japanese traditional notation (see above). The eight columns are divided into two columns of four, and at every fourth column the clapper punctuates (see the letter, 拍, which means "clapper," in music examples 1 and 11). The clapper, the letter 拍, in the Korean traditional notation is equivalent to the large dot of the Japanese traditional notation, except that the clapper comes in at every fourth column while the large dot comes in at every third dot.

To sum up, the musical structure of *Nagyang ch'un*, being of two musical sentences of equal length which consist of four musical phrases of equal length, might be said to be quite symmetrical.

Hyang-ak, Korean Music

(a) *Samogok* (Song of the Kind Mother) 思母曲 : The text of the Korean song in the Korean language is in three verses (see music example 3, column 1-6; 8-13; 15-17.) The musical structure is made up of three musical sentences based either on the identical cadential progression terminating on *ha-o* 下五 (literally lower five, meaning an octave below the central note, *kung* 宮), or both on the text and on the interlude (see music example. 3, column 7) and the postlude (see music example 3, column 14). If the latter criterion is accepted, both the first and the second sentences consist of six phrases (six columns of the notation) respectively, and the concluding sentence is in three phrases.

Equally significant is the irregular length of the musical phrase as well as the irregular length of the musical sentences; the length of the last musical phrase of each musical sentence is longer than that of its preceding phrase by three squares (see music example 3, column 6; 13; 17).

All in all, the musical structure of *Samogok* is made up of three musical sentences, that is, odd-numbered sentences, instead of two sentences as in *Nagyang ch'un*. Both the length of the musical phrases and that of the musical sentences are irregular. In a word the musical structure of *Samogok* is asymmetrical, distinct from the symmetrical structure of *Nagyang ch'un.*

(b) *Chŏngsŏk-ka* (Live Long, Gracious King) 鄭石歌 : The text of the old song is in a single verse of six lines. The musical structure of this song is of a single musical sentence marked by the cadential progression terminating on *ha-o* 下五, followed by the short postlude (see music example 4). It consists of the second phrase extending over 40 squares; the last phrase 45 6-9). It is to be noted that the last musical phrase does not begin from the top (strictly speaking, the fourth square from the top) of the column as its preceding musical phrases do (see music example 4, column 1 and 4), but starts from the bottom (the fifth square from the bottom) (see music example 4, column 6). Consequently the length of the musical phrases differ; the second phrase extending over 40 squares; the last phrase 45 squares.

Thus the musical structure of *Chŏngsŏk-ka,* made up of three musical phrases of irregular length, is also asymmetrical, distinct from the Chinese music.

(c) *Sŏgyŏng pyŏlgok* (Song of Sŏgyŏng) 西京別曲 : The text is made up of two lines followed by a line of nonsense syllables. Its musical structure is of a single musical sentence of three musical phrases with the postlude (see music example 5, column 1-2; 3-4; 5-7; 8). The lengths of those three musical phrases are different; the opening phrase occupies 32 squares (two columns), the second phrase, the shortest, 29 squares (two columns minus three squares), and the last phrase with nonsense syllables, the longest, 50 squares (three columns plus three squares).

To sum up, the musical structure of *Sŏgyŏng pyŏlgok* with its odd-numbered phrases of irregular length is distinct from that of *Nagyang ch'un* which has even-numbered phrases of equal lengths.

(d) *Kasiri* (Song of Parting) 가시리: The text of the shortest song is in three lines. The musical structure is of a single musical sentence of three musical phrases without postlude.

(see music example 6, column 1-2; 3-4; 5-6). The last musical phrase beginning from the bottom of its preceding musical phrase, makes it longer and makes its preceding phrase shorter (see music example 6, column 4, third square from the bottom). This is another example of the music structure of odd-numbered phrases of irregular lengths.

(e) *Ch'ŏngsan pyŏlgok* (Song of the Blue Mountains) 靑山別曲 : The musical structure is of a single musical sentence of three music phrases of irregular lengths without prelude (see music example 7, column 1-4; 5-7; 8-10).

(f) *Yugu-gok* (song of Cuckoo) 維鳩曲 : The musical structure is apparently made up of two musical sentences; the first musical sentence has four musical phrases, and the second sentence is the repetition of the last cadential musical phrase of the first preceding sentence (see music example 8, column 1-2; 3-4; 5-6; 7-8; 9-10). However the musical structure will be examined in connection with the following item, *Yasim-sa.*

For the purpose of comparison with the following item, *Yasim-sa,* it should be mentioned that this song has the identical melodic lines of the latter halves of the second and the third phrases (see music example 8, column 4 and 6), the equal lengths of the five phrases, and no postlude.

(g) *Yasim-sa* (All through the Night) 夜深詞 : The musical structure of this song is similar to that of *Yugu-gok* in many ways; it is apparently made up of two musical sentences or cadences. The first musical sentence has four phrases and the second one is a repetition of the cadential phrase of its preceding sentence (see music example 9, column 1-2; 3-4; 5-6; 7-8; 9-10). The melodic lines of the latter halves of the second and third phrases are identical (see music example 9, column 4 and 6). The lengths of the five phrases are equal. There is no postlude.

The problem arises whether the musical structure of this song should be regarded as being made up of two sentences based on two cadences (see music example 9, column 1-8; 9-10), or as being a single sentence in two parts (see music example 9, column 1-6; 7-10). For the repeated cadential phrase is too short to be an independent musical sentence and the repetition of the cadential phrase is also found without any change of melodic line in the repetition of the cadential phrase of the other song named *P'ung-ipsong* 風入松 (*Siyong hyang-ak-po* p. 42) giving an impression of an independent set phrase serving as a coda for several songs. This problem needs further investigation.

From the study we have made of *Nagyang ch'un* and several Korean songs from *Siyong hyang-ak-po* it might be concluded that the difference between *Hyang-ak* and *Tang-ak* with respect to the musical structure is as follows: As far as Chinese music introduced into Korea is concerned, it has two musical sentences of equal length which consist of four musical phrases of equal length as well. On the other hand most, if not all, Korean music has odd-numbered sentences of odd-numbered phrases of irregular length. In a word, while the musical structure of Chinese music is symmetrical, that of Korean music is asymmetrical.

Such asymmetrical musical structure is also found in Korean songs of today as well. The classical lyric song *kagok* 歌曲 is made up of five phrases of irregular length as follows;

Phrase 1: 32 beats (which is divided by the caesura into 11 and 21 beats).
Phrase 2: 27 beats (11 plus 16 beats).
Phrase 3: 37 beats (16 plus 21 beats).
Phrase 4: same as phrase 2.
Phrase 5: 48 beats (16 plus 32 beats).

Such asymmetrical musical structure is also to be found in *Nasori (Ha)* 納曾利 (破), one of *Komagaku* 高麗樂 (Music from Korea) of Japanese court music. The cadential phrase, *hyoshi* 11 and 12 (measure 29-32; 45-48) is also to be found in *hyoshi* 7 and 8 (measure 25-28; 29-32) (see music example 10 which is copied from Mr. Sukehiro Shiba's transcriptions in the staff notation 芝祐泰; 五線譜による雅樂總譜卷四). Therefore

Nasori can be divided into two music sentences of different lengths; the first sentence is from the beginning to measure 32, and the second one is from measure 33 to measure 48.

Moreover, *Nasori* has phrases of irregular lengths. The cadential phrase of the first sentence is shorter than its preceding phrase by three beats (in *ryūteki* part) or two beats (in *hichiriki* part) (see music example 11, the part marked with ﹁ ﹁). Consequently its following musical phrase comes to increase its length; it is longer than the regular length by three or two beats.

As far as *Nasori* is concerned, its musical structure is as asymmetrical as that of Korean music; the lengths of the musical phrases as well as those of the musical sentences are different. Further investigation is needed for discovering to what extent the criteria of the asymmetrical musical structure for the distinction of Korean music from Chinese music can be applied to *Komagaku*.

Example 1

Example 2

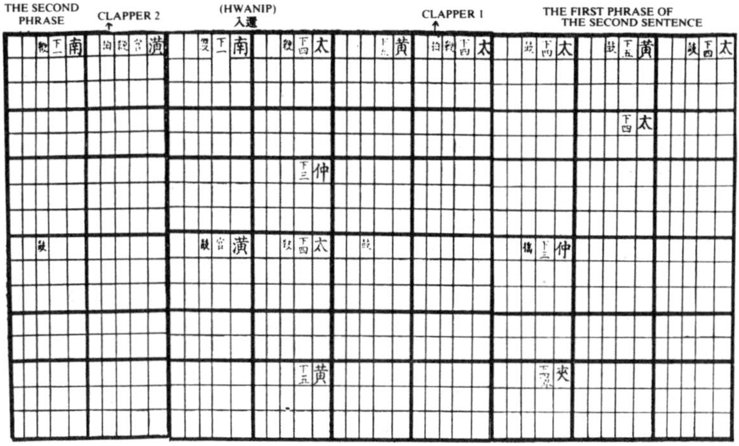

Example 3

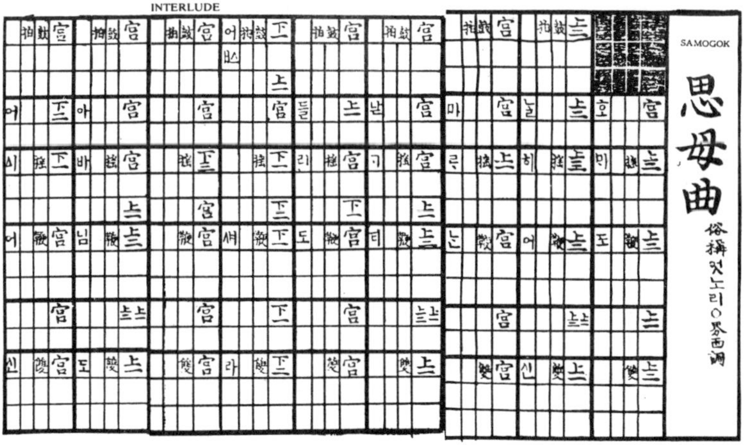

Example 3

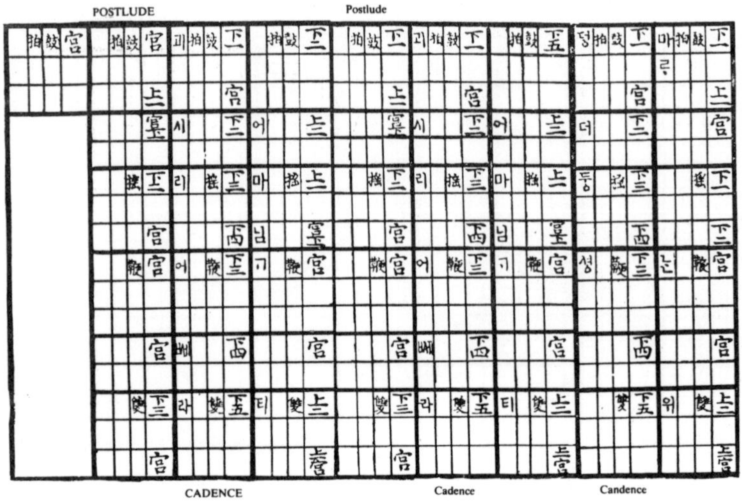

Example 4

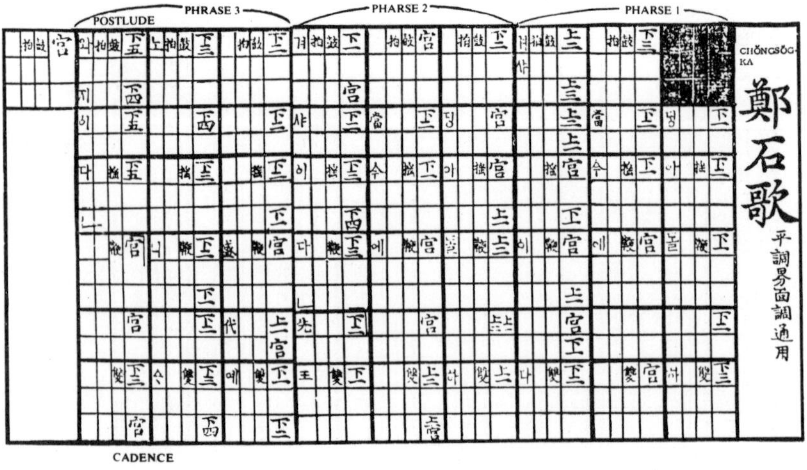

Example 5

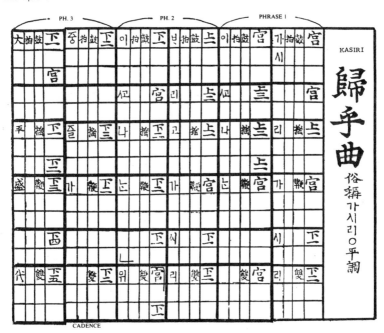

Example 6

Example 7

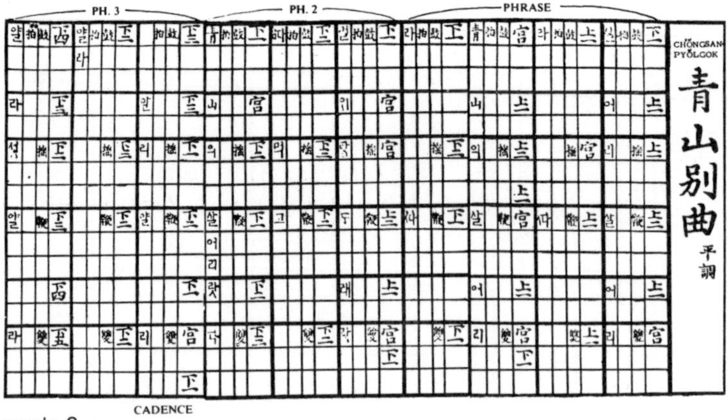

Example 8

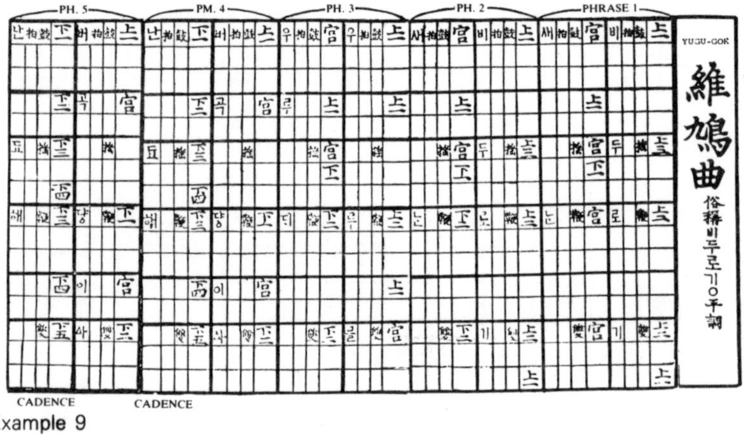

Example 9

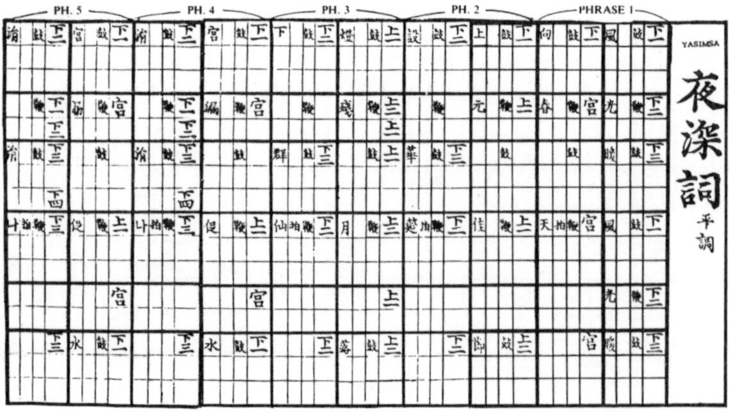

Example 10

Sejong and the Preservation of Chinese Ritual Melodies

ROBERT C. PROVINE, JR.

Much has already been said about the immense cultural accomplishments during the reign of the justly renowned King Sejong, who ruled from 1418 to 1450. One such accomplishment, the invention of *han'gŭl,* is still honored with a national holiday. Historical and legal studies were many and valuable; many such documents are still available today and attest to the skill and development of printing in Sejong's time. Music is usually mentioned as something to which Sejong paid especial attention, but detailed examples of this royal patronage have not yet been made available in English. This article examines some aspects of an important musical document, the *Treatise on Ceremonial Music* (雅樂譜), prepared in 1430 on the orders of Sejong.

The *Treatise* gives a distinct interpretation of the history and theory of Chinese ritual music. The historians and musicians who prepared the book took a strongly neo-Confucian approach to their work, as would be expected at this point in Korean history. Confucian scholars had always been concerned with the proper reconstruction of ancient Confucian music, and the Koreans were no exception. But the *Treatise* is no carbon copy of earlier Chinese efforts, and it differs in several significant ways from the kind of work done in China.

The Korean scholars openly admitted that the fundamental

task was impossible: genuinely ancient music, lamentably, had perished irrevocably. But unlike Chinese music theorists, the Koreans showed an inclination toward the practical, and decided to do the next best thing. First, they steeped themselves in orthodox music theory, relying on ancient Chinese sources and neo-Confucian commentaries. Then, in accord with their interpretations of the theory, they "corrected" the oldest music they could find, hoping to recreate melodies with at least certain features of antiquity. In so doing, they managed to preserve a collection of early Chinese ritual melodies which have since been lost in China itself.

Excellent material on the Chinese background is available in Rulan C. Pian's *Sonq (sic) Dynasty Musical Sources and Their Interpretation* (1967). Professor Yi Hye-gu of S. N.U. has written several first-rate articles on music in the Sejong period, including "Musical Accomplishments of Pak Yŏn" (1959) and "On the Preface to A-ak-po in the Chronicle of King Sejong" (1971). Also valuable is Professor Yi's study of the modern-day remnants of some of the music, "Comparison of the Extant Confucian Music in Korea and China" (1973). (See Bibliography)

Background and Purpose of the Treatise on Ceremonial Music

The *Sejong Annals* (世宗實錄), printed in 1454, contains 163 extensive chapters, of which the first 127 are written in the normal chronicle form of the *Annals*. The 36 remaining chapters comprise four appendices devoted to specific studies. The longest of these studies, 12 chapters, concerns music and consists of several works. The first, Chapters 136-137, is the *Treatise on Ceremonial Music* of 1430, which describes and notates ceremonial music of Chinese origin.

Sejong had in mind two specific ceremonies for which he

desired correct, Confucian music: the Royal Audiences (朝會), when he met with his government officials in the Royal Audience Chamber; and the Sacrificial Rites (祭祀), when he and his officials obeyed ceremonial etiquette in offering sacrificial food to divine spirits. This was to be purely instrumental music, performed by two orchestras in alternation. However, the actual instrumentation, apart from sets of bells and chimes, was of tangential relevance in the preparation of the musical scores and will not be considered in detail in this article.

Scholars and Their Source Materials

Inspired by a lecture on Chinese music theory and the discovery of sonorous stone in Korea, Sejong assigned various scholars to the task of preparing the ritual music. These men included Chŏng In-ji, author of the *History of the Koryŏ Dynasty* (高麗史), and Pak Yŏn (朴堧), a man of many talents who has since been considered one of Korea's three sages of music. Chŏng In-ji's introduction to the *Treatise on Ceremonial Music* describes the task in some detail, but the technical and cosmological information is too complex for thorough examination here. The present discussion will concentrate on some of the more important points.

First of all, in trying to reconstruct Confucian music, it was necessary to accurately reproduce an absolute basie pitch, *huang-chung* (黃鐘), from which all the other pitches could be obtained by a circle of fifths method. Only if the proper pitches have been (re-)established will melodies have the desired effect when performed. The Korean scholars had two ways to obtain the *huang-chung* pitch: they could construct a pitch pipe according to specifications contained in ancient Chinese sources, or they could assume that instruments that had been bestowed by the Ming court had accurate pitches and could be used as models.

Pak Yŏn, always the believer in the ancient sources (or at least his own interpretations of them), set about building a *huang-chung* pitch pipe. The Chinese specifications were in terms of length and volume, based upon numbers of grains of a particular kind of "black millet." Pak got apparently appropriate grain from Haeju and constructed the pitch pipe. The resultant pitch, unfortunately, was slightly higher than the corresponding one on the instruments bestowed by the Chinese, and the decision still had to be made.

Despite its fidelity to ancient Chinese sources, the pitch pipe was rejected: who was to say that the size of the black millet grain was identical to that of Confucius' time, with all the variables of climate and soil fertility? The decision to use the *huang-chung* pitch on the Chinese instruments was a rather extraordinary decision, considering that the specifications of antiquity (however inaccurate) were rejected in favor of an instrument of recent origin. Chŏng In-ji's introduction puts it this way: "These instruments have a long tradition and, furthermore, they are gifts of the Chinese court." This suggests that Korea was also reluctant to inform the Son of Heaven that his pitches were inaccurate.

The Korean decision indicates a practical tendency absent in the work of earlier Chinese music theorists: the Chinese had seldom been concerned with the pitches that performing musicians actually made, but rather with the propriety of theoretical precision. The Koreans' practicality is even more evident in the next process they followed in their effort to reconstruct ancient music: even though the genuine ancient music itself was irretrievably gone, certain features of it could be deduced from careful study of the musical theories of the neo-Confucian Chu Hsi (1130-1200) and his close friend Ts'ai Yüan-ting (蔡元定, 1135-1198). If one should take the oldest surviving Chinese music and "correct" it according to these features of antiquity, many accumulated impurities would be removed, and music which at least resembled that of the ancients could again be performed.

This procedure was imminently practical, providing a means of transforming talk into action, or theory into music. The remaining problem, of course, was to locate reliable sources of relatively old music suitable for revision. The Koreans had access to Sung dynasty music of a more popular nature, such as pieces for the Ch'in (琴) or settings of Tz'ŭ poetry (詞), since we can verify that they had copies of the Chinese sources. Though Chŏng In-ji fails to mention this sort of music, it is clear the Koreans rejected any such "popular" music for these serious ritual purposes.

The scholars concluded that only two sources contained music that could reliably be considered old: Chu Hsi's *General Survey of Ritual* (儀禮經傳通解, ca. 1220), which records twelve songs attributed to the K'ai-yüan (開元) period of the T'ang dynasty (i.e. 713-742); and the *Music for the Confucian Temple* (大成樂譜, 1349) by one Lin Yü (林宇) of the Yüan dynasty, recording sixteen melodies for Confucian ceremonies.

Chu Hsi's twelve settings of texts from the *Classic of Poetry* (詩經) are well enough known and have been studied in detail by Laurence Picken (1956) and Rulan Pian (1967). These melodies were preserved primarily through copies made by later scholars, though one of the original prints of the *General Survey of Ritual* does survive in Taiwan. In that print, some of the musical notes are missing and there are also emendations by a later hand. The copy made by the Koreans in 1430 (printed in 1454) is relatively early, and is very likely a copy made from the first edition. Unfortunately, its value as an early copy is diminished by several errors made in preparing the printing blocks.

On the other hand, the sixteen melodies recorded by Lin Yü are virtually unknown outside of their appearance in the Korean *Treatise on Ceremonial Music*. Lin Yü is not to be found in any of the many indices to Chinese historical biography consulted by the present author; similarly, the *Music for the Confucian Temple* has not been located in any of the historical bibliographies. Indeed, there is nothing to suggest that the work was any more than a handwritten record of certain rituals, and its fate in China has been total oblivion. In Korea, too, the work itself has perished; we now have only the musical notations copied into the *Sejong Annals*.

The only information we have about Lin Yü is given in the *Sejong Annals* (Chapter 57), where it says he was a man of Hsin-an (新安), a district in present-day Hopeh province in northeast China, and that he wrote the *Music for the Confucian Temple* in 1349.

Chŏng In-ji states, however, that the sixteen melodies were also recorded in a work entitled *Regulations of Chih-cheng* (至正條格) from the late Yüan dynasty. He points out errors in the melodies of this version, and chooses to rely upon the more trustworthy *Music for the Confucian Temple*. But even the less accurate *Regulations of Chih-cheng* was to perish: it was included in a Ming dynasty literary compendium of 1408, the *Yung-le Tatien* (永樂大典). All copies of the relevant chapters of the compendium have evidently been destroyed, the last one when the British and French sacked Peking in 1860. We know of their former existence through surviving indices. The compilers of the mammoth literary compendium *Ssu-k'u Ch'üan-shu* (四庫全書) of the late eighteenth century did not include the *Regulations*, though the index to the compendium describes it in some bibliographic detail: like Chŏng In-ji, the *Ssu-k'u* compilers considered the book unreliable.

Aware that they were dealing with many musical and historical variables, the Korean scholars did something of extraordinary foresight and modesty: they included exact copies of their original sources, thereby subjecting their process of "correction" to the scrutiny and criticism of later generations. As Chŏng In-ji says, "These two sets of ["corrected"] melodies comprise two volumes. In addition, we have written out the relevant passages from the original sources so that latter day scholars may have this material. It is lamentable that ancient music books are so few. . . ."

Process of "Correction"

The Chinese system of musical modes was immensely complex; even worse, it was variously interpreted from period to period, so that inconsistencies and errors were common. The names of some modes are recorded in the ancient Chinese *Rituals of Chou* (周禮), though, of course, no musical examples are given. Differing meanings were given to the same modal nomenclature by the Northern Sung and the Southern Sung. The Korean scholars preparing the *Treatise on Ceremonial Music* also had to come to grips with the immense problems of the modal system and its cosmological implications. Right or wrong, they made a decision about interpretation of the modes in the pieces written down by Chu Hsi and Lin Yü. Later in the century, in the reign of Sŏngjong, their decision was officially reversed as the modal controversy raged on.

Having decided which modes were proper and which were unacceptable, the scholars found that six of Chu Hsi's songs and three of Lin Yü's melodies were in improper modes and discarded them as being beyond repair. Another of the Lin Yü melodies contained notes foreign to its mode (accidentals), and it was also discarded.

Thus, the scholars were left with six of the Chu Hsi songs and twelve of the Lin Yü ritual melodies. These needed further correction, based upon a strict interpretation of theoretical observations of Chu Hsi. According to Chŏng In-ji, Chu Hsi states that although there are twelve pitches, only seven are used at a time. The Koreans interpreted this to mean that proper ritual melodies should be limited to seven notes, or a range of just less than an octave. Accordingly, the Koreans reduced the melodies to only seven pitches, lowering by an octave the notes that were too high. For example, the first of Lin Yü's melodies was originally as given in Example a) below.

The notes marked with an asterisk lie outside the proper seven-note range and were therefore lowered an octave, to

Example 11

give the Korean revision shown in Example b):

The Koreans also intended to transpose the revised melodies to begin on each of the twelve pitches in the octave. Transposition of this sort was traditional, and, more practically speaking, it was a means of stretching considerably the small amount of old music available. But the principal instruments for use in ritual music, the *P'yŏn-jong* (編鐘) and *P'yŏn-gyŏng* (編磬) (sets of metal bells and stone chimes, respectively), had a range of only sixteen notes. That is, they could sound the twelve notes of the primary octave and the first four chromatic tones of the next higher octave. Most of the transposed versions proposed by the Koreans would lie outside this available range. Hence, in the transposed versions, the Koreans lowered by an octave and note which would otherwise lie above the highest of the sixteen available pitches. Example c) above shows the melody of Example b) transposed up a major sixth, with resultant octave alterations. Clearly, the original melodic *gestalt* has been entirely transformed.

Since instrumental, not vocal, music was needed for the Royal Audiences and the Sacrificial Rites, the original texts associated with the Chu Hsi and Lin Yü pieces were discarded. Sejong was presented with this resultant body of instrumental music, and the *Sejong Annals* mentions its performance (Chapter 51).

The Korean "corrections" were intended, in some sense, to antiquate the Chu Hsi and Lin Yü melodies. It was a most practical scheme, and resulted, after orchestration, in a usable body of ritual music. In addition, every step of the correction process was justified on the basis of a consistent interpretation of Chinese writings on music from the *Rituals of Chou* down to Sung dynasty neo-Confucian theories. Unfortunately, there is no compelling reason to believe in any step of the correction process: the modal problem was hopelessly complex, and even today scholars squabble among themselves about it. Chu Hsi's statement that only seven notes are used at a time might easily be interpreted to mean that such music is written using heptatonic scales, without restriction to a single octave.

The exciting matter here is that, in the course of their research and revision, the Korean scholars managed to preserve sixteen ritual melodies lost in their native China. We have already noted that they were copied from a Chinese source, the *Music for the Confucian Temple* of 1349. That date alone puts these melodies in a select class, since the known Chinese melodies predating 1349 are not many. We turn now to a further study of the sixteen melodies of the *Music for the Confucian Temple.*

Antecedents and Descendants

The Korean copy of Lin Yü's *Music for the Confucian Temple* contains seventeen melodies, two of which are identical. They are as follows:

SACRIFICE TO CONFUCIUS
1. Welcoming the Spirits (Nine sections)
   a) Played three times
   b) Played two times
   c) Played two times
   d) Played two times
2. The Cleansing
3. Ascending into the Temple

4. Libations and Gifts (Five times)
5. Offering of Sacrificial Food
6. First Offering to Confucius at the Tablet
7. First Offering to Yen Hui, the Prince of Yen
8. First Offering to Tseng Tzu, the Prince of Ch'eng
9. First Offering to Tzu Szu, the Prince of Yi
10. First Offering to Mencius, the Prince of Chou
11. Middle and Final Offerings
12. Removing the Vessels of Sacrificial Food
13. Ushering out the Spirits
14. Sacrifice to the Dead (Music same as II)

Lin Yü's *Music for the Confucian Temple* (i.e. the Korean copy of it) is the earliest source of both music and text for the pieces above. However, the music belongs stylistically to a period at least as early as the Sung dynasty, and it is unlikely that Lin Yü actually composed the music. He probably just copied down some ritual tunes that he had come to know. The music can be identified with the set of Confucian texts and modal prescriptions recorded in the *History of the Yüan Dynasty* (元史), compiled in the later fourteenth century. At the end of the texts, the following comment is inserted: "The preceding sacrificial texts are all old (舊). The Yüan dynasty once intended to edit and change them, but they were not adequate for use" (Chapter 69). Most of the texts are also to be found in the *History of the Sung Dynasty* (宋史, Chapter 137), but the lack of modal prescriptions and the absence of a few texts makes at least the musical relationship uncertain. An attempt to trace the music or texts further back in Chinese history quickly becomes conjecture: the book titles recorded in the dynastic bibliographies and the known functions of government offices might suggest a trail leading as far back as the reign of Huitsung, in the period between 1111 and 1118. But this is unnecessarily fanciful.

The sixteen Lin Yü melodies bear a very close stylistic relation to certain pieces by the late Sung dynasty composer

Hsiung P'eng-lai (1246-1323). Hsiung recorded thirty-one
ceremonial songs which have been transcribed by Rulan Pian
(1967). Of these, the last nine are settings of texts for the
sacrifice to Confucius and have practically the same titles as
nine of the Lin Yü pieces. The poetic and musical styles are
identical. In fact, Lin Yü's first piece (given in the musical
example above) is identical in music and text to one of
Hsiung's pieces. Otherwise, the two sets of melodies are
essentially independent. The melodies recorded by Lin Yü,
then, are either of Sung (or earlier) origin or represent a
conscious stylistic paraphrase of Sung ceremonial music.

A very few of the Lin Yü melodies occur in scattered sources
postdating the *Sejong Annals*. The first melody, also recorded
by Hsiung P'eng-lai, is given in a pentatonic version by Prince
Chu Tsai-yü in his *Yüeh-hsüeh Hsin-shuo* (樂學新説 , 1595). At
least two later Korean sources contain some of the Lin
Yü music: both the famous treatise *Akhak Kwebŏm* (樂學軌範,
1493) by Sŏng Hyŏn and the encyclopedia *Munhŏn Pigo*
(文獻備考, first prepared 1770) record the first melody in
twelve transpositions and the last melody in three transpositions.

Closing Observations

The Korean *Treatise on Ceremonial Music* of 1430 was an
extraordinary accomplishment. The combination of theory
and musical examples is already unusual in the history of east
Asian musical theory. Abstract theory is present, but the
Korean approach is practical and yields a usable product. In
their research process, the Korean scholars showed an amazing
willingness not only to confront traditional theory with actual
practice, but even to overrule it. As a gesture of scholarly
honesty and humility, they admitted to their uncertainties and
preserved their source material for posterity's judgment. Even
such a work is only one example of the musical achievements

under the supervision of the great King Sejong.

But was it correct? History can be cruel, and before the fifteenth century was out, the music produced in the *Treatise* had been criticized and replaced in the ceremonies for which it was intended. Only two of the Lin Yü pieces remain in the modern repertoire, at the ceremonies of the Royal Confucian Shrine. We can take a little comfort in the fact that those two melodies have been preserved in the Korean "corrected" versions of 1430.

BIBLIOGRAPHY

Yi Hye-gu
1959   "Pak Yŏn i huse e chun ŭmak yusan," reprinted in his *Han'guk Ŭmak Sŏsŏl*. Seoul, 1967.
1971   "Sejong sillok sojae aak po sŏ," *Han'guk Ŭmak Yŏn-gu*, I (Seoul, 1971).
1973   "Han'guk kwa Chungguk ŭi hyŏnhaeng Munmyo-ak pigyo," in *Tonggyo Min T'ae-sik Paksa Kohŭi Kinyŏm Yugyo-hak Nonch'ong*. Seoul, 1973.
Rulan Chao Pian
1967   *Sonq (sic) Dynasty Musical Sources and Their Interpretation.* Cambridge, Mass., 1967.
Laurence Picken
1956   "Twelve Ritual Melodies of the T'ang Dynasty," *Studia Memoriae Belae Bartok Sacra*. Budapest, 1956.

"Chinese" Ritual Music in Korea: The Origins, Codification, and Cultural Role of A-ak

ROBERT C. PROVINE

A-ak (雅樂) is one of the great treasures in the corpus of Korean traditional music. It was performed during the Yi dynasty in a number of the sacrificial rites (*chesa* 祭祀) observed by the royal court, as well as in certain other government ceremonies requiring the highest elegance and decorum. *A-ak* may still be heard today in the semi-annual Sacrifice to Confucius(*Sŏkchŏn* 釋奠) held at the Shrine of Confucius (*Munmyo* 文廟) in Seoul,[1] as well as in concept performances by the National Classical Music Institute (*Kungnip Kugagwŏn* 國立國樂院).

The term *a-ak* is Korean pronunciation of the same Chinese characters pronounced *ya-yüeh* in Chinese and *gagaku* in Japanese, meaning "elegant music." Recently, the word has been used in Korea to refer to the whole repertory of court music[2] (much as *gagaku* does in Japan), but historical sources always use *a-ak* to mean one specific type of ritual music which forms an important, though small part of the court repertory. It is in this latter, restricted sense that the term is used here.

This paper surveys the origins of the Korean *a-ak* tradition in the early twelfth century, the reform and codification of the music in the fifteenth century, and the cultural role of *a-ak* over the ensuing centuries. It is beneficial, before examining the Korean tradition itself, to take a brief look at the Chinese backdrop against which the Korean tradition arose. Later, it may be asked to what extent *a-ak* may be considered music in a Chinese style.

Introduction: the Chinese Background

The Chinese philosopher Confucius, who lived in the sixth and fifth centuries B.C., once heard some ancient music in proper performance and was so profoundly affected by the experience that for three months afterward he was unaware of what he was eating. He said, "I did not picture to myself that any music existed which could reach such perfection as this."[3] He referred to such uplifting and perfect music as *ya-yüeh*.[4]

Confucius held the view that music is primarily educational: good music promotes virtue, its harmony and good order reflecting the concord between members of a smoothly functioning society. While ancient odes stir the mind and proper decorum in social conduct develops the character, it is music which applies the final polish.[5]

Ever since the time of Confucius, China's loftiest music, performed during such important ceremonies as sacrifices to imperial ancestors, has continued to be called *ya-yüeh*. The Chinese dynastic histories devote many pages to the theory and history of this *ya-yüeh* and to the instrumentation of ensembles used to perform it. The sources reveal that the music itself was modified from time to time or even replaced altogether, the term *ya-yüeh* simply being applied to whichever kind of ceremonial music was currently in fashion.

The decline and fall of a ruling Chinese dynasty was mirrored by a loss of propriety by its *ya-yüeh*. If a government had become permeated with undesirables, then its *ya-yüeh*, no doubt, had similarly fallen prey to intrusion by popular, foreign, or other misbehaved music. Each new dynasty re-

codified the music, starting with a fresh determination of the
fundamental pitch from which all others could be derived by a
mechanical method based on the circle of fifths. Time and
again the sources lament the loss of genuine ancient music.
Time and again new or modified *ya-yüeh* replaced the
disgraced music of an earlier period, only to eventually suffer
the same fate itself. The musical alterations were usually
justified by citations of abstruse theoretical passages from
canonical texts thought to reflect the wisdom of Confucius
himself.

The eleventh-century philosopher Chou Tun-i (周敦頤 1017-
1073), writing on government, summarized the musical problem in context as follows:

> In ancient times, sage-kings instituted ceremonies and
> promoted moral education.... Consequently, all people
> were in perfect harmony and all things were in concord.
> Thereupon the sage-kings created music to give expression to
> the winds coming from the eight directions and to appease the
> feelings of the people. This is the reason why the sound of
> music is calm and not hurtful, and is harmonious without
> being licentious. As it enters the ear and affects the heart,
> everyone becomes calm and peaceful. Because of calmness,
> one's desires will be appeased, and because of harmony, one's
> impetuousness will disappear. Peace, calmness, and modera-
> tion — these are the heights of virtue. As the world is
> transformed and brought to completion, government reaches
> its perfection. This is what is meant by moral principles which
> match Heaven and Earth and which are the ultimate standard
> of the ancients.
>
> Later generations have neglected ceremonies. Their govern-
> mental measures and laws have been in disorder. Rulers have
> indulged their material desires without restraint, and conse-
> quently the people below them have suffered bitterly. Rulers
> claimed that ancient music is not worth listening to and re-
> placed it by or changed it into modern music, which is seduc-
> tive, licentious, depressive, and complaining. It arouses desires
> and increases bitterness without end. Therefore there have

been cases of people destroying their rulers, casting away their fathers, taking life lightly, and ruining human relations, and it has been impossible to put an end to such atrocities. Alas! Ancient music appeased the heart but modern music enhances desires. Ancient music spread civilizing influence but modern music increases discontent. To hope for perfect government without restoring ancient ceremonies and changing modern music is to be far off the mark.[6]

The history of Chinese *ya-yüeh* is fascinating, immense, and complex, but it is also, in a sense, a hopeless pursuit. Of the music itself, we have little which antedates the fifteenth or sixteenth centuries. The Chinese theorists and dynastic histories almost never supply us both theory and pieces of music, and, as a result, it is virtually impossible to decipher unambiguous definitions for musical terminology found in the sources. Interpretation of the Chinese theorists requires, at the very least, the generous application of a lively imagination.

Origins of the Korean A-ak Tradition

In the twelfth century, a portion of the Chinese *ya-yüeh* tradition was exported to Korea, and, with music codified in the fifteenth century, performances survive in Seoul even today. As often happens when foreign culture is adopted in a new land, this *ya-yüeh*, or *a-ak* tradition became more clearly defined and rigidly observed in its new home than in its birthplace. Korea provides us ample theoretical and historical sources, together with music, both notated and performed, for studying this tradition. Since the Korean case is distinct and well-documented, it may eventually provide a musicological springboard for re-examination of the larger *ya-yüeh* tradition in China.

Popular books in East Asia, and even a few in the west, make the understandable claim that the *a-ak* now heard in Korea is Chinese in style and origin and perpetuates authentically a tradition long lost in its motherland.[7] This claim requires investigation in light of available historical sources. There are two basic matters to consider: first, the beginning of the *a-ak* tradition in the early twelfth century, and, second, the early fifteenth-century codification of the surviving music.

The story begins with the eighth emperor of the Chinese Sung dynasty, Hui-tsung (徽宗, who reigned from 1100 to 1125. At this time, the Korean peninsula was under King Yejong(睿宗)of Koryŏ, who ruled from 1105 to 1125. According to the *Koryŏ-sa* (高麗史 History of the Koryŏ dynasty), emperor Hui-tsung sent to Korea two large gifts of music: the first, in 1114, consisted of 167 instruments such as tuned iron slabs, plucked lutes, harps, and shawms, to be used in entertainments at court banquets.[8] The second, in 1116, included the staggering total of 428 exquisitely crafted and richly decorated instruments, together with costumes and dance properties, all for use in *a-ak*;[9] among other things, this enormous

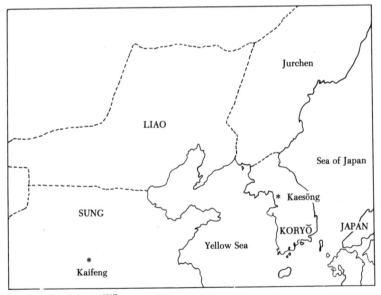

Northeast Asia, ca. 1115

collection had twenty sets each of tuned bronze bells and stone chimes. The second bequest was the beginning of the Korean *a-ak* tradition.

Emperor Hui-tsung sent the following message to King Yejong:

> Since the Three Dynasties [Hsia, Shang, and Chou] ritual has been scattered and music destroyed. If we search out ancient [sources], explain and elucidate them, [we see that rites and music] reach their greatest splendor after developing for a hundred years. A thousand years later we, reflecting upon the pitches and tunes of the Former Kings, have arrived at notes with such style and refinement as to fill the whole country, making visitors feel settled and giving pleasure to strangers. From far away in your country, expressing compassion from the Eastern Sea, you have asked permission to send officials, and these are now at court. In olden days when the teachings of feudal lords were honourable and their virtue outstanding they were rewarded with music, having instruments bestowed on them for the performance of sacrificial music. For "changing the evil customs of a place" there is nothing like this. Now we answer your request, and are sending [this gift] to your country. Though our borders are different and our lands separated, fundamentally there is great harmony [between us]. Is this not good? We are now presenting you with *Ta-sheng ya-yüeh*.[10]

The preceding description of the two gifts is, at least on the surface, what we learn from the Korean sources. The Chinese sources maintain a stony silence on the matter of the huge musical gifts to Korea. Keith Pratt, Spaulding Lecturer in Chinese at the University of Durham, has investigated the questions of *why* the emperor of China would send such imposing and expensive gifts to Korea and *why* the voluminous Chinese historical sources fail to mention them.[11] The following paragraphs draw heavily from Mr. Pratt's important research.

First of all, it is essential to understand the geo-political situation in early twelfth-century East Asia (see Map). On Sung's northeast border was a small Mongol state named Liao; beyond Liao lay a belligerent Tungusic tribe called the Jurchen who were threatening to overrun both Liao and Sung. The Korean peninsula lay south of the Jurchen in a strategically important position. The Korean court tried to maintain neutrality vis-à-vis the disputes going on in the north, wishing to offend neither the powerful and barbaric invading Jurchen hordes or the huge Sung empire, which was the center of world culture.

The Sung emperor Hui-tsung ruled over an empire already weak from past fiscal mismanagement. As a great patron of the arts, he contributed to Sung's decline by supporting a luxurious court and further straining the state coffers. He was unequal to the military task of defending China from outside encroachment.

After 1108, both the Jurchen and Sung approached the Korean court for alliance, but Korea was noncommittal. The extravagant gifts of music in 1114 and 1116 (which, due to the political situation, must have been transported across the turbulent sea) were but part of a massive Sung effort to secure Korea's loyalty and support. But the Koreans remained neutral, and, as far as the Korean sources are concerned, their response to Sung was deep cultural gratitude and nothing more. Sung was left to fight its own battles.

Eventually, Emperor Hui-tsung abandoned hope of Korean support, and he formed an ill-conceived alliance with the Jurchen against Liao, hoping that annexation of Liao territory would satisfy the Jurchen. In tandem, they defeated Liao in 1125, at which point the Jurchen simply turned their forces on their supposed ally, Sung, being no longer constrained by the inconvenience of a buffer state. The Sung capital, Kaifeng, fell in 1127, the court fleeing south to pick up the southerly remains of its empire and forming what is now termed the "Southern" Sung dynasty. Korea, for its part, had already cast its lot with the winning side in 1126.[12]

The enormous 1116 gift of music which set the long-lived Korean *a-ak* tradition on its way was, in short, an unsuccessful political bribe. Such a colossal diplomatic failure was not likely to find its way into official Chinese dynastic histories, and readers of Chinese history, therefore, have been unaware of the extent of Emperor Hui-tsung's ill-contrived scheme to purchase Korea's loyalty. Chŏng In-ji, writing the *Koryŏ-sa* during a period of good relations with Ming China, would hardly have dared to describe a Sung emperor as engaging in such unscrupulous practices. As a result, neither Chinese nor Korean sources speak directly about the real reasons for the musical gifts, and indeed the Chinese sources fail to mention them at all.

Matters are further complicated by the fact that the musical gifts were made at a rather curious moment in Chinese musical history. Emperor Hui-tsung supported the founding and development of the Ta-sheng Institute (*Ta-sheng fu* 大晟府), a music bureau masterminded by a Taoist named Wei Han-chin (魏漢津) and operated from 1105 to 1125.[13] The unusual theories, music, and instruments produced by this Institute were both novel and short-lived in China itself.

Two examples will show the unorthodox nature of the Institute's activities. First, the famous scholar's instrument of China, the zither ch'in (琴 Korean *kŭm*), traditionally had seven strings;[14] those constructed by the Ta-sheng Institute had variously 1, 3, 5, 7, or 9 strings. Seventy-three of these unconventional instruments were included in the 1116 gift to Korea.[15]

The second example concerns the process of pitch reform. According to ancient sources, grains of a certain type of millet should be used as units of measurement in constructing a pitch pipe for the fundamental pitch from which other pitches are derived. The length of the pipe was 90 grains and its capacity 1,200.[16] Wei Han-chin's substitute method, which pleased Emperor Hui-tsung immensely, was to use the lengths of certain of his majesty's fingers as the standards of measurement.[17]

In sum, the Korean *a-ak* tradition began as a political bribe, and its musical content derived from a peculiar, albeit colorful, period in Chinese musical history. It would appear that *a-ak*, at its inception, was simply Chinese music transferred to Korea. In succeeding centuries, Koreans continued to perform and modify the imported Sung music. We know, for example, that the constitution of performing ensembles varied and that native Korean music became irretrievably mixed with the music from China.[18]

Musical Reform and Codification in Early Yi Dynasty

For a number of reasons, it became necessary to reform Korean *a-ak*. One was the gradual assimilation of native music already mentioned. Another was the deterioration over time of many of the original instruments: for example, gourd, used for making the sound boxes of mouth organs, was especially prone to rot,[19] and bamboo, used for flutes, dried and cracked with age. A greater necessity for rebuilding instruments resulted from the Red Turbans' invasion of Koryŏ: the capital, Kaesŏng, was sacked in 1361, and all the musical instruments from Sung were destroyed, except for a set of bells and a set of chimes which an old musician had thrown into a pond.[20]

Ming replaced Yüan in 1368, and in 1370 the first emperor sent a gift of ten musical instruments to the Korean king, including bells and chimes.[21] These new instruments were coarsely made and crude in sound. According to one source, "those who could appreciate it listened only to the [remaining] instruments bestowed by Sung."[22] The small number of instruments may indicate that the Chinese emperor intended them merely as models upon which the Koreans could fashion some new ones.

In 1392, the Yi dynasty supplanted Koryŏ and subsequently held sway until the present century. The change in dynasty necessitated, after the Chinese example, a reform of *a-ak*, which was now thought to be impure and diluted. The first three rulers of Yi, however, were more concerned with consolidation of power and reorganization of governmental institutions than with musical reforms. Their success in setting up a workable administration made it possible for the fourth king, Sejong, to pursue cultural development in political stability. One significant musical event during the reign of King T'aejong, however, was the arrival in Seoul in 1406 of yet another imperial gift of fourteen musical instruments for use in *a-ak*.[23]

Music in general flourished under the patronage of King Sejong. A chief instigator of reform and codification of *a-ak* was the theorist, Pak Yŏn (朴堧 1378-1458).[24] Pak was an intransigent Sinophile, and he based his musical proposals on authoritative Chinese writings ranging from Confucius up to philosophers and theorists of the twelfth century. He pursued the rectification of *a-ak* with a relentless determination that his colleagues occasionally found more irritating than admirable,[25] but his dedication produced a musical legacy whose effects are still felt five centuries after his death.

It is not possible here to give more than a basic outline of the fifteenth-century Korean reform of *a-ak*. The sources are voluminous, and, for example, the extant writings of Pak Yŏn alone would fill several volumes of translation and commentary.[26] A comparison of the Korean reforms with the activities of the early seventeenth-century Florentine camerata may be helpful. Members of the so-called camerata, in attempting to revive the legendary effectiveness of Greek music, created the initial forms of western opera. The Koreans, similarly, sought to restore the effectiveness of the music which caused Confucius to forget his sense of taste. In the process, they created a *new* kind of music which, like western opera, has proved to have remarkable longevity. One suspects that the Korean creation bears as little resemblance to ancient Chinese music as the early seventeenth-century operatic style does to ancient Greek music.

Pak Yŏn's renovation of *a-ak* was in three basic parts. First, he set about determining the correct fundamental pitch and constructed pitch pipes to be used as standards for tuning other instruments.[27] Second, he supervised the construction of hundreds of musical instruments for use in *a-ak* performing ensembles.[28] Finally, he and others revised some notated Chinese ritual melodies, that is, antiqued them, for use by the new ensembles. The following paragraphs describe a few sample details of this mammoth project: Pak's construction of a basic pitch pipe, his source of notated Chinese music, and some aspects of music theory.

A. As already mentioned, the pitch pipe for the fundamental frequency should be determined by using grains of millet as units of measurement: 90 grains for the length, 1,200 for the capacity. Pak made a pitch pipe by this method, sounded it, and discovered something rather unnerving: the pitch he obtained was different from that on the instruments bestowed upon Korea by the Chinese emperor. Who was Pak Yŏn to find fault with a gift from the Son of Heaven? Reconsidering his project, Pak reasoned:

> Taking millet nourished in the East Royal Fields (*Tong chŏkchŏn* 東籍田), I lined up the grains and made a fundamental pitch pipe. When I blew it, the pitch was a half-tone higher than the Chinese fundamental pitch. I fear that because of infertile land and dry weather, the millet had lost its accord. It seems to me that, given a single kind of seed, the rice grown in the southern provinces comes out shiny, moist, plump and big; the grains of the central areas are withered, dry, emaciated, and tin; and those of the northeast region are still more emaciated and thin. Millet is subject to the same reasoning.
>
> I wish to choose millet entirely from the types grown in the south and classify it into three grades. Lining up the grains, I would make pitch pipes and see if there is one that matches the Chinese fundamental pitch. If so, the other eleven pitch pipes could be made by the circle of fifths method, and we could use

these for tuning purposes; also, we could use them to find the standards for capacity, weight, and length. But the fact is that in each period of history they made pitch pipes on the basis of millet and the pitches varied somewhat from age to age. For all we know,the present Chinese pitches may not be the genuine article, and the use of our [own] country's black millet might yield the proper result.

But these pitches, dimensions, and weights are affairs of the Son of Heaven and not something conjured by vassal states according to their own whim. So if the present project does not, in the end, agree with the Chinese pitch, then in the meantime we should follow a temporary expedient, borrowing and using a different kind of millet. We would line it up and make a pitch pipe that agrees with the Chinese pitch. Following the circle of fifths, we would be able to rectify the pitches.[29]

Following this line of reasoning, Pak produced a pitch pipe measured on the basis of artificial beeswax "grains of millet"; it matched the Chinese pitch, and he was then able to make eleven more pipes by the circle of fifths.[30] Pak was successful on two important counts: he made a pitch pipe according to the ancient method and at the same time maintained proper Confucian filiality toward the Chinese emperor. Parenthetically, the fundamental pitch brought from China and carefully maintained in Korea until the present is C.[31]

B. Locating some ancient, or even just comparatively old, Chinese ritual melodies to revise for use in Korean *a-ak* was made difficult by the annoying fact that there was virtually nothing available. As Chŏng In-ji observed, "It is lamentable that ancient music books are so few and that rules of notation were not passed on, letting the music fall in ruin. Genuine ancient music is no longer to be seen."[32] Not to be thwarted, the Koreans simply took the oldest music they could locate: twelve tunes written down by the famous twelfth-century philosopher Chu Hsi (朱熹 1130-1200) and printed in his posthumous *I li ching-chuan t'ung-chieh* (儀禮經傳通解 General

Survey of Ritual) (ca. 1220), and sixteen melodies recorded by one Lin Yü (林宇) in a 1349 work entitled *Ta-sheng yüeh-p'u* (大晟樂譜) [Music of the Ta-sheng Institute].[33] The Koreans "corrected" these tunes according to their interpretation of ancient Chinese music theory, and produced the raw material for *a-ak*. Happily, they also made copies of the two original sources, expressly for the benefit of "future scholars,"[34] and we are therefore able to compare the original and revised versions, deriving clear meanings for a variety of technical terms imprecisely defined in their native China.

The twelve tunes written down by Chu Hsi are well known and have been studied by Laurence Picken and Rulan Pian.[35] The sixteen melodies in Lin Yü's *Ta-sheng yüeh-p'u*, on the other hand, have all but vanished in their native China and are now known only through their survival in Korea. Is this source of 1349 in fact a record, as its title suggests, of music used in the notorious Ta-sheng Institute of the early twelfth century? How appropriate it would be for the Koreans to re-introduce in 1430 some ritual melodies which may have formed part of the original *a-ak* tradition begun as a Chinese bribe over three centuries earlier!

Evidence establishing the origin of Lin Yü's melodies is as yet incomplete. In an article published in 1974, I stated that any connection to the Ta-sheng Institute was "pure conjecture,"[36] but materials subsequently unearthed suggest the relationship might be quite direct. Since no music from the Ta-sheng Institute is otherwise known to exist,[37] these melodies could prove to be very important in the study of Sung dynasty court music. I hope to examine all the evidence in the near future.

C. I would like now to look briefly at several aspects of the music theory used by the Koreans in their "corrections" of source melodies. While these aspects reflect strongly the hierarchical nature of Chinese Confucian music theory, they are Korean interpretations and not necessarily the same as Chinese interpretations.

First of all, the basic scales are pentatonic (five-tone) and heptatonic (seven-tone), and are obtained by a uniform procedure: starting from a basic pitch, the remaining notes in the scale are acquired mechanically through the circle of fifths. The scale degrees thus derived have important extra-musical associations; the five degrees of the pentagonic scale, for example, are related to the five elements (earth, metal, wood, fire, and water), the five dircetions (north, south, east, west, and center), and, significantly, to a hierarchy of ruler, minister, people, affairs, and objects.

Suppose there is a melody which begins and ends on a note associated with minister or people. Then the all-important concluding position is not occupied by the "ruler" note, and the proper hierarchy is violated. From this, the Koreans reasoned that all correct *a-ak* melodies must cadence on the "ruler" note, and they simply discarded those of the Lin Yü and Chu Hsi melodies which did otherwise.

Suppose there is a melody having a wide range. Then it is likely that there will be two "ruler" notes an octave apart. Just as two sovereigns are unacceptable in a single nation, two different "ruler" notes are unacceptable in a single melody. Therefore, no proper melody in *a-ak* can be permitted to have a compass large enough to allow such duplication. In revising the melodies of Lin Yü, the Koreans simply lowered any offending notes into a basic octave and prevented any possibility of hierarchical difficulty.

The Korean process of reforming *a-ak* in the early fifteenth century is remarkable in a number of ways. For example, while music theorists in China had almost been content to discuss theory as theory, without interference from actual music, the Koreans made a workable interpretation of ancient theory and applied it to the revision of actual pieces of music. Both their methods and their practical results are well documented.

But the Koreans' methods may strike the modern western musician as being oddly devoid of musicality, which is something aesthetic and emotional. What does an association of notes with ruler and minister have to do with the *musical* style and effect? One does suspect that some aspects of the theory, such as the limited melodic range, are determined in part by practical matters such as voice and instrument capability, and that the hierarchical associations are post facto philosophical justifications. On the other hand, the theory is not *so* remote that an alert Confucian could not base his aesthetic appreciation of the music upon it.

An essential point is that virtually everything about the Korean re-creation of *a-ak* was based upon the written page. It can hardly be claimed that the music preserves Chinese performance practice and that what is to be heard in Korea today is the same or similar to what was heard in ancient or even twelfth-century China. There is some evidence that Korea studiously *avoided* known Chinese performance practices: in 1430, for example, a Korean musician sent to China by King Sejong reported back that Chinese musical performances were faulty in a number of ways, and Sejong was convinced that Chinese practices were questionable.[38]

It should be noted that the instruments manufactured by the Koreans for use in *a-ak* performing ensembles *were* in fact modelled upon exemplars from China, so that the instruments themselves demonstrably continued a Chinese tradition of construction (which remains unbroken in Korea to this day). But music performed upon the piano is not Italian just because an Italian invented the instrument, and Korean *a-ak* is not Chinese, just because it is played on instruments of Chinese heritage.

Korean *a-ak*, in short, is no more Chinese than seventeenth-century opera is Greek or all piano music is Italian. I fear this view will not be welcomed by those who consider Korea a cultural dependency of China and who like to think that it is authentic Chinese *ya-yüeh* which now survives in Korea.

Observations and Conclusions

The Korean *a-ak* tradition began in the early twelfth century as the by-product of an unsuccessful political bribe from the Chinese emperor to the Korean king. At its inception, *a-ak* was simply Chinese ritual music performed on Chinese musical instruments on Korean soil. The music came from the Ta-sheng Institute, that is, from an exceptional and colorful period in Chinese musical history, and it can hardly be considered either ancient or a main-stream development.

Almost as soon as they began to play *a-ak*, Koreans started to modify it. After three centuries, King Sejong and Pak Yŏn attempted to rectify the accumulated errors in *a-ak* by constructing newly-researched instruments and giving them a new body of music to play. Apart from the skeletal melodies, the musical style of *a-ak* has been entirely Korean ever since.

The Chinese origin of *a-ak*, in other words, is musically quite remote. It cannot be maintained that the style is Chinese or even that the style predates the fifteenth century. This means that *a-ak*, by East Asian standards, is fairly recent. Some Japanese *gagaku*, for example, derives from pieces transmitted orally to Japan from T'ang China; it comes from China musically as well as spiritually. In any event, pretensions to Chinese heritage in no way magnify the worth of *a-ak*. Rather, the power of the *a-ak* tradition is amply proven by its survival for over five centuries which included some of Korea's most trying moments.

This argumet that *a-ak* is almost totally Korean in musical style is based on the evidence of written sources and extant performed music, examined in accordance with modern western methods. It is, however, undeniably true that Koreans have for centuries considered *a-ak* to be Chinese in origin, style, and spirit, and this view has been the operative one in terms of *a-ak*'s role in Korean culture. The music might as well be Chinese, since that is how it has been treated since the fifteenth century.

Even King Sejong, who knew perfectly well that the *a-ak* codified during his reign was essentially a Korean creation, had a lingering suspicion of *a-ak* as being foreign. In 1430, for example, he observed:

> A-*ak* is fundamentally not Korean music. It is, in fact, Chinese music and what Chinese people ordinarily hear, so it is appropriate for performance in [their] sacrificial rites. When the people of our nation are alive, they listen to Korean music (*hyangak* 鄉樂), but after they die, [Chinese] *a-ak* is performed [in sacrificial rites]. What is the explanation?[39]

The feeling that *a-ak* was Chinese persisted, and King Sejo observed his father's sentiments by replacing the *a-ak* performed at the Royal Ancestral Shrines (*Chongmyo* 宗廟) with native music (*hyangak*), while keeping *a-ak* in the other sacrificial rites, which mostly served the spirits of Chinese.

Since the Koreans have felt that this native creation remained somehow irrevocably foreign, they have given it special, untouchable status since the fifteenth century. While they have not hesitated to modify and alter music considered to be native, they have been reluctant to tamper with the "imported" *a-ak*. The Korean piece *Yŏmillak* (與民樂), for example, is known in notated versions from the fifteenth century to the present and is still performed. The fifteenth-century version could have only lasted a few minutes, but after centuries of slowing down, accretion of extra decorative notes, and further slowing down, the piece now runs over an hour and twenty minutes. It is only through detailed analyses of several notated scores that any connection between the present version and the fifteenth-century original may be demonstrated.[40]

Present-day *a-ak*, on the other hand, is note-for-note the same as in fifteenth-century scores. There is no evidence of musical tampering of the sort encountered in *Yŏmillak*, and this tells us that the performance of *a-ak* has been highly conservative since its codification under King Sejong. Modern performances of *a-ak* are probably closer to fifteenth-century style than are performances of pieces of "native" court music like *Yŏmillak.*

In conclusion, *a-ak* is almost purely Korean in musical style, but it has been accorded Chinese status and preserved conservatively for over five centuries. The grandeur of the music and the strength of the tradition far outweigh any musical loss of face that might result from scholarly conclusions about *a-ak*'s native origins. *A-ak* is uniquely and admirably Korean, and for that reason a heritage to be treasured all the more.

NOTES

1. For a description of *a-ak* in this modern rite, see my article, "The Sacrifice to Confucius in Korea and Its Music," *Transactions of the Korea Branch of the Royal Asiatic Society,* 50 (1975), 43–69.
2. As in the general description of Korean court music by Sŏng Kyŏng-nin (成慶麟), *Chosŏn ŭi a-ak* (朝鮮의 雅樂, The *A-ak* of Korea) (Seoul: Pangmun ch'ulp'ansa 博文出版社, 1947).
3. *Lun yü* (論語, Analects), Ch. 7, p. 46a (*Ssu-pu pei-yao* ed.); translation from Arthur Waley, *The Analects of Confucius* (New York: Vintage Books, 1938), p. 125.
4. *Lun yü*, Ch. 17, p. 114b.
5. *Lun yü*, Ch. 8, p. 53b.
6. Translation from Wing-tsit Chan, trans., *Reflections on Things at Hand: The Neo-Confucian Anthology Compiled by Chu Hsi and Lü Tsu-ch'ien,* Records of Civilization Sources and Studies, 75 (New York: Columbia Univ. Press, 1967), pp. 218–219.
7. See, for example, *Survey of Korean Arts: Traditional Music* (Seoul: National Academy of Arts, 1973), p. 142.
8. Chŏng In-ji (鄭麟趾 1396–1478) et al., comps., *Koryŏ-sa* (高麗史, History of the Koryŏ Dynasty), 139 chapters (1451), 13.33b (1114/6). A detailed list of instruments is given in *Koryo-sa* 70.28a–29b.
9. *Koryŏ-sa* 14.15b (1116/6). Instruments listed in 70.5b–9b.
10. *Koryŏ-sa* 70.5ab. Translation from K. L. Pratt, "Music as a Factor in Sung-Koryŏ Diplomatic Relations," *T'oung Pao,* 62, No. 4–5 (1976), 209.

11. See K. L. Pratt, "Music as a Factor," and also his "Some Aspects of Diplomatic and Cultural Exchange Between Korea and Northern Sung China," in *Chang Sa-hun paksa hoegap kinyŏm tongyang ŭmakhak nonch'ong* (張師勛博士回甲記念東洋音樂學論叢, Articles on Asian Music: Festschrift for Dr. Chang Sa-hun) (Seoul: Han'guk kugak hakhoe 韓國國樂學會, 1977), pp. 313-323.

12. For more information on this period of Korean history, see Michael C. Rogers, "The Regularization of Koryŏ-Chin Relations (1116-1131)," *Central Asiatic Journal*, 6, No. 1 (1961), 51-84.

13. On this, see Ling Ching-yen (凌景埏), "Sung Wei Han-chin yüeh yü Ta-sheng-fu" (宋魏漢津樂與大晟府, The Music of Wei Han-chin and the Ta-sheng Institute of the Sung Dynasty), *Yenching Journal of Chinese Studies*, 28 (Dec., 1940), 105-132.

14. R. H. van Gulik, *The Lore of the Chinese Lute: An Essay in the Ideology of the Ch'in*, rev. ed., Monumenta Nipponica Monograph (Tokyo: Sophia Univ. Press, 1969), p. 4.

15. *Koryŏ-sa* 70.6a and 7b-8a.

16. See, for example, Pan Ku (班固 A.D. 32-92), comp. *Han shu* (漢書 History of the Former Han Dynasty), 120 chapters, 21.9b and 11a (Pona ed.).

17. Ling "Wei Han-chin," 105-108.

18. The modifications are examined in Yi Hye-gu (Lee Hye-ku 李惠求), "Koryŏ Taesŏng'ak ŭi p'yŏnch'ŏn" (高麗大晟樂의 變遷, Transformation of *Taesŏng'ak* during the Koryŏ Dynasty), in his *Han'guk ŭmak sŏsŏl* (韓國音樂序說, Topics in Korean Music), Sŏul taehakkyo haksul ch'ongsŏ (서울大學校學術叢書) 9, (Seoul: Seoul National Univ. Press, 1967), pp. 139-150.

19. As described, for example, in *Sejong Changhŏn taewang sillok* (世宗莊憲大王實錄, Annals of King Sejong), 163 chapters (1454) (printing of 1603-1606), 26.25b (1424/11) (hereafter *Sejong*).

20. *Sejong* 59.1a (1433/1).

21. *Koryŏ-sa* 42.9b (1370/5) and 70.15ab.

22. *Sejong* 59.1a (1433/1).

23. *T'aejong kongjŏng taewang sillok* (太宗恭定大王實錄, Annals of King T'aejong), 36 chapters (1431) (printing of 1603-1606), 12.10ab (1406/int 7).

24. A biographical sketch and an incomplete collection of Pak's writings appear in his posthumously collected works, *Nan'gye yugo* (蘭溪遺藁 Literary Remains of Pak Yŏn), 1 vol. (1882). The remainder of Pak's writings are scattered in the early Yi dynasty *Annals*. A modern study of Pak's historical importance is Yi Hye-gu, "Pak Yŏn i huse e chun ŭmak yusan" (朴堧이 後世에 준 音樂 遺産, Musical Accomplishments

of Pak Yŏn), in his *Han'guk ŭmak sŏsŏl,* pp. 169–180.

25. See, for example, the objections to Pak's work reported in *Sejong* 59.1b (1433/1).
26. An ongoing project of the present author.
27. Various passages in the *Annals* which deal with Pak's pitch pipes are examined in Yi Hye-gu, "Pak Yŏn ŭi yulgwan chejak ŭi yŏndae" (朴堧의 律管制作의 年代, Chronology of Pak Yŏn's Pitch Pipes), in his *Han'guk ŭmak nonch'ong* (韓國音樂論叢, Essays on Korean Music) (Seoul: Sumundang 秀文堂, 1976), pp. 289–301; English trans. by R. C. Provine, ibid., pp. 387–402.
28. Most of the essays in Pak's collected writings (note 24) are devoted to studies of instrument construction.
29. *Sejong* 47.17b (1430/2).
30. *Sejong* 59.1b (1433/1).
31. The history of musical pitch in the Yi dynasty is examined in Pak Hung-su (朴興秀), "Yijo ch'ŏkto e kwanhan yŏn'gu" (李朝尺度에 관한 研究, Studies on Yi Dynasty Standards of Measurement), in his *kugak ŭi iron chŏgin yŏn'gu nonmunjip* (國樂의 理論的인 研究 論文集, Collection of Articles on Korean Music Theory) (Seoul: Sŏnggyun'gwan Univ. Press, n.d. 1970?) pp. 55–84.
32. *Sejong* 50.37b (1430/int. 12).
33. Date from *Sejong* 57.24a (1432/8).
34. *Sejong* 131.6b and 137.22a–27b.
35. Laurence Picken, "Twelve Ritual Melodies of the T'ang Dynasty," in *Studia Memoriae Belae Bartók Sacra* (Budapest: Aedes Academiae Scientiarum Hungaricae, 1956), pp. 147–173; Rulan C. Pian, *Sung Dynasty Musical Sources and Their Interpretation,* Harvard-Yenching Institute Monograph Series, 16 (Cambridge: Harvard Univ. press, 1967), pp. 9–10 and 154–173.
36. "The Treatise on Ceremonial Music (1430) in the Annals of the Korean King Sejong," *Ethnomusicology,* XVIII (1974), 11.
37. Pian, *Sources,* p. 6.
38. *Sejong* 49.32a (1430/9).
39. *Sejong* 49.31b-32a (1430/9).
40. On *Yŏmillak,* see Jonathan Condit, "The Evolution of *Yŏmillak* from the Fifteenth Century to the Present Day," in *Chang Sa-hun paksa hoegap kinyŏm tongyang ŭmakhak nonch'ong,* pp. 231–262.

Education in Classical Korean Music, Past and Present

CHANG SA-HUN

The Educational and supervisory organizations of traditional music have existed over 1,000 years from the Three Kingdoms period to the present. This paper attempts to examine the functions of these organizations and pedagogy of music in comparison with present institutions.

Organizations and Educational System of the Past

The supervisory organizations and educational systems devoted to classical music can be chronologically summed up as follows: the Three Kingdoms, Koryŏ dynasty, and the Chosŏn dynasty.

1. Three Kingdoms period

The classical music of the Koguryŏ, Paekche and Silla kingdoms shared a common feature, but the music of each kingdom retained its own character.

A scene of a processional music performance can be seen in the mural of the tumulus in Anak dating from the mid-fourth century. Another remarkable fact is that Korean musicians and dancers participated in concerts in Sui during the end of the sixth century and the beginning of the seventh century.

In the mid-fifth century, meanwhile, Paekche dispatched a group of four musicians to Japan for music education. These musicians requested the Paekche government to replace them with a new group.[1] In the beginning of the seventh century, Mimaji from Paekche was naturalized in Japan and taught *gigaku* (masked mime)[2] there.[3]

These facts suggest that there existed some organizations governing music, though no records are available to confirm this assumption.

In the middle of the seventh century there existed *Ŭmsŏng-sŏ*[4] (Institute of Music) in the court, which administered musical events, the various ceremonies, rituals and banquets.

The name of the Music Institute was changed to *T'aeakkam* (Board of Great Music) during the reign of King Kyŏngdŏk (742-765). However, the original name was restored during the reign of King Hyegong (765-780).[5]

In 552, King Chinhŭng of Silla sent three musicians to Urŭk, a *kayagŭm* maestro.

The three Silla musicians learned 12 numbers from Urŭk. Of the 12 numbers, five were adopted as *T'aeak* (an official court music répertoire) of Silla.

2. Koryŏ Period

In the Koryŏ period, there were offices in charge of music such as *Chŏnaksŏ*, *T'aeaksŏ*, *Kwanhyŏnbang*, and *Aaksŏ*. *Chŏnaksŏ* was responsible for education and supervision, *Aaksŏ* for Royal Ancestors' shrine music. All these organizations are believed to have had both educational and supervisory functions. According to the historical account, the court music teachers were comprised of: one dancer-vocalist, two lute and drum players, two flutists, one lute player, one harpist, one bamboo instrumentalist, and one dancer.[6]

No further records on the development of music education are available. But there is little doubt music education was conducted by a certain specialized organization in the Koryŏ court.

3. Chosŏn Period

Two musical institutes, *Aaksŏ* and *Chŏnaksŏ*,[7] were established at the time of the reformation of the ranking system of civilian and military officials in 1392. Subsequent changes were made in the field of musical administration toward the end of the Chosŏn period. But such official organizations have continued to exist in the form of *Changakwŏn* (Bureau of Court Music).

The *Aaksŏ* and *Chŏnaksŏ* inherited the system of musical education that existed at the end of the Koryŏ period.

During the reign of King T'aejo, musical organizations belonged to the Ministry of Protocol and Education together with such fields as Confucian studies and medical science. The musical organizations under the Ministry of Protocol and Education included *Pongsangsi, Aaksŏ, Chŏnaksŏ, Kwansŭptogam* and *Akhak-togam*.[8]

(1) *Pongsangsi*

This organization was devoted to musical affairs related to ceremonies held at Chongmyo, the Royal Ancestral Shrine.[9]

Members of the *Pongsangsi* were classified into *Chaerang* and *Mugong. Chaerang* was further classified into *Chwabang* (Left chamber) and *Ubang* (Right chamber).

Members of *Chwabang* performed ritual chants of the Terrace; while those of *Ubang* performed ritual dance; members of *Mugong* performed Military dance at the court rituals.

Chaerang comprised 300 members and *Mugong* was made up of 150 members.[10] *Chaerang* members were selected among young boys of the Ministry of Protocol and Education and *Mugong* members were selected among young boys of the Ministry of War.[11]

(2) *Aakso*

Aakso was founded in the first year of King T'aejo for the performance of ritual music. Members of the *Pongsangsi* performed ritual chants or dance to the accompaniment of music performed by musicians of the *Aakso*.

(3) *Chonakso*

This organization was also founded in the first year of King T'aejo. It provided royal banquets musics.[12]

According to records[13] dating from the times of King Munjong and King Sejong, the musicians of this organization were employed on a wide range of occasions, such as ritual services at the Munso-jon and Hwidok-jon, royal procession, and entertainment music concerts, acrobatics, and the Civilian and Military dance.[14]

The number of musicians of this group was increased from 230 to 300 in 1438.[15]

(4) *Akhak-togam*

This organization governed music which was one of ten kinds of discipline.[16] The main function of this organization was to select and train promising talents as members of the *Pongsangsi*, *Aakso*, and *Chonakso* and to train *Chaerang* and *Mugong* of the *Pongsangsi* and musicians of *Aakso*.

(5) *Kwansup-togam*

The function of this organization was mainly to train musicians in the field of the court entertainment music, blind musicians employed on the occasions of royal banquets and female singers and dancers. Most of the musicians, dancers, and singers were trained in this organization except the musicians of the *Aakso*. Members of this organization were well trained to the extent that King Sejong once stated:

"The performers of the *Pongsangsi* are inferior to those of the *Kwansup-togam*. They have to be trained by those of the

Kwansŭp-togam.[17]

As I have already mentioned, members of the *Pongsangsi* and *Aaksŏ* specialized in Chinese court music and related singing and dancing. The *Akhak-togam* was in charge of selecting talents, whereas the *Pongsangsi* and *Aaksŏ* provided training in music, singing and dancing. The *Kwansŭp-togam* trained artists with emphasis on Korean tradition. As a result, the mainstream of traditional Korean music was inherited by members of the *Kwansŭp-togam.*

After the reign of King Sejo, music was governed by the *Changakwŏn* (Bureau Board of Musical Affairs). This organization had also Left and Right chambers, the functions of which were different from those mandated since Koryŏ dynasty. This system of musical activities continued to the end of the Chosŏn period. After the Reform of 1894 the organization was replaced by similar organizations of different names, such as *Kyobangsa, Changakkwa, Aaktae,* and *Aakbu.*

4. System of Music Education

Though no detailed records are available, a music education system is believed to have existed during the Three Kingdoms and Koryŏ periods. But here this subject is confined to the Chosŏn period.

(1) *Selection of aksaeng and akkong*

Aksaeng is a musician specializing in Chinese-style court music (*Aak*) and *akkong* is a musician specializing in Chinese-style folk music and traditional Korean music.

The répertoire and the musical instruments in selecting these musicians varied according to each period.

1) The musical instruments used in selecting musicians

According to the records covering March of the 12th year of the reign of King Sejong, the musical instruments used in selecting these musicians in the fields of Chinese-style court music, Chinese-style folk music and traditional Korean music were:

Some 33 different musical instruments were used in the field of court music. They included zithers, bells and instruments made of metal, stone, bamboo, wood, and leather.

Some 15 instruments were used in the field of Chinese music. They included lute, zither, flute, pipe, chime, and drum.

Some eight instruments were used in the field of traditional Korean music. They included *hyŏn'gŭm* (a six-stringed zither), *kayagŭm* (a 12-stringed zither), hour-glass-shaped drum, lute, and fiddle.

2) The répertoire used in selecting musicians

According to *Kyŏngguk Taejŏn* published in 1471, the examinees were asked to perform the following numbers:

Candidates for *aksaeng* were to perform three court music numbers, a song and a civilian and military ritual dance.

Candidates for *akkong* specializing in Chinese-style folk music were to perform *Samjinjakbo*, *Yŏminnaklyŏng*, *Yŏminnakman*, *Nakyangch'un* and *Oun'gaedanjo* and other numbers.

Among the numbers to be performed by those who wanted to specialize in traditional Korean music were *Samjinjakbo* *Yŏminnaklyŏng*, *Yŏminnakman*, *Chinjak*, and *Sagi*.

Thus *aksaeng* trainees were required to perform only 3 numbers, in addition to singing and dancing. But the requirements for those who wanted to specialize in Chinese-style folk music were 41 numbers and the requirements for those who wanted to specialize in traditional Korean music were 31 numbers. This indicates that those who specialized Chinese-style folk music and traditional Korean music received more elaborate artistic training than those who specialized in court music. But *aksaeng* were higher than *akkong* in social standing. While the latter were from the low class, the former were from the commoner.

3) Musical instruments and répertoire for *Chwabang* and *Ubang* during the end of Han empire

According to the classical records entitled *Chŭngbomunhŏn-bigo* the requirements for musicians in the categories of *Chwabang* and *Ubang* were as follows.[18]

a. *Chwabang*

The musical instruments required to perform included zithers, metal and wooden instruments.

Fifteen numbers including *Hawangjonggung* were required to perform.

Additional requirements were 41 ritual chants.

b. *Ubang*

Trainees in Chinese-style folk music:

The required musical instruments included chime, flute, and Chinese fiddle.

The numbers required included *Pot'aep'yŏng, Chŏngdaeŏp, Pohŏja, Yŏminnakman, Yŏminnaklyŏng* etc.

The additional musical instruments required included Korean style *pip'a, hun, tang,* etc.

Trainees in traditional Korean music:

Such instruments as *taegŭm, kŏmun'go, kayagŭm* and *changgo* were required to perform.

The required numbers were *Pot'aep'yŏng, Chŏngdaeŏp, Chŏngdongbanggok, Pohŏja, Yŏminnakman, Yŏminnaklyŏng, Akchang, Chŏngŭp, Mihulak,* etc.

The additional requirements were *p'yŏn'gyŏng, p'yŏngjong,* Korean fiddle, and singing and dancing.

The musicians also provided musical accompaniments to the performance of such dances as *ch'omu* and *ch'ŏyong-mu* on the occasions of banquets. The music for the inner banquets was provided by blind musicians.

(2) *Education of Female Musicians and Female Physicians*

Originally, training of female musicians was associated with training of female doctors who were needed in the treatment of female patients.

The education of female physicians began in 1406 at the suggestion of officials of *Chesaengwŏn* (Office of Medical

Affairs). Female physicians belonged to the *Naeŭiwŏn* or *Hyeminsŏ*.

While these female physicians practised diagnosis and acupuncture, the needlewomen of the *Sangŭiwŏn* (Office of Dresses) made dresses for the royal household. But all these women were also trained in singing and dancing as well.

After medical education at the *Chesaengwŏn*, the female doctors were sent home to serve in their home towns.[19] Candidates for female doctors were first trained in Chinese classics in their home towns. They were further educated at the *Chesaengwŏn* before taking lessons in medicine.[20]

Sejong Sillok (Records of the Period of King Sejong) states: "Performing arts require elaborate training. But singers and dancers of the *Kwansŭp-togam* were of an extremely poor class."

For this reason, the training of these female singers and dancers was conducted between February and April and between August and October.[21]

They were trained in such musical instruments as *kŏmun'go*, *kayagŭm*, *changgo*, and *ajaeng*. They were also trained in singing and playing the lute. Those who were slow in learning were punished by *Chejo*(music director) or expelled from the organization. Negligent teachers were also punished and those who had no talent were sent home.[22] The female students were trained by leading musicians of the *Changakwŏn*.[27]

The female musicians were trained by a designated specialist and after training in singing and dancing they served for royal entertainments on various occasions.

The musicians of the *Naeŭiwŏn* were called *yakbang gisaeng*, while the musicians of the *Sangŭiwŏn* were called *sangbang gisaeng*. These *gisaeng* continued to serve together with the *gisaeng* of *Hyeminsŏ* and *Kongjo* (Department of Construction and Engineering) till the end of the Han Empire.

These *gisaeng* institutes were merged by Sin T'ae-hyu, who was *Kyŏngmusa* (director of the police department), into the *Sanghwasil* in Kwangmu period. For the welfare of *gisaeng*,

Cho Chung-ung organized the Sinch'ang Union, and Song Pyŏng-jun founded the Kwanggyo Union.[23]

(3) *Blind Musicians*

Blind musicians were trained to perform orchestral music and to provide musical accompaniment to singers and dancers for the inner banquets.

They were needed during royal parties because ordinary musicians were not allowed to be present and because *gisaeng* were unable to provide musical accompaniment.[24]

But the blind musicians were temporarily used until *gisaeng* became proficient enough to provide musical accompaniment. Records of the Sejong period state:

"Now *gisaeng* are able to perform both Chinese and Korean music. Blind musicians are no longer needed, but they are still in the official list. They must be discharged from the court."

Records state that King Sejong accepted this recommendation.[25]

But it was still difficult for women to perform such difficult instrument as flute to provide accompaniment to dancers. After all, blind musicians were still employed to perform instruments that *gisaeng* chiefly played string and percussion instruments, blind musicians played wind instruments.

Education in Classical Korean Music from the End of Han Empire to 1945

According to Kim Yŏng-jae (1883-1954), Ham Hwa-jin (1883-1948) and Ch'oe Sun-yŏng among the leaders of the *Changakwŏn* in the 1930s, there existed, toward the end of the Han Empire, two musical organizations—*Aksach'ŏng* and *Chŏnakch'ŏng*. The *Chŏnakch'ŏng* was made up of four categories of different standards called *Adongbang*, *Changnaebang*, *Sŏngjaebang*, and *Ch'amsangbang*, and *Osangbang*, which was devoted to teaching the classical Korean dance called *Ch'ŏyong-mu.*[26]

While *Aksach'ŏng* was largely an administrative organization, the *Chŏnakch'ŏng* was devoted to teaching music.

Adongbang (children's class) gave music lessons to children of 12 to 13 years of age. When they became 16 to 17 years old they took lessons in the *Changnaebang* (future class). Then they were admitted to the *Sŏngjaebang* (adult class), then to the *Ch'amsangbang* (advanced class).

Lessons were given in two forms — *Changp'ae* and *Soyŏpbang*. The *Changp'ae* lessons were given by the *Changakwŏn* for six months from March 3 to September 9. The *Soyŏpbang* lessons were given during night hours in wintertime, from November 1 to December 14. The *Soyŏpbang* lessons were given either at the *Changakwŏn* or the teacher's house (private lessons).[27]

In 1911, the *Changakwŏn* degenerated into *Aaktae* (court music band). The director and members of the band had the lowest official status, *kowŏn* and *yongwŏn*, respectively. Furthermore, 81 members of the band were fired in 1911, 84 in 1915, 48 in 1917 and finally reduced to 57.

Thus it became a critical problem to preserve the traditional Korean music. For this reason the Royal Yi Household founded the Court Music Training Institute in 1919. Nine students received training in the first year. And the musicians were promoted to higher official ranks in 1921.

In 1926, the institute provided the students with the general curricula of middle school as well as major courses in traditional music. It was mainly aimed at preserving traditional music rather than at further development. This tradition has been handed down to the present.

Education in Traditional Music after 1945

New developments in traditional Korean music were

premature immediately after the 1945 Liberation of Korea from Japan. Little development was made until 1954 due to the Korean War. Education in classical music was gradually resumed from 1945 onward.

1. The National Classical Music Institute as Successor of *Changakwŏn*

After 1945, the Yi Household discontinued to provide the *Aakbu* with financial assistance. On December 17, 1948, the National Assembly passed a bill to place the *Aakbu* under government control. The National Classical Music Institute was founded in April, 1951.

2. Education in Classical Music

While the National Classical Music Institute is aimed at preserving the original forms of traditional Korean music, classic music education at various levels of schools is aimed at promoting theory and new national music.

(1) *Education at High School Level*

 1) The National Classical Music High School
This school was reorganized from the former Classical Music Training Institute (1955) affiliated with the National Classical Music Institute.
 Inauguration: 1972
 Status: Three-year High School
 Annual Admittance: 120 students
 Major Subjects: *kŏmun'go* (a six-stringed Korean zither), *kayagŭm* (a 12-stringed Korean zither), flute, Korean harps, and songs
 2) The Classical Music School (Private)
 Inauguration: 1960
 Status: Three-year Middle School and Three-year High School

Admission: 180 students
Major Subjects: *kŏmun'go, kayagŭm*, flute, harps, *p'ansori*
(narrative songs), and folk songs
  3) Yerim High School (Private)
Inauguration: 1973
Status: Three-year High School
Admission: 50
Major Subjects: *kŏmun'go, kayagŭm*, flute, harps, *p'ansori*

(2) *Education at College Level*

Tŏksŏng Women's College established a Department of
Classical Music in 1954 and admitted 30 students majoring in
such subjects as *kŏmun'go, kayagŭm*, and flute, but this
department was closed in 1956. Sŏrabŏl Arts College also
opened a Department of Classical Music in 1964, but this
department was closed after two years.
  1) The Department of Classical Music at the College of
Music, Seoul National University
Inauguration: 1959
Status: Four-year College
Admission: 25
Major Subjects: *kŏmun'go, kayagŭm*, flute, harps, theory
and composition
Graduate School: Established in 1963
  2) The Department of Classical Music at the College of
Music, Hanyang University
Inauguration: 1972
Status: Four-year College
Admission: 30
Major Subjects: *kŏmun'go, kaya'gŭm*, flute, harps, theories
and composition
  3) The Classical Music Department at the College of
Music, Ewha Womans University
Inauguration: 1974
Status: Four-year College
Admission: 30

Major Subjects: *kŏmun'go, kayagŭm*, flute, harps, and
   fiddle
4) The Department of Classical Music at Ch'ugye Arts
Institute
   Inauguration: 1974
   Status: Four-year College
   Admission: 40
   Major Subjects: *kŏmun'go, kayagŭm*, flute, harps, com-
      position and *p'ansori*

3. Education in Ordinary Middle and High Schools

Since 1979 five textbooks have been authorized for
education in classical music at high school level. The curricula
have been increased from the previous 30 percent to 50 percent, and this reflects the importance of education in classical
music based on national identity.

But in general, the teachers have not been fully qualified.
To improve the qualifications of teachers, the government has
provided the teachers with a retraining program each-year.

Meanwhile, many schools are becoming active in teaching
classical Korean music as a compulsory or secondary subject.

Among the schools that teach classical music as a regular
subject are Chungang Girls High School, Kŭmnan Girls High
School, Hongik Girls High School, Kimch'ŏn Agricultural
High School, and Kup'o Girls Commercial High School.
Among the schools that each the subject as an extracurriculum
subject are Chinmyŏng Girls High School, Tongdŏk Girls
High School, Anyang Girls Middle School, Sillim Girls Middle
School, and Yŏngdŭngp'o Girls High School. And among the
schools that have a classical music orchestra are Chungang
Girls High School, Kup'o Girls Commercial High School, and
Tongsan Primary School, Kwangju.

Among the universities that have students majoring in
classical music are Kyemyŏng College, Teachers' College of
Chŏnnam University and Ch'ŏngju Teachers' College.

4. The Korean Classical Music Education Association

The Korean Classical Music Education Association was founded in 1975 with the aim to promote the development of education in classical music and to promote the interest of music teachers of primary, middle and high schools across the country.

The association, with its headquarters in Seoul, has branches in provincial cities. It annually publishes a journal entitled *Education in Classical Music* and sponsors a classical music contest for primary, middle and high school students each year.

As we have already observed, traditional Korean music has been supervised and promoted by national organizations for nearly 1,000 years. Schools of various levels across the country have come to emphasize the importance of education in classical music ingenuous to Korea.

The statistics resulting from a survey based on written queries addressed to a total of 1,500 primary, middle and high schools revealed:

1. Education in classical music is necessary by all means.

2. Over 70 percent of students who have received lessons in classical music showed interest in the subject.

3. Forty five percent said that teachers specializing in classical music are needed.

4. The survey favored an increase of classical music lessons in the teachers' retraining programs.

5. The survey favored more elaborate explanations about classical music in textbooks.

6. The survey favored the necessity of materials on classical music and support of school principles in this regard.

NOTES

1. *Nihon Shoki,* Vol. 50, Chapter of February, 15th year of Kinmei Tenno (Emperor Kinmei) of Japan.
2. Korean Masked Dance Play, the prototypes of *Yangju Sandae* Masked Dance Play and *Pongsan* Masked Dance Play.
3. *Nihon Shoki,* Vol. 54. The fifth year of Suiko Tenno.
4. Established in the fifth year of the reign of King Chinhŭng (555) and renamed *T'aeakkam* during the reign of King Kyŏngdŏk (742–765). It was renamed *Ŭmsŏng-sŏ.*
5. *Samguk sagi,* Vol. 38.
6. *Koryōsa,* Vol. 80, Sikhwa-ji.
7. *T'aejo sillok,* Vol. 1, July, 1st year.
8. *T'aejo sillok,* Vol. 9, March, 5th year.
9. *T'aejo sillok,* Vol. 1, July, 1st year.
10. *Sejong sillok,* Vol. 53, September, 13th year.
11. *Sejong sillok,* Vol. 47, February, 12th year.
12. *Ibid.,* Vol. 47, February, 12th year.
13. *Munjong sillok,* Vol. 4.
14. *Sejong sillok,* Vol. 120.
15. *Ibid.*
16. *T'aejong sillok,* Vol. 12, November, 6th year.
17. *Sejong sillok,* Vol. 46, September, 12th year.
18. *Chŭngbomunhŏnbigo,* Vol. 106. Music Chapter 16.
19. *Sejong sillok,* Vol. 22, December, 5th year.
20. *Ibid.*
21. *Ibid.,* Vol. 10, September, 25th year.
22. *Ibid.*
23. "*Yŏmyŏng-ŭi tongsŏ ŭmak* (The Dawn of Music) by Chang Sa-hun, pp. 11–40, Pojinjae, 1974.
24. *Sejong sillok,* Vol. 116, April, 29th year.
25. *Ibid.*
26. The terms *ch'ŏng* and *pang* in musical organizations denote group or class.
27. *Kukak kaeyo* by Chang Sa-hun, pp. 283–284, Chŏngyŏn-sa, 1961.

Performing Style of
Korean Traditional Music

YI PO-HYŎNG

Today most traditional music of Korea is performed indoors, such as in music halls and theaters. But up to the end of the Chosŏn dynasty most forms of traditional Korean music had been performed as accompaniment to rites, banquets and farm work, and accordingly the motivation, place and style of performance had been different from those today. Even when the music was strictly for the enjoyment of players and listeners, it was performed in a village square or in a room.

In this paper, I will discuss why, when, where and how traditional Korean music was performed, and by whom. To do this for every piece of music would be a tremendous task. So my discussion here will be limited to the music performed in the court and the magisterial office, the music performed in the royal shrine, the music performed in the Buddhist temple, the music performed in shamanist exorcisms, the music performed in the room, the music performed for enjoyment in the village square or the front yard of a big house and the music performed during work.

Music in Court and in the Magisterial Office

Court ceremonies and rites were usually accompanied by various pieces of ritual music and court dance. On the occasion of the morning court meeting with the king, the royal reception of a foreign emissary, the birth of a prince, the investiture of the crown prince and the birthdays of the king and the queen, the court band consisting of percussion, string and wind instruments performed pieces of court music such as *Sujech'ŏn*, *Pohŏja*, *Yŏminhŭng* and *Yŏngsanhoesang*, while court dancers did various dances to the accompaniment of these tunes. The music was usually slow, solemn and peaceful, and the dances were also slow, elegant and graceful.

The royal procession was usually with the court band playing such march tunes as *Yŏminak* and *Nakch'unch'un*. The march of soldiers was also accompanied by music. The military parade was generally with two bands; one consisting of big percussion and wind instruments, such as bugle, trumpet, cymbal and drum, in front of the columns and the other consisting of small instruments such as the fife and drum in the back of the columns. The most popular pieces for a march were *Kilkunak* and *Kilt'aryŏng*.

The music performed in the magisterial office were usually exorcist and Buddhist tunes called *Kutkŏri* and *Yŏmbult'aryŏng*, and these pieces were played with wind and percussion instruments in the office's front yard. As in the case of the court, these tunes were also accompanied by dances. In addition, the magistrate's procession was accompanied by a band playing march tunes.

Music in the Royal Shrine

The tunes of royal shrine music remaining today are *Munmyojeryeak* and *Chongmyojeryeak*. There also were tunes, though not appeared today, for the rite to pray for national prosperity, the rite to pray for a bumper crop and the rite to pray for a big sericultural production increase.

The *Munmyojeryeak* is performed in the rite to commemorate such Chinese Confucian great men as

Confucius and Mencius, as well as Korean Confucian great men, such as Sŏl Ch'ong and Ch'oe Ch'i-wŏn. The music of this rite, originated from China, was performed by court musicians, and was accompanied by dances in the shrine yard. The piece welcoming the deceased souls of Confucian great men, called *Ŭianjiak*, was performed with instruments originated in the ancient Chinese court, and dancers, holding a short pipe instrument in the left hand and a pheasant's feather in the right hand, did a dance called *Munmu* to the accompaniment of this tune. This music was followed by another one called *Myŏnganjiak* and a dance. Then *Sŏnganjiak* highlighted the rite with a sort of martial dance in which the dancer held an ax in the left hand and a shield in the right hand. The rite is then concluded with *Ŭianjiak*, the same tune as the starting music of the rite.

Chongmyojeryeak was the music for the rite to commemorate the deceased kings of the Chosŏn dynasty. This music was also accompanied by dances. Originally China-originated music was used for this rite, but in the middle of the 15th century the music was changed to pure Korean tunes such as *Pot'aepyŏng* and *Chŏngdaeŏp*. As in the case of the Confucian rite, a court band consisting of percussion, string and wind instruments performed *Hŭimun* of *Pot'aepyŏng* in the lower side of the shrine yard, and dancers did the same dance as the starting dance of the Confucian rite, using a short pipe instrument and a pheasant's feather. With the performance of *Hŭimun* in the upper side of the yard a singer sang to signal the start of the dance. This *Hŭimun* tune was followed by *Chonp'ye-Hŭimun* and a dance suitable to this tune. Then nine tunes of *Pot'aepyŏng* were played, along with dances. This rite also included martial dances using spears and swords to the accompaniment of nine tunes of *Chŏngdaeŏp*, including *Somu* and *Tokkyŏng*.

Music in Buddhist Temples

Buddhist music, as played in Korea, can be divided by performance style into two; one is the music performed in indoor services and the other played outdoors.

Indoor services vary in scale from small regular morning and evening prayer services through big services such as *Yŏngsanje*. Small services were usually accompanied by simple songs, but big ones included various tunes and dances.

The word '*je*' in *Yŏngsanje* was a service leading the soul of a deceased man to the Buddhist Paradise called *Kŭngnak*. There were many kinds of *je*, such as *Yŏngsanje*, *Suryukje*, *Sipwangkakpaeje*, etc. In this service, the temple's chief priest shaking a small bell, chanted Chinese or Sanskrit sutra in free rhythm, while professional Buddhist singers were invited to the service and sang Buddhist songs in the yard of the temple where the service was held. These songs varied; some were short in the poetic form and others were long in the prosaic form. These songs were sung also in free and slow rhythm to evoke a solemn feeling among the listeners. The professional singers also sang Buddhist hymns arranged in the melody of folk music or for humming so that laymen could enjoy them. These Buddhist songs of professional singers were usually accompanied by various Buddhist dances.

Mendicant monks, visiting laymen's houses for alms or donations for building a new temple, chanted prayers in Korean. This was often accompanied by folk songs or exorcist music played with a drum and a gonglike instrument. These songs were also sung by *kŏlip'ae* (farmer's music band) playing farm music, thus indicating that there were some relations among farmer's music band, mendicant monks and *kŏlip'ae*. These songs were all in Korean, those of quick tempo such as *Myŏngdangp'uri* and *Kwagŏp'uri* were first sung, and followed by the slower ones such as *P'yŏngjoyŏmbul* and *Panmaegi*.

Music in the Room

The most artistic room music of the Chosŏn dynasty was the music heard in the gentlemen's salon. This music was called *Pangjungak*, chamber music. The salon was usually in a detached building or in a far-end wing of a gentlemen's house, he met his friends and guests there. It had a beautiful garden in the front and was furnished with calligraphic works and paintings, as well as with stationery goods and musical instruments, such as drum, harp and flute. Meeting in such a room were poets, calligraphers, musicians and artists. As they had an eye for art, they usually enjoyed an artistic play. The poet first made a poem, and the calligrapher wrote it on paper. Then the musician musicalized it in one of the 12 tunes of *Yŏngsanhoesang*, which is a sort of suite consisting of seven to 12 pieces for play with various instruments such as harp, zither, flute, and drum. But the music in the gentlemen's salon was usually played with harp and zither. After this music, singers and songstresses sang songs called *Kagok* in solo or in chorus. In general, men's songs were solemn and imposing and women's tender and charming, and they sang in turn to end in a duet or in chorus.

Whereas the music in the gentlemen's salon was instrumental and vocal, the music in the meeting room of merchants and craftsmen was only vocal. The songs and ballads for craftsmen and merchants were folk music and other styles of song such as *kasa*, and *sijo* which were also for gentlemen, and *chapka*. They sang in turn, but the first part songs were usually slow *kasa* or *sijo*. Then came moderate *chapka* or songs of *p'ansori* (a sort of opera). In the last part quick folk songs or quick *chapka* were sung.

The way of singing in the room of merchants and craftsmen differed by area. In the Kyŏnggi area slow *chapka*, such as *Yusan'ga* and *Soch'unhyangga*, were first sung, followed immediately by quick *chapka* tunes, including *Kombot'aryŏng*, and then by folk songs such as *Hangangsut'aryŏng* and

Opongsant'aryŏng. In the Western part of the country, slow *chapka*, such as *Kongmyŏngga* and *Chohan'ga*, came first, and this was followed by slow folk songs — *Susimga, Nanbongga* and *Sanyŏmbulga* — and then by quick songs — *Chajin-Nanbongga* and *Sasŏl-Nanbongga*. In the southern part, moderate *tan'ga* or songs of *p'ansori* were first sung, and then came slow folk songs such as *Yukchabaegi* and *Hŭngt'aryŏng*. Quick songs of *Kaegurit'aryŏng* and *Chindo-Arirang* were sung last.

Music in Shamanist Exorcism

There were three folk rites in Korea; one was for the peace and prosperity of a family, another for the soul of a deceased person and the last for the peace of a village. These rites were performed by the villagers or shamans.

The family rite was usually held in the front yard or on the veranda of a house. The shaman, standing by the rite table with many kinds of food, sang and danced to the accompaniment of the music played by his or her assistants using drum and gong. This shamanist band differed in composition by area; in the central and southwestern parts of the country the band had pipe instruments in addition to drum and gong. The family rite consisted of three prayers; the first was for a long life for family members, the second for family wealth and the last for family peace.

The rite for the soul of a deceased person was almost the same in style as the family rite, though it was usually held after the family rite. This rite was for rest in peace of the deceased person's soul in paradise and for the purification of the soul from any devilish things.

The village rite was held in the village shrine or in the village square. When the rite was held in the village shrine, its style was the same as the family rite. After that a shaman and his or her assistants visited all the families of the village to bless them after the rite. This visit was accompanied by a march tune played by the shaman's band of flute, drum and gong. But when the rite was held in the village square, the style was different. In this case, the shaman, his or her band and village folks first visited the village shrine to the accompaniment of a march, and they played shamanist music before the shrine and then visited door to door all the families of the village again to the accompaniment of a march to bless them. After this they went to the village square to start the main program of the rite which was the same as the family rite in style. In this rite, prayers were offered to the gods of family peace, village peace, farming, fishing and hunting. Then in the last, a clownish play was performed to please the miscellaneous gods of the village. In some areas, the village rite was accompanied by music, dance, play and stunt.

Many shamanist songs were similar in melody to folk songs but some shamanist songs had a rhythm that could not be found in folk music.

In case the rite was held without a shaman officiating, the village head officiated at it and village folks played the ritual music using drum, flute and gong. The size of this village band varied by village; some villages had a band of five members and others a band of as many as 30 members, including dancers and clowns. As in the case of the rite with a shaman participating, the rite without a shaman also started with a procession of village folks to the village shrine to the accompaniment of farm music, not a shamanist march. In the shrine, the people prayed and danced to the accompaniment of music. After this, they proceeded to the common well of the village for another prayer and then visited every house in the village. In the evening, the main event of the rite was held in the village square, followed by performance of dance, music, play and stunt which often continued until late in the night in a festival mood.

Music for Enjoyment in the Village Square

In Chosŏn dynasty the village square was also used as a playground and performed here were music, dance, play and stunt forming a suite. This village square suite of play was originally performed in village festivals such as village rites and village parties. But the suite was sometimes performed for money in late Chosŏn dynasty.

There were five kinds of groups performing such suites — *Chaein-Kwangdae, Sadang, Kŏllip, Sodaejaengi, P'unggak-jaengi* and *Ch'orani.* The *Chaein-Kwangdae* was good at shamanist songs and dances and folk songs as well as fancy performances, thus contributing to the development of folk art. It played not only in village festivals but also in banquets of local government offices and even of the court. The play of this group usually started with rope dancing. Dancing on a tight rope, the dancer exchanged witty jokes with a clown on the ground, and then the rope dancing continued to the accompaniment of music played with flute and drum. The rope dancing was followed by clown play also with witty jokes and then by a sword dance and monk dance to the accompaniment of flute and drum music. The play ended with *p'ansori* such as *Ch'unhyangga, Simch'ŏngga, Hŭngbuga, Sugungga* and *Chŏkpyŏkka. P'ansori* was later separated from this kind of play to develop as an independent Korean-style opera for indoor performance. Today *p'ansori* has developed into a refined genre of traditional Korean music, and its music changes in rhythm and melody, depending on the dramatic effect of the story, so that the music and the story (drama) are in harmony.

The *Sadang* originated from the group of Buddhist singers and dancers for the propagation of Buddhism and collection of alms and donations. This group also played in a big ground such as the village square. Woman members were called *sadang* and they sang *p'anyŏmbul* (Buddhist song) and danced to the accompaniment of music played by male members called *kŏsa.* The *Sadang* arranged Buddhist songs for alms and donations in the tune of folk music, such as *Sŏnsori* and *Sant'aryŏng*. These arranged songs were sung by male members with small drum. The songs were always sung in standing position, and they slightly differed in rhythm by area. Originally the songs were very amusing, but the songs arranged by *Sadang* for folk music were stirring, especially when sung by a man.

Music during Work

Although Korea is a peninsular country, agriculture has been the chief industry of the people, and accordingly farm music is most popular. In addition, there are fishermen's music, funeral music, carpenter's music, woodcutter's music, daily laborer's music and weaver's music.

As it is today, rice was the main agricultural product of country in Korea, and in the southern part of the country there were many farm songs. Farmers had different songs for different farm work, such as plowing, harrowing and irrigating. Singing such songs, farmers could endure the hard work. Especially, the songs for rice transplanting were unique; the song leader starts a song to the accompaniment of a drum and others sing the refrain in chorus planting the rice. These songs for rice transplanting are in dance rhythm so that farmers can forget the hard work. These songs were heard everywhere in the country, especially in the southern part of the country, in spring.

In summer, weeding is the main farm work, and farmers did this work three to four times in summer. In the weeding season, a bugler woke up village people at dawn and they got together in the village square. After a roll call, they walked to the field in columns to the accompaniment of drum, bugle and gong. They usually carried a farm streamer. Reaching the field, they put the streamer at a corner while to the accompaniment of farm music before starting weeding work.

The weeding songs were led by the song leader, as in the case of transplanting songs. The songs in the morning were slow, those in the afternoon moderate and those in the evening quick. Finishing a day's work at sunset, they walked back to the village also in columns to the accompaniment of a march. On the last day of weeding work, farmers let the best farmer of the season ride an ox on the way back to the village after work, and they followed him singing songs in chorus. Reaching the best farmer's home, they were treated to food and wine in exchange for congratulatory music and dance. In the seventh month of the lunar calendar when a year's weeding work is completed, a day was set for a rite in the village shrine to pray for a bumper crop. In this rite the village people enjoyed music and dance.

In the harvest season of autumn, farmers sang different songs. There were songs for reaping, thrashing and milling. These songs, together with those for plowing, harrowing, irrigating and weeding, still remain as folk songs of the country, though only reaping and milling songs are quite popular today.

Fishermen had their own songs and ballads. Before going to sea, they put the boats in the waters and held a rite to pray for a good catch. This rite was accompanied by music and dance, using drum, flute and gong. The highlight of the rite was the chorus led by the song leader. After the rite the fishermen pulled up anchor and set sail for the fishing grounds. Of course, rowing was also accompanied by songs led by the leader. When they pulled up the fishnets in the sea, they sang in chorus, too. In the case of a big catch, fishermen celebrated it with ballads and songs to the accompaniment of drum, flute and gong on their way home, putting up the flag of a big catch on their boats. These big catch songs were also led by the song leader.

All funeral processions were accompanied by music, too. On the eve of the burial day, bier bearers usually carried an empty bier around the village, singing a song called *Tadaegi-*

sori. On the funeral day, the bier bearers also sang songs after the song leader throughout the procession to the grave. In southern Korea, the funeral songs were often accompanied by flute, drum and gong. When the coffin was removed from the bier in the grave yard, diggers put the coffin into the grave and earth on the coffin, singing in chorus. This burial song was also led by the song leader.

Trends and Developments
in Korean Traditional Music Today

CORALIE J. ROCKWELL

For the student of Ethnomusicology — broadly speaking, "world music" — who, in the 1970s, embarks on an examination of a specific musical tradition, whether it be jazz, "rock," classical or folk, court music, temple music, eleventh century plain chant or twentieth century computer music, there are two basic principles which should be recognized and applied in his study. First, the music selected should itself be studied, performed and analyzed in detail, and second, the music should be considered closely in its cultural and social context.

As a student trained in Western music and Western musicological methods, I have come to Korea in an attempt to apply these Ethnomusicological principles to a study of some aspects of Korean traditional instrumental and vocal music, in particular the *kayagŭm*, *sijo* and *kagok* repertoires.

For me, the entire world of music is vitally important as a means of communication between peoples. Music, as the product of human creative genius, sensitivity and emotion is indeed a reflection of the society into which it is born. It is an expression not only of abstract musical ideas, but also a medium for the transmission of philosophies, beliefs and daily events in people's lives.

How many of these aesthetic ideals, however, can still be found to apply to present-day Korean traditional music? So

106

far I have found little change in the actual music. Rather it is the environment that is changing.

It is quite apparent that the desire to perpetuate earlier musical traditions waxes strong amongst traditionally trained musicians, composers and scholars, but wanes in Korean society at large because of the tremendous changes that have taken place in the life style of the Korean people, particularly in the last two decades. With rapid westernization, their attitudes, value judgments and priorities are being transformed so quickly that with each succeeding generation ties with the past are becoming more tentative.

Traditional buildings such as the National Classical Music Institute complex, which was once located in the heart of the historic royal palace and shrine area in Seoul, have been destroyed and relocated in modern buildings in a less accessible area. Court music, court dancing and "gentlemen's chamber music" repertoires have dwindled to a standard abbreviated performance program presented largely for tourists at irregular intervals. The time-honored art of singing the three line poem *sijo*, its more elaborate version with a larger instrumental ensemble, *kagok*, and the narrative *kasa* and *p'ansori* repertoires is slowly disappearing amongst the younger generation. Confucian temple ceremonials, which may still be witnessed twice a year in the Sŏnggyun'gwan University Confucian Shrine, lack certain instruments which were lost during the Korean War and have not been replaced with good copies of the original ones.

On the brighter side, however, the more popular and dynamic form known as *kayagŭm-sanjo* — solo, semi-improvisational music for the long twelve-string zither — is at present experiencing a considerable revival, especially among high school girls and female college students. Performances of folk music, folk dance, mask plays and farmers' music, too, may often be seen in a variety of situations, from national folk arts contests to television competitions for amateurs, and in the most exotic surroundings of Seoul's hotels and night clubs.

It is inevitable that the importation of Western music and methods of composition should penetrate the traditional Korean music environment, but not without some considerable detriment to both. Attempts to combine Korean and Western instruments are very large unsatisfactory except in rare cases, where a solo *kayagŭm* may be featured in a concerto-type composition with Western symphony orchestra,[1] or when new compositions are written for solo instruments or small groups of traditional instruments only.

Surely, one might argue, the greatest strength of any country's art lies in the projection of a unique style and beauty as expressed through its own distinctive characteristics. Just as garlic and pepper are indispensable ingredients in Korean food, so the use of special ornamental techniques is essential in traditional Korean music.

The scales and tunings of instruments such as *taegŭm* (large flute), *p'iri* (double-reed 'oboe'-like instrument) and *kŏmun'go* (6-string long fretted zither) bear no relation to the Western music equal tempered tuning system based on pitch A = 440 cycles per second. Measured scientifically, according to the Ellis cent system where 100 cents equal one half tone, it has been found that the intervals of the *U* and *kyemyŏn* keys and their various modes are quite irregular.[2] When placed in the context of a traditional music composition, these intervals and their many ornaments combine to create a phenomenon of aural splendor that cannot be reproduced in the same distinctively "Korean" way outside the Korean repertoire.

It might be said that it is not the size, shape or number of instruments and associated vocal and dance styles alone that define the basic musical characteristics of one culture as compared to another. Rather it is the combination of mode, tunings, ornamentation, rhythm, mood and dynamics.

Some of the present Korean *chŏng'ak* (court music) repertoire, for example, is distinguished by the use of the *U* key and pentatonic *U* or *sol* mode, with E flat as the "central tone."[3] On the other hand, much of the *kayagŭm-sanjo* repertoire, and the *sijo, kagok, p'ansori* and *minyo* genres use the *kyemyŏn* (*la*) mode in its various forms. In seventeenth century notation books for court music and *kagok*, this mode was originally pentatonic (in cipher notation 1, 3, 4, 5, 7), but during the next three centuries the third and fourth pitches experienced a kind of fusion, and pitch seven took on a secondary role, so that the basic mode consisted of three notes only with additional ornaments (that is, intentional pitch variation) acting as subsidiary tones.

In an excellent brief survey of the modes of Korean music today, Professor Han Man-yŏng wrote the following about pitch variation.[4]

The type and position of vibrato ("shaking")[5] *and glissando ("sliding") can determine not only mode, but also whether the music is folk or upper class, and even the musicality and character of the performer. It may not be an exaggeration to say that an understanding of these pitch gradations is an understanding of the essence of Korean music.*

From an examination of the *sijo* music in *chŏnggan-bo* notation (mensural notation using *yulcha-bo* — Chinese characters — for specifying pitch), it can be seen that the mode of the music is *kyemyŏn-jo* in its "reduced" or tritonic form (pitches E flat 黃, A flat 仲, Double B flat 林). Pitch A flat, or *chung*, receives the widest vibrato, while E flat (*hwang*), a fourth lower, is vibrated to a lesser extent. According to the research of Korean musicologist Dr. Chang Sa-hun, it is the central or basic tone of the mode that receives the widest vibrato.[6] The third pitch, B flat (*im*) usually receives a wide vibrato, but it is the most flexible and variable tone of all three, and is often found to merge very closely with pitch *chung*, approximately a minor second lower, by a combination of vibrato and sliding.

As with all of the court music repertoire, the vibrato used in *sijo* begins from the written pitch and not from any pitch above. On the other hand, folk music, and forms derived from it, such as *kayagŭm-sanjo*, display a wide variety of vibrato, glissando (sliding) and other delicate ornaments that often begin three or even five pitches above the basic tone being produced.

It is the belief of many Ethnomusicologists that the most fundamental examples of any musical idiom can be found first in the vocal music. Dr. Mantle Hood has referred to the "highly developed sense of pitch discrimination"[7] among the Sundanese singers of west Java, whom he heard moving with ease from one tuning system of the *gamelan* orchestra to another, by means of "vocal tones" — tones that occur halfway between the fixed pitches of the bronze metallophones that play the main nuclear melody. Korean vocalists, too, have an equally advanced sense of pitch discrimination, especially *kagok* performers, because the pitch of all the accompanying instruments (string zither, flute and double reed) is more flexible than the instruments of the Javanese *gamelan*. Focusing on the fundamental structure of the mode of the *kagok* song (either *p'yŏng-jo* or *kyemyŏn-jo*), the singer prepares and resolves each individual pitch with the appropriate vocal tone ornaments that are imitated and elaborated on by the *taegŭm* (flute) and *p'iri*.

Some of the most characteristic ornaments of the *kayagŭm-sanjo* repertoire are borrowed directly from the vocal techniques of *p'ansori* and *minyo* (folk songs). The general term for either vibrato or glissando, *nong-hyŏn*, refers particularly to the wide vibrato that occurs on the *hwang*, *chung* and *im* strings (pitches 1, 4 and 5, or E flat, A flat and B flat). The upper pitches of the *kyemyŏn* mode in *kayagŭm-sanjo* (C and B flat) are much narrower than a whole step, and in fact this upper tone (C) is a kind of rapid "crushing note" or *appoggiatura* with almost indeterminate pitch. It is a very abrupt sound, and like many of the cadences or final endings in the vocal repertoires, it might be compared to "the final jab of pressure given at the end of a brushstroke in calligraphy."[8]

Another of the most distinctive characteristics of *kayagŭm-sanjo* music, as borrowed from the *p'ansori* repertoire, is a rapid microtonal "sliding" preparation of the upper tone, B flat of the *kyemyŏn* mode. The *kayagŭm* player calls this ornament *mibun-ŭm*. It is this sound, perhaps, more than any other in the *p'ansori* and folk song styles that is the most noticeable characteristic of the *kyemyŏn* mode to an outside listener. It could be described subjectively as a· "tragic, weeping" sound, but it bears little or no relation to the actual subject material of the folk narratives. The combination of an extraordinarily husky vocal quality and the ornaments described above, particularly the "breaking" or sharp jabbing sound and the microtonal sliding *appoggiatura*, has led one writer to liken the *p'ansori* style in the *kyemyŏn* mode to electronically produced "white noise."[9]

So far I have discussed only mode and its related ornamentation as the most characteristic aspects of Korean traditional music both past and present, but no Korean music exists without a rhythmic framework.

The *sijo* and *kagok* notation books show in the right hand column of each page, or against every column of notation if the number of beats changes, the basic rhythmic pattern to be interpreted on the *changgo* (hourglass drum). These rhythmic columns are in groups of 16(11 + 5) or 10(7 + 3) for *kagok*, and groups of 5 + 8 + 8 + 5 + 8 for *sijo*. They are "regular" or even beats in terms of distance between strokes, but the total groupings are made up of uneven combinations. Such combinations are known as "additive rhythms" in Ethnomusicological terminology, in that the meter is formed by adding unit groupings, rather than dividing them into a whole (for example, four beats) as is often the case in Western music.

Meter for much of the Chinese-influenced court music *(T'ang'ak)* is slow, even and "four square" (built on rhythmic units of four, like a slow march), but the *Hyang'ak* (Korean indigenous court music) repertoire is built on metric units of three (like "waltz time").

Whereas the *p'ansori, minyo* and *sinawi* (group folk-style improvisation) genres have influenced the modes and ornamentation *of kayagŭm-sanjo,* the same is not equally true of the rhythmic patterns. While the folk songs have one rhythmic pattern only for each song, and the *p'ansori* repertoires have extraordinarily complex drumming patterns that are flexible and are dictated to some extent by the speed of the narrative, the *kayagŭm-sanjo* repertoire is built around a variety of separate rhythmic cycles that move from compound and simple triple divisive meters (⅜, ¹²⁄₄) to additive meters (¹⁰⁄₈). When performed in entirety, a *kayagŭm-sanjo* can have up to ten sections or movements, each distinguished by a gradual increase in tempo and change of meter. The first section, *chinyang-jo,* is very slow (♩. = 35) and the meter is ⅜; by the final sections, *chajinmori* and *tanmori,* the tempo increases to a very fast speed (♩ = 208-230) and the meter changes from ¹²⁄₈ (compound time) to a fast ¼ (simple time) at the end.[10]

All of these rhythms, particularly the faster ones, create complex asymmetrical patterns with the melodic line, so that syncopation and cross-rhythms occur. This type of "rhythmic cycle" is unique in Far East Asia, and may possibly stem from earlier traditions in the Middle East and India. Combined with rapid changes in dynamics — from loud to soft — or with subtle and gradual crescendos, especially in long vibrato passages, *kayagŭm-sanjo* demonstrates some of the most outstanding and distinctive characteristics of Korean music.

For the Western or Korean students learning to sing and play Korean musical instruments, the task is therefore not an easy one. To obtain an aesthetic understanding of *sijo* and *kagok,* for example, it is first of all essential that previously learned musical concepts which may prejudice one's hearing be eliminated by strict ear training and performance. Only by *making* music can the student really discern what the essential characteristics, subtleties and nuances of the music are. After many months and often years of disciplined study, performance skill can increase to such an extent that the student's comprehension of the musical norms of the tradition becomes sophisticated.

Such training obviates the necessity for a consistently satisfactory study environment and the availability of the best possible teachers. Unfortunately, as I have already shown, it is becoming more difficult every decade in Korea to find traditional performers and teachers of the highest calibre. With the death of the famous *kagok* singer and compiler of *sijo* and *kagok* notation books, Mr. Yi Chu-hwan, a great gap has occurred both in the study and performance of the *kagok* repertoire. Members of the Kagok Institute in Seoul, a small group of private individuals, including some distinguished professors, teachers and performers, meet at rather erratic intervals to practise *kagok*, but without complete instrumental ensemble, and at present without any definite plans for regular performances. Although the Music College of Seoul National University includes *kagok* in its curriculum, it is only studied for four hours each week (two hours for vocal instruction and two hours for instrumental ensemble) in the final year of the undergraduate degree course. There is no provision for *kagok, sijo, kasa, kayagŭm-pyŏngch'ang* or *p'ansori* to be studied as a major subject for the degree.

While it is understandable that music degree these days should be preparing students to teach, either privately or in schools, there should also be a broadening of the traditional performance aspects. If this is not possible within the scope and time limits of the semester program, then the opportunity to study the vocal repertoires should be available to those students who wish to do so at other institutes of traditional music.

I am offering, therefore, some opinions and ideas dedicated to the revival of much that is being lost, especially in the Korean "classical" music repertoire, as a result of changes in the socio-cultural environment. It is my belief that through careful reconstruction of the necessary environmental factors, and with a consistent program of education, the music that I as a Western student have come to appreciate so much may be widely disseminated not only amongst the Korean people who have the right to inherit it, but also amongst other world people, particularly musicians, students, scholars and teachers who have the right to learn about it.

What are some of these "environmental factors" that are necessary for a completely satisfactory study of a highly complex and delicate art such as the singing of *sijo* and *kagok*— or any of the other traditional repertoires? Dr. Yi Hye-gu once mentioned this vital aspect of aesthetics and the relationship of much Korean traditional music to the natural environment, in a chapter on the *sijo* in his book *Han'guk Ŭmak Yŏn'gu* (Studies in Korean Music, 1957). As a young student he often went into the mountains and listened to the wind sighing in the pine trees and the sound of water dropping at irregular intervals from damp rocks. The mountain environment created a feeling of calm, pleasant stillness — a stillness that was occasionally disturbed by the wind blowing the pine needles in sudden gusts.

Dr. Yi's point is made very clearly. Although the rhythm of much of the "classical" repertoire of Korean music is slow, and the modal and melodic variations seem monotonous, the greatness of the music lies in a powerful stillness and tranquility that is enhanced by essential ornaments and dynamics creating temporary tension, then release.

It is my impression, then, that the most desirable environment for studying any traditional art is one that is quiet, conducive to concentration, and one that will enhance the best aspects of the art. Placed in such an environment, the artist will not only improve his performance technique and desire to perform well, but will feel that his art is not being lost and regarded as something "old-fashioned" in a modern world. With better practice and study conditions, more performances and more desirable aspects of publicity will emanate.

I need hardly say, therefore, that present conditions I have seen at the National Classical Music Institute are what have prompted me to offer these suggestions for a correction of environmental facilities for traditional musicians there. This large team of researchers, instrumentalists and dancers who are now housed in the rear of the new National Theater suffer from cramped conditions, lack of soundproof offices and training rooms and other essential facilities, such as separate teaching rooms for specific instruments and ensembles, an adequate library, museum, and recording and transcription laboratories and equipments. If the traditional architectural environment cannot be re-created, then at least the benefits of modern technology and learning can be put to good use in an attempt to correct the present situation.

Members of the Institute are also concerned about the future of their national art, and as a result there has been recent collaboration with the government Ministry of Culture and Information and the Ministry of Education to put into effect a five-year plan for the arts. Nowhere else in Far East Asia has such a plan been proposed, and nowhere else in the Far East is it more likely to succeed than in Korea.

Last month I discussed the plan with the director of the National Classical Music Institute, Mr. Kim Ki-su, and members of his staff, and my thanks go to them for their assistance and permission to outline briefly some of the details of it.

The plan is based on a need to re-define "historic Korean nationalism in traditional music." The main objects are:

1) intensification of traditional music education;
2) increase and spread of traditional music and the retention of original forms and styles;
3) enhancement of artistic talent and ability of musicians by increased training and performance.

In the educational policy it is planned that every school in Korea will make provision for a "traditional music environment" by allocating definite periods of study each week to Korean music (30 percent of all music teaching time). All school teachers are to be educated for "the correct and effective instruction of the students" by musicians at the National Classical Music Institute and in other selected institutions throughout the country. Schools that do not have internal support for the purchase of instruments will be supplied with *kayagŭm* and *tanso* (notched flute) in the first instance. These will be followed by additional instruments at a later date.

It is further proposed to try to preserve the original aspects of traditional music by systematic investigation and excavation (i.e. field work), recording, making discs, transcription, notation and publication.

By systematic organization of "theory, history and scales and instruments" it is hoped to spread the music more widely.

Finally, by raising the standards of musical training and performance, it is intended to announce and publicize the excellence of Korean traditional music by many public performances. Further in the interests of the public, demonstrations and displays of instruments, music books and costumes are planned for the National Information Center, and classes for any interested members of the public will be held in two-week sessions on eight occasions throughout the year at the National Classical Music Institute.

Given the necessary and desirable changes in environment, and sufficient public and government support, the members of the small traditional music teaching and performing community in Korea should be able to restore much that is being lost in their art. Then it can be studied and performed by Koreans themselves, and by other people outside Korea who regard a knowledge of this unique culture as vital to an understanding of world music at large.

NOTES

1. In this case, the *kayagŭm* can be tuned equidistantly to the Western orchestra tuning.
2. Rockwell, C.J. *Kagok, a Traditional Korean Vocal Form.* Providence, Rhode Island: Asian Music Publications, 1972.
3. For the purpose of this article, the *U* and *P'yŏng* modes can be generally described as "bright," and may be represented in cipher notation as 1 2 4 5 6.
4. *in* Yi Hye-gu et al. *Survey of Korean Arts. Traditional Music.* National Academy of Arts, Seoul, 1973, p. 93.
5. Author's parentheses.
6. Chang Sa-hun. *Kug'ak Non'go* (Studies of Korean Music). Seoul: Seoul National University Press, 1967.
7. Mantle Hood. *The Ethnomusicologist.* N.Y.: McGraw Hill, 1971, p. 37.
8. Han Man-yŏng. "Theory" *in Survey of Korean Arts. Traditional Music,* ibid; p. 100.
9. Malm, William P. *Music Cultures of the Pacific, the Near East and Asia.* Prentice-Hall, 1967. pp. 130–34.
10. Yi Chae-suk. *Kayagŭm-Sanjo.* Seoul, Korean Musicological Society, 1971.

Korean Musicology:
Its Historical Development
and Problems

SONG BANG-SONG

It is evident that one needs an extensive and profound understanding not only of Korean music but also of the music of other Asian countries in order to attempt any systematic study of Korean musicology. Moreover, it is clear of that one would be required to have a substantial and concrete knowledge of the history and the theories of Korean traditional music. Then, why do I dare undertake a task as formidable as that? The reasons are as follows:

First, I think that a serious and systematic examination of the growth pattern and imminent problems of Korean musicology is so urgently needed that one may be excused for attempting it even without all the preparations he feels he needs for the undertaking. Second, the sporadic concerns shown by Korean musicologists about the problems and prospect of Korean musicology have been far from being satisfactory. Third, in my opinion, Korean musicology is passing from one phase to another at this point, and it is important for us to reevaluate the past achievement and redefine the future direction of Korean musicology immediately.

In short, the present essay is an attempt to outline an historical development of Korean musicology, together with a suggestion which may be relevant to the perspective of Korean musicology.

The Terminology of Korean Musicology

Conceptually, the term 'Korean musicology' means the range of scholarly concerns that have as their object of study all the different spheres of Korean traditional music. There is, however, another term applied to the same field of musical study, 'national musicology.'[1] The reason I prefer the term 'Korean musicology' to 'national musicology' is given below:

> People often call *kugak* (national music) the Korean music. Likewise, the term Korean musicology is substituted for the term 'national musicology.' In a broader sense of the term, of course, Korean musicology includes not only the study of traditional Korean music but also the study of Western music as long as it is undertaken in Korea. However, it is an undeniable fact that, in a narrower sense of the word, the term Korean musicology means the study limited to Korean traditional music. The reason why I am using the term 'Korean musicology' instead of the term 'national musicology' is that the latter suggests the Korean music of the past while the former has a greater future-orientedness in its connotation.[2]

Apart from the reasons pointed out in the above, I can give the following reasons in addition for my choice of the term.

The term 'national music' has been used as an antonym to the term 'Western music' which was introduced into our country at the end of the 19th century. National music in this context means all branches of music that have originally developed in this land from the past to the present. In this light, it is natural and proper to call the department of a university where Korean traditional music is studied the 'department of national music' and such a study the 'national musicology.' In my opinion, however, there is a definite technical difference between the term 'national musicology' and the term 'Korean musicology.' For an explication of my assertion, I suggest that we examine a rather peculiar phenomenon in the terminological customs of Korean musicological circles.

When a Korean student of music studies the historical and theoretical aspects of Western music, he is said to be studying not 'Western musicology' but just simply 'musicology.' Why is this? Why is he not called a 'Western musicologist' in the same way as a Korean who studies traditional Korean music is called a 'Korean musicologist'?

This question, however, brings us to another problem: What is the definition of musicology?

We may say that the broader meaning of the term 'musicology' is 'a study of music in general.' But we must admit that the narrower sense of the word as it is commonly used in Korea is 'the study of Western music.' In this context, it becomes interchangeable with the term 'historical musicology' — the branch of study in the West which has its focus on the study of the history of Western music. Then, 'historical musicology' becomes an antonym of the study of all non-Western music and Western folk music as well. That is, the term becomes an antonym of the term 'ethnomusicology.'[3] The prefix 'ethno' indicates that the definition of the term 'ethnomusicology' was decided by the self-centered standard of Western musicologists. From the viewpoint of Oriental musicologists, there is a grave contradiction in these terminological practices. If oriental musicologists were to decide by a standard as self-centered as that of Western musicologists, all Oriental musicologists who are studying Western music of any kind would become 'ethnomusicologists.' The contradiction in musicological terminology becomes even clearer when we consider this. That is, a study carried out by a Korean musicologist studying Korean traditional music with a historical approach is not included within the category of historical musicology but is called ethnomusicology. It was for a rather simple reason, however, that this kind of absurdity has had its impact on the Korean musicological scene. The reason is that the branch of study we call musicology first assumed a recognizable concept, framework, and some sort of a working system entirely through a direct adoption of Western standards and arrangements when Western music first came into Korea toward the end of the 19th century. Unfortunately, Koreans failed to make necessary changes and adaptations when putting Western conceptual and technical principles into their own use. But now, with a new era in musicology opening up before us, we must at once recognize the existence of these negative consequences of an unreflective adoption of what was foreign to us through a thorough-going reevaluation of what we have adopted from the West.

First of all, we must admit the inaccuracy of the term 'ethnomusicology' as applied to the study of our traditional music. Secondly, it is to be insisted that the term 'musicology' as meaning 'historical musicology' be freed from its West-Oriented usage. It should eventually be applied to the study of each national music of the countries of the world regardless of their national or racial backgrounds. Therefore, whatever musical field a Korean musicologist may have adopted for specialization, it is proper to call him a 'musicologist,' and all the scholarly pursuits by Korean musicologists may, and should be considered as proper concerns of Korean musicology.

As I have already pointed out, it has been a general custom to name the study of our traditional music 'national musicology.' By the same rule, the studies of different countries in the Orient, whether it be Japan, China, or any other Oriental country, would be called the 'national musicology' of each respective country.

What I would like to propose at this point without going into a further examination of inadequate usage of certain terms in the field of musicology for a constructive rearranging of musicological terminology is that instead of some inaccurate and awkward terms we have been using in referring to musical studies carried out in different parts of the world, we use such terms as Korean musicology, Japanese musicology, Chinese musicology, American musicology and so on.

Of course, there is much room and need for further consideration and improvement in all theoretical domains of Korean musicology. For instance, we have yet to make definitive decisions about the basic concept, scope and methodology of Korean musicology. It is not the present writer's intention however, to go into a discussion of these questions here. What I have been discussing so far is no more than a rationale for my adoption of the term 'Korean musicology' as applying to all musical studies and researches done on Korean traditional music.

Perhaps in the future some Korean musicologists may take interest in studying the music of such hitherto unexplored regions as Eskimo music or Indonesian music, and so on, which will make it inevitable for Korean musicologists to make some conceptual and terminological modifications. When such a time comes the term 'Korean musicology' may take on a meaning different from the one it has now. Until such a change occurs in the general conditions and climate of Korean musicology, however, I feel that we are safe to use the term 'Korean musicology' in the sense I took some pains defining so far; that is, as the study of Korean traditional music.

An analysis of the studies and activities of Korean musicology will show that it has concerned itself with both the classical and folk music of Korea. To put this differently, the Korean musicologists have engaged themselves with both what the Western musicologists might call the historical aspect and the ethnomusicological aspect of Korean musicology. I will come back to this subject later (in Chapter 4).

The Developmental Process of Korean Musicology

For expediency's sake, I will classify the period during which Korean musicology has developed from its simple beginning into its present scholastic and social stature into four periods. The first period, which I consider a long cradle period for Korean musicology, lasts to Korean Liberation from Japan in 1945 (August). During this period, Korean traditional music was not even considered properly as an object of serious study.

The second period begins from Korean Liberation, and cotinues through the 1950s. This was a time when Korean musicology acquired its basic form as a serious study. It may be said that before this period ended, the foundation of Korean musicology as a modern scholarly discipline was established.

The third period may be called the maturation period of Korean musicology as a science. The beginning of the period coincided with the first installation of the department of national music as an independent program at the College of Music, Seoul National University.

The fourth period began in the first part of the 1970s and continues through the present time. During this period, Korean musicology has gone through a remarkable expansion thanks to the active contributions of the newly rising generation of musicologists of Korea.

The first period which coincided with the occupation of the country by the Japanese was characterized by the effects of cultural as well as political repression by the Japanese. However, the musicological records of this period shows that at least nominal scholarly activities were maintained in the form of historical analyses or general surveys.

The second period is a time when Koreans experienced all sorts of after-the-Occupation and postwar (the Korean War also took place during this decade) confusions and economic instability. During this period, Korean musicology was barely kept alive by scattered individual efforts of a relatively small

number of scholars and it may be safe to say that the decade
was characterized by a general stalemate in the development
of Korean musicology.

It was therefore with the beginning of the third period that
Korean musicology first acquired its foothold and prestige in
the cultural foreground of Korean society. Most of all, it was a
big advance for Korean musicology to be taken into the
boundary of an educational institution of such a solid
academic standing as Seoul National University. (I mentioned
before that SNU incorporated the study of national music into
their curriculum in this decade). We may say that now the
groundwork was fully laid for Korean musicology to grow and
transform to the fullest of its capacity. I will now discuss each
of these four developmental stages in more detail. The focus of
my discussion will always stay on the actual works and
contributions made by scholars and institutions.

Korean Musicology during the Occupation

From the beginning of Japanese Occupation, Korean
traditional music had to subsist on a very strenuous as well as
precarious existence level. Apart from the cultural and
political repressions suffered because of the foreign occupation
of the land, traditional music had to cope with the onrush of
Western music which occurred about the same time as the
Occupation. Even so, as I mentioned above, Korean
traditional music managed to keep alive through this difficult
time. Court music was sustained by the *Yiwangjik aakpu*
(李王職雅樂部, Royal Music Institute of Yi Household), and folk
music was preserved mainly through the stage performances
given by the professional artists of the *Chosŏn sŏngak yŏn'guhoe*
(朝鮮聲樂研究會). Under the circumstances, it was quite natural
that our traditional music was exposed to the public only in its
most fragmentary and oversimplified aspects.

Korean musicology of this period can be classified into two
branches. One was the studies and researches done by Korean

scholars and the other by foreign scholars. Among those Korean scholars who made contributions to the growth of Korean musicology during this period, we may include Ham Hwa-jin, An Hwak, Song Sŏk-ha, Yi Hye-gu, Kye Chŏng-sik, and Chŏng No-sik.

Ham Hwa-jin was the *aaksajang* (雅樂師長, head-musician of the Royal Music Institute of Yi Household) and in that capacity, he both acted as a spokesman of the circle of court musicians and wrote a number of books related to Korean court music.[4] An Hwak who carried on his study of the cultural history of Korea wrote numerous articles on Korean traditional music in the monthly magazine *Chosŏn* (朝鮮).[5] Song Sŏk-ha who was one of the first to take a scholarly interest in Korean folklore, introduced an annotated bibliography of old music manuscripts of Korea.[6] Yi Hye-gu, in charge of the national music program at Kyŏngsŏng Broadcasting Station, the National network, toward the end of the Japanese Occupation, published a theoretical work on Korean music in 1943.[7] Kye Chŏng-sik who was a violinist obtained his doctoral degree in music while studying in Germany, and the subject of his dissertation was Korean folk songs. He was the first to receive a doctorate for a study on Korean music.[8] Chŏng No-sik may be said to have laid the foundation of the study of Korean folk music as a scholarly subject. He published *Chosŏnch'anggŭksa* (朝鮮唱劇史) on the basis of the materials he could collect from the interview with *p'ansori* (similar to *ch'anggŭk* with a more of plebeian nature) singers. There were also Yi Sang-jun's *Collection of Korean Folk Songs* (1929), Yi Ki-yŏl's *Interpretation of Musical Writings* (1932), and Yi Sŏn-yu's *Complete Collection of Five Songs* (1929), all contributing their share to the growth of Korean musicology under the oppression of a foreign dictatorship.

The foreign scholars who made contributions for the development of Korean musicology during this period may be divided into two groups, Western scholars and Japanese scholars. A Frenchman named Maurice Courant is the first Western scholar who introduced Korean music in his work in 1913.[9] In 1930, a German musicologist named Andreas Eckardt wrote a book on Korean music,[10] and again in 1940, an American, J.L. Boots, wrote a long essay.[11] Sara May Anderson, an American, received her master's degree with a thesis on Korean folk music in 1940.[12] Of Japanese scholar, we may mention Shimizu Fumio,[13] Kishibe Shigeo,[14] Tanabe Hisao,[15] Naito Torajiro,[16] Takahashi Toru,[17] Taki Ryoichi,[18] Iwaya Takeichi,[19] Hiraga Ryojo.[20] One more significant event that took place in 1933 was the facsimile publication of *Àkhak kwebŏm* (樂學軌範) known as the Mt. T'aebaek edition (1610), which came out in three volumes and became a valuable source material for Korean musicology.

Korean Musicology in the 1950s

The main features of Korean Musicology of this period are: a) All the studies, researches, and activities related to Korean musicology were carried out exclusively by Korean scholars b) A substantial amount of writings and research materials managed to be published in book form in spite of the social and economic instability of Korean society over a good part of this period.

The main scholarly association through which Korean musicologists carried on their activities during this period was the *Han'guk kugak hakkhoe* (韓國國樂學會, Korean Musicological Society) founded in 1948. The Society held monthly meetings which gave opportunity to the more studious Korean scholars to present the results of their studies or new findings. Among those who presented papers at the Society during the year of 1948 were: Min Yŏng-gyu, Sŏng Kyŏng-nin, Yi Pyŏng-gi, Yi Chu-hwan, Yi Hye-gu, Pak Sang-gūn, Chang Sa-hun, and Kim Po-nam[21]. The Society has held over 200 meetings since then and thus has played a vitally important role in establishing the foundation of Korean

Musicological Society.

Of the considerable number of books that were published during the short period between Korean Liberation and the Korean War, the more important were: Ham Hwa-jin's *Chosŏn ŭmak t'ongnon* (朝鮮音樂通論, Seoul, 1948), Chang Sa-hun's *Chosŏn ŭi minyo* (朝鮮의 民謠, Seoul, 1949), and *Minyo wa Hyangt'o akki* (民謠와 鄕土樂器, Seoul, 1948), Sŏng Kyŏng-nin's *Chosŏn ŭi aak* (朝鮮의 雅樂 Seoul, 1947) and *Chosŏn ŭmak tokpon* (朝鮮音樂讀本, Seoul, 1947) and *Chŏng-ok's Chosŏn minyo yŏn'gu* (朝鮮民謠研究, Seoul, 1949). These works, which were published one after another as if in a sudden burst of joyful feeling over the liberation of the country from Japanese rule, were mostly general survey or analysis of Korean music written with the intention of educating the Korean public about the history and tradition of their musical past and also to teach the young generation at elementary and middle schools the basic knowledge of traditional music. The book on Korean folk songs written by Ko Chŏng-ok cannot be said to belong to the category of musicological study, strictly speaking, but is important in that it offered a new perspective for the study of Korean folk music.

In 1957 Yi Hye-gu set a new landmark in the development of Korean musicology by publishing the *Han'guk ŭmak yŏn'gu* (韓國音樂研究). Among the number of articles by Chang Sa-hun "A Study of *Pohŏja* (步虛子論攷)" was especially notable, and he compiled the *Kugak haesŏl sajŏn* (國樂解說辭典) in 1960. In addition to these there were publication of books by Yi Chu-hwan[22] and Sŏng Kyŏng-nin.[23] In the 1950's there were also a considerable number of facsimile editions of old music manuscripts such as *Siyong hyangakpo* (時用鄕樂譜, Seoul 1954), *Yanggŭm sinbo* (梁琴新譜, Seoul, 1959), and *Kyoju kagokpo* (校注歌曲譜, Seoul, 1951), all of these source materials gave new incentive and scope to the study of Korean traditional music. Kim Ki-su's *Han'guk minyo osipkokchip* (韓國民謠五十曲集, Seoul, n.d.) and Yi Chu-hwan's *Kagokpo* (歌曲譜, Seoul, 1960) and *Kasabo* (歌詞譜, 1960), Chŏng

Kyŏng-t'ae's *Aakpo* (雅樂譜, Chŏngju, 1950) and *kugakpo* (國樂譜, Chŏnju, 1953) were all publications that prompted musicological interest. The *Minsok akpo* Vol. I (1958) and Vol. II (1959) by the Ministry of Education also made a contribution to improving the transcription of Korean music into staff notation, which in turn helped to speed up the modernization of Korean musicology. There were also phonograph records that were produced to serve as research materials. For instance, the Korean Broadcasting Station produced a set of Korean music including six discs.

In 1956, Kim Sun-ae, an active composer, received a master's degree with her thesis on Korean traditional music at Eastman School of Music in Rochester.[24] As I have repeatedly pointed out, the establishment of the department of national music at Seoul National University was an immeasurably important and meaningful event in that it provided Korean musicology with a necessary framework within which the growing young scholars could strive to bring Korean musicology into a mature modern science.

As we can see studies and researches were carried out with diligence and devotion on the part of Korean musicologists right through the 1950s. Thus, in spite of the conditions of the period which was socio-economically the most difficult time in recent Korean history, Korean musicology moved step by little step forward. The academic and scholarly works along with the research materials made available during this period provided the musicology of the new decade with the necessary springboard and I do not doubt that it was thanks to these preparatory efforts of the earlier musicologists that now we have competently-developed theories and solidly-structured activities strongly supported by their affiliation with the universities.

Korean Musicology in the 1960s

Korean musicology during the period of the 1960s was

definitely university-oriented, and consequently had a highly academic overtone in its activities and new plannings. It was also characterized by an experimental diversity and a spirit of rediscovering the national identity in music. As a result, the scope of academic and scholarly interests expanded immensely and the growth of Korean musicology became faster and socially more significant than ever before.

The major musicological events of this period may be examined in three different categories. One of these is the field of publication of books, another the publication of musical scores and manufacturing of phonograph records, and the third, the studies and researches that have affiliation with foreign countries.

The representative publication during this period include: Yi Hye-gu's *Han'guk ŭmak sŏsŏl* (韓國音樂序說, Topics in Korean Music, 1967), Chang Sa-hun's *Kugak non'go* (國樂論攷, Studies in Korean Music, 1966), and *Yi Hye-gu paksa songsu kinyŏm ŭmakhak nonch'ong* (李惠求博士頌壽記念音樂學論叢, Essays in Ethnomusicology: A Birthday Offering for Yi Hye-gu, 1969) by Korean Musicological Society. Aside from these, the publications of this period included noteworthy studies such as: Yi Hye-gu's *Han'guk akki torok* (韓國樂器圖錄, Seoul, 1962), Chang Sa-hun's *Kugakki yŏnjubŏp* (國樂器演奏法, 1963); *Han'guk akki taegwan* (韓國樂器大觀, 1969); *Kugak sa* (國樂史, 1965) and *Han'guk akki tosŏl* (韓國樂器圖說, 1966) by Korean Musicological Society, Yi Chu-hwan's *Sijoch'ang ŭi yŏn'gu* (時調唱의 研究, 1962), *Kugak kaeyo* (國樂概要, 1961), Glossary of Korean Music (Seoul, 1961).

Among the source materials, the outstanding contributions made in this period were: *Kyŏngin akhak kwebŏm* (景印樂學軌範, Seoul: Yonsei University Press, 1968); *Yuyeji* (遊藝志, Seoul: Korean Musicological Society, 1969); Kim Kŭn-su's *Kyobon akhak kwebŏm* (校本樂學軌範, 1965) and *Hyŏprul taesŏng* (協律大成, 1969). Transcription of Korean music into Korean notation or Western notation include: *Han'guk ŭmak* (韓國音樂) 16 volumes (1968-1978) by National Classical Music

Institute; *Sinkug akpo* (新國樂譜) vol. I (1962) and Vol. II
(1965); Kim Ki-su's *Taegŭm kyobon* (大笒敎本, 1061), *Tanso
Kyobŏm* (短簫敎範, 1963), *Hŭngboka* (興甫歌, 1970); Yi Chu-
hwan's *Kagokpo sok* (歌曲譜 續, 1961), Kim Yŏn-su's *Ch'angbon
Ch'unhyang ka* (唱本春香歌, 1967); Cho Wi-min's *Hyŏn'gŭm
sanjobo* (玄琴散調譜, 1965); and Han Man-yŏng's *Pŏmp'ae:
Sangju kwŏn'gong* (梵唄：常住勸供, 1967), *Han'guk minyojip*
(國韓民謠集, 1967), and *Sibi chapka* (十二雜歌, 1967). The best
of the phonograph records that came out during this period
were: *Kugak tae chŏnjip* (國樂大全集, Anthology of Korean
Traditional Music: 30 discs) by Sinsegye Record Co. in 1968;
Minyo samch'ŏlli (Anthology of Korean Folk Song: 10 discs) by
Sŏngŭm Record Co. in 1968; and *Kugak chŏngsŏn* (國樂情選,
Selected Anthology of Korean Traditional Music: 6 discs) by
Universal Record Co. in 1968. The musicology of the period is
distinguished from that of the preceding period in that it was
partially supported by musicological pursuits undertaken
abroad. Kim Chin-gyun, although he was a Korean, studied in
Austria receiving his doctorate at Vienna University in 1964,
the first to receive a doctorate in music.[25] He continued to
write on Korean folk music after his return to Korea and thus
contributed to the growth of Korean musicology with what he
learned through a foreign training.[26] Among the foreign
musicologists, we can name Walter Kaufmann who introduced the method of notation in Korean traditional music in
his *Musical Notations of the Orient* (1967), Andreas Eckardt
who in his *Musik, Lied, Tanz in Korea* (1968) introduced
Korean music in its general aspects to Westerners.

There were also records made by foreign record companies.
These include *Folk and Classical Music of Korea* (1951) and
Korea: Vocal and Instrumental Music (1965) produced by
Folkways company, *Music from Korea; The Kayagŭm* (1965)
by East-West Center, and Disque Vogue's *Musique Boud-
dhique de Corée* (1968).

In 1963, a program for master's study was started at Seoul
National University, and from 1966 on, the school has issued

master's degrees to numerous young musicologists who wrote competent dissertations.[27] All of these happenings point to the fact that the 1960s saw a new era in the growth of Korean musicology. Among other things, the decade brought about the emergence, gradual though it was, of a new generation of musicologists. Young musicologists with master's degrees became active in different branches of musicology and continued adding new dimensions to the study and activity of musicology. Now there was no doubt that Korean musicology would develop in its full-fledged capacity to become an enterprising science in the modernized cultural scene of Korean society.

Korean musicology in the 1970s

The musicological study and activity of this decade has been as fruitful and vigilant as the preceding decade. But the new period began with a few conditions related with musicological pursuits which the former period did not have. One of these was that from the beginning of this period, the young musicologists who had done their graduate studies at SNU became markedly active in the musicological vista. Fortunately for this ambitious and energetic young generation the Korean Musicological Society started a magazine: *Han'guk ūmak yŏn'gu* (韓國音樂研究) in 1971 and the Institute for Oriental Music which was founded as an attached institution of SNU, started to publish an annual academic journal called *Minjok ūmakhak* (民族音樂學) in 1976. The second noteworthy feature was the increase in number and scope of college level academic institutions with Korean music in their curriculum. In such educational institutes as Hanyang University (1972), Ewha Womans University (1974) and Ch'ugye Art College (1974), departments were newly installed to receive music students specializing in Korean traditional music. This was big advance in position and opportunity for those interested or engaged in musicology. Now there could be no doubt that

Korean musicology was soundly incorporated in the main body of intellectual and cultural life of Korea. The third distinguishing feature, which, although it was not exclusive to this decade, made enough difference in the general musicological climate to be mentioned in this context, was the fact that the publication of musical scores including old materials became more animated than in the preceding period. This helped create a new intellectual atmosphere which was more stimulating than ever before to both the established and growing population of musicologists. The fourth special feature of this decade was that with the foundation of the Society for the Korean Music Education (*Han'guk kugak kyoyuk yŏn'guhoe*, 韓國國樂教育研究會), promoting the importance of educating school children in elementary and secondary schools was institutionalized. The fifth characteristic was that Korean traditional music was widely introduced to foreign countries during this period through the efforts of Korean musicologists residing either abroad or in the country.

In summary, I would like to emphasize again the fact that Korean musicology of the 1970s was the concern mainly of younger generation musicologists. The general prospect is that it will continue to depend on them not only for its stable existence in the Korean academic and cultural world and continuation of activities but also for the eventual realization of its ideals. With this fact established, I will proceed to discuss briefly the individual works accomplished during this period.

The theoretical publications or essay collections of this period include: *Chang Sa-hun paksa hoegap kinyŏm tongyang ŭmak nonch'ong* (張師勛博士頌壽記念東洋音樂論叢, Articles on Asian Music: Festschrift for Dr. Chang Sa-hun, 1977) by Korean Musicological Society: Pak Hŭng-su's *Kugak ŭi ironjŏgin yŏn'gu nonmunjip* (國樂의 理論的인 研究論文集, 1971); Chang Sa-hun's *Sijo ŭmak non* (時調音樂論, 1973), *Han'guk chŏnt'ong ŭmak ŭi yŏn'gu* (韓國統傳音樂의 研究, 1975); Yi Hye-gu's *Han'guk ŭmak nonch'ong* (韓國音樂論叢, Essays on Korean

Music, 1976). The publications by Yi Hye-gu, Chang Sa-hun and Pak Hŭng-su were mostly essay collections they had published in various academic journals during the 1960's. As theoretical and historical studies and analyses, they were a remarkable contribution to the development of Korean musicology in its most active stage.

During this decade, publication was prolific in the field of basic reference materials also. For instance, Yi Hye-gu's *Akhak kwebŏm yŏkchu* (樂學軌範釋註, 1972); Ch'a Chu-hwan's *Koryŏsa akchi* (高麗史樂志, 1972); *Kugak munhŏn charyo chipsŏng* (國樂文獻資料集成) by Asian Music Research Institute in 1978 and 1979; facsimile edition of *Taeak hubo* (大樂後譜) by National Classical Music Institute in 1979; facsimile edition of *Sogak wŏnbo* (俗樂源譜, 1970-1972), *Kŭmhap chabo* (琴合字譜, 1974), *Ŏŭnbo* (魚隱譜, 1978) by Korean Musicological Society. In 1975 Yi Tong-bok issued xerox copies of a considerable number of old musical manuscripts including *Hŭkhong kŭmbo* (黑紅琴譜), *Kŭmbo* (琴譜), *Paegunam kŭmbo* (白雲庵琴譜 *Wŏngaek yuŭm* (園客遺音), *Yanggŭmbo* (洋琴譜), *Hwigŭm kagokpo* (徽琴歌曲譜), *Han'gŭm sinbo* (韓琴新譜), *Hyŏn'gŭm oŭm ch'ongnon* (玄琴五音總論) and *Hyŏn'gŭm tongmun yugi* (玄琴東文類記).

The accomplishments in the field of creative composition were also important feature of the 1970's. Representative works are Hwang Pyŏng-gi's *Ch'imhyangmu* (沈香舞, 1974), and Yi Sŏng-ch'ŏn's *Norit'ŏ* (1977) and *Supsok ŭi iyagi* (1977). While the pieces in these compositions were mostly for *kayagum* solos or duets, *Kugak ch'angjak kokchip* (國樂創作曲集, 1974) by the Korean Culture and Arts Foundation included some orchestral pieces.

Transcription of Korean music into Western or traditional notations was also significant accomplishment during this decade: for instance, Kim Chŏng-ja's *Chŏngak kayagŭmbo* (正樂伽倻琴譜, 1976); Kim Ki-su's *Wŏlha chŏngga sŏn* (月荷正歌選, 1971) and *Namch'ang kagok paeksŏn* (男唱歌曲百選, 1979); Kim In-je's *Chŏngak kayagŭmbo*

(正樂伽倻琴譜, 1979); Han Pŏm-su's *Han Pŏm-su taegŭm sanjo* (韓範洙大笒散調譜, 1975); *Kugak chŏnjip* (國樂全集, 1974-present) by National Classical Music Institute; Yi Chae-Suk's *Kayagŭm sanjo* (伽倻琴散調, 1971); Sin K'we-dong's *Hyŏn'gŭm-gok Chŏnjip* (玄琴曲全集, 1977); Yi Yang-gyo's *Sibi kasa chŏn* (十二歌詞全); Ku Yung-guk's *Hyŏn'gŭm chŏng'ak* (玄琴正樂, 1979); Yi Ch'ang-bae's *Han'guk kach'ang taegye* (韓國歌唱大系): and Pak Kwi-hŭi's *Hyangsa Pak Kwi-hŭi kayagŭm pyŏngch'ang kokchip* (香史 朴貴姬 伽倻琴倂唱曲集, 1979).

Aside from these publications, there were a number of books written with the purpose of being used as textbooks for undergraduate students and also to provide the Korean public with the basic knowledge of Korean traditional music. These include Chang Sa-hun's *Han'guk ŭmak sa* (韓國音樂史, 1976), *Kugak ch'ongnon* (國樂總論, 1976), and *Kugak kaeron* (國樂概論, 1975); Kim Ki-su's *Kugak immun* (國樂入門, 1972); Yi Sŏng-ch'ŏn's *Kugak sa* (國樂史, 1976); Kim Yong-jin's *Kugakki haesŏl* (國樂器解說, 1976); Sŏng Kyŏng-nin's *Kugak kamsang* (國樂鑑賞, 1976), *Han'guk ŭmak non'go* (韓國音樂論攷); Pak Ki-hwan's *Kugak t'ongnon* (國樂通論, 1976); Pak Hwang's *P'ansori sosa* (판소리 小史, 1972), and *Ch'anggŭksa yŏn'gu* (唱劇史硏究, 1976); and Pak Kŭm-ae's *Kugak* (國樂, 1972).

One of the distinctive features of the 1970's was English publications on Korean music. Representative of these are *An Annotated Bibliography of Korean Music* (Providence: Brown University, 1971) and *The Korean-Canadian Folk Song: An Ethnomusicological Study* (Ottawa: Canadian Centre for Folk Culture Studies, 1974) by Song Bang-song; *Kagok: a traditional Korean vocal form* (Providence: Brown University Press, Coralie Rockwell 1972 and *Drum Rhythms in Korean Farmers' Music* (Seoul, 1975) by Robert C. Provine. During this period, a number of master's degrees were given to both Korean and American students in different academic institutes in the United States for their work on Korean music. Pak Chong-gil received his degree at the Washington University with his thesis on Korean court music in 1970,[28] and Yi Pyŏng-wŏn received his degree also at the Washington University with his study of Korean Buddhist chant in 1971.[29] Sŏ In-jung received his degree at Indiana University in 1972 with his thesis on Korean instruments.[30] Among American students, Lenore K. Smith received her degree from Wesleyan University in 1970[31] and Coralie Rockwell received her degree from University of California at Los Angeles in 1969.[32]

A number of doctoral dissertations were submitted to American universities and other academic institute during this decade: for instance, Yi Pyŏng-wŏn's "An Analytical Study of Sacred Buddhist Chant of Korea" (Washington University, 1974), Song Bang-song's "*Kŏmun'go Sanjo*: An Analytical Study of the Style of Korean Folk Instrumental Music" (Wesleyan University, 1975), Yi Kang-suk's "The Development and Trial of Korea-Based Musical Activities for the Classroom" (Michigan University, 1975), Chi Ch'ŏl-yŏng's "The Influence of Chinese Music on Korean Music" (North Colorado University, 1976), Jonathan Condit's "Sources for Korean Music, 1450-1600" (Cambridge University, 1976), and Robert C. Provine's "Chinese Ritual Music in Korean Sacrificial Rites: Musical Polygenesis in the Fifteenth-Century Korea" (Harvard University, 1979).

In the meantime the National Academy of Arts carried out a project for introducing Korean music abroad, and under this project published were *Survey of Korean Arts: Traditional Music* in 1973 and *Survey of Korean Arts: Folk Arts* in 1974. The Korean National Commission for UNESCO, on the other hand, published an introductory book, *Traditional Performing Arts of Korea*, in 1975. In 1978 the Society for Asian Music in New York issued *Asian Music: Korean Music Special Issue* Vol. IV. No.2. All these English publications on Korean traditional music may be further ample testimony to the ever widening scale and ever growing strength of Korean musicology in its present developmental stage.

Production of records and tapes played no less a role during this period than the publication of books in promoting the substance of Korean musicology what they are now. The most outstanding production of records of the decade were *Han'guk ŭmak sŏnjip* (韓國音樂選集, Anthology of Korean Classical Music, 1972-present) by National Classical Music Institute; *Han'guk ŭi ŭmak* (韓國의 音樂, Anthology of Korean Traditional Music, 40 discs, 1976) by Bureau of Cultural Properties; and *Han'guk minyo tae chŏnjip* (韓國民謠大全集, Anthology of Korean Folk Music, 15 cassette tapes, 1978) by Academy Sounding Manufacturer. There are also discs made by foreign record companies: for instance *Korean Social and Folk Music* (1970) by Lyrichord, *P'ansori: Korea's Epic vocal art and instrumental music* (1972) by Nonesuch, and *Korean Music* (1973) by Philips.

I have in the above surveyed the developmental stages of Korean musicology on the basis of actual works and contributions made in various branches of the field. The prospect in the 1980s is that there will continue to be sincere efforts of musicologists to study and make new discoveries about the music of their forefathers with their final objective in bringing Korean musicology into a fuller realization of its possibilities and dreams. However, in spite of the eagerness, intellectual capacity, and professional strength of musicologists, there still seems to be something lacking in the preparations of our scholars for their lunge into their final race for the completion of the modernization process in Korean musicology. My honest belief is that there are still areas in Korean musicology which need improvements ranging from a minor modification to a more drastic rearrangement in order for the discipline to acquire a self-consistent and efficient system to control, and give an overall direction to, the various efforts of musicologists. I think this process is not to be avoided if Korean musicology is to take a responsible role in enhancing the cultural level of our society and also in promoting the progress of music on an international level. A reevaluation of the musicological achievements up to the present, finding a practical and sensible methodology, and directions for various changes are necessary steps to take in our search for a good scientific system of musicology. I will have occasion to deal with these points in the course of my examination of the problems of Korean musicology in the following chapters.

The Problems of Korean Musicology

The present writer once made the following statement about the problems Korean musicologists are facing at the moment:

> What has to be done most urgently is: 1) We must set up a clear definition or concept of Korean musicology, that is, we must make sure what Korean musicology really is. 2) We must organize the musicological materials so that they may be most profitably utilized by students and scholars. 3) We must train ourselves to have better critical and analytical mind than before. 4) We must pay special attention and care to assure precision in the recording of musicological data as well as in making analytical or critical points in our musicological writings.[33]

It is not my intention to repeat, or give extensive explanations about, the four points mentioned here. What I am going to do instead is merely to add a few more points to those already mentioned. However, before I go into this discussion, I would like to attempt a quick summary of musicological achievements. I want to make it clear here that my approach this time will be directed by an analysis of the dominant tendencies of musicological studies and activities and that I will adopt an angle different from the one I had adopted before for my survey of happenings and facts in the developmental stages of Korean musicology.

In the course of my discussion about the developmental process and characteristics of Korean musicology, I have examined the scholarly and social achievements of Korean musicologists in some detail. After all, however, all those works and activities were merely an end product of the intense concern and effort of individual musicologists to arrive at a proper understanding of their traditional past through music, that is the rediscovery of national identity and artistic integrity. In as much as their enthusiasm and concern for Korean musicology were sincere and strongly motivated, it is proper and imperative that we define the problems of Korean musicology strictly on the basis of what they have done and want to do.

From the works published and concerns manifested by Korean musicology over the years of its development into its present maturity, I think it is possible to detect two dominant tendencies of musicological participation. One of them is what one might call a linear, or a historical, approach to musicology, and the other is what one might call a horizontal, or present-oriented, approach. To put it more simply, the former represents the approach of historical musicology and the latter, that of ethnomusicology.

In general analyses, the former, that is, the approach of historical musicology places its major concern on the examination of documents of all times in musicological history; the latter, that is, the ethnomusicological approach, relies heavily on findings made through field work and new exploration of old materials.

What I would like to emphasize at this point is that the important fact is that these two branches of musicological concern are not separate and independent fields of study in relation to each other but rather spheres of research and study possibilities that could, and should, be mutually complementary and dependent.

I would like to point out here that the terms 'historical musicology' and 'ethnomusicology' as applied to Korean musicology are adopted by the present writer only in the second chapter of the present thesis. However, whatever terms may be used, they can do nothing but give fixed names to the things that have been done from time immemorial in Korean history of music. The only meaningful point that may be made about the classification of Korean musicology into these two groups is that historical musicology as a discipline seems to interest the older generation of musicologists and has a longer history whereas the ethnomusicology seems to attract the younger generation of musicologists and has a shorter history, behind it. I will now proceed to discuss these two groups separately with my focus of attention, however, on exposing the problems Korean musicology of the present time faces in the course of my discussion of the groups.

Korean Historical Musicology

Throughout the half century during which Korean musicology has continued its developmental struggles, the majority of contributions to musicology have been made in the sphere of historical musicology as I briefly pointed out elsewhere in the present paper. This becomes evident even in an examination of the earlier musicological writings of such scholars as Yi Hye-gu and Chang Sa-hun. The essay collection called *Han'guk ŭmak yŏn'gu* (1957) by Yi Hye-gu, for example, comprises over 20 articles which are significant proofs of this point. His essays, "The Four Modes in *The Yanggŭm sinbo Manuscript*", "The U Mode in *Kagok*" explicate the process through which Korean musical mode has changed since the 17th century in terms of theory: the essay "The Music of Koguryŏ Kingdom and Central Asia" and "The Buddhist Music of Silla Kingdom" are evidence of the earlier efforts of Korean musicologist's interest in historical examination of an ancient era. Such essay as "A Comparative Study of the *Sandae* Mask Drama to the Japanese *Gigaku*" or "*Kunanhaeng of* Master *Mogŭn*" (牧隱先生의 驅儺行) or "Song Man-jae's *Kwanuhŭi*" (宋晚載의 觀優戲) shows historical interest in finding out the historical facts about the performing arts related with Korean folk music. "A Study of *Pohŏja*" included the essay collection, *Kugak non'go* (國樂論攷) by Chang Sa-hun analyzes the historical development in which *saak* (詞樂) of Sung dynasty has gone through changes in the process of being incorporated into Koran music. A Study of *Ch'ŏngsan pyŏlgok* (青山別曲), *Sŏgyŏng pyŏlgok* (西京別曲), *P'ungipsong* (風入松), *Manjŏnch'un* (滿殿春) were comparative and historical study of Koryŏ songs in the early Chosŏn period, based on examination of old musical manuscripts. There were also studies of *Samhyŏn hwanip* (三絃還入), *Yŏmbul* (念佛), and *Kunak* (軍樂), which were all historical analysis of instrumental music of the late Chosŏn period. In addition to these *Maehwajŏm changdan ko* (梅花點長短考) and other essays on *sijo* music were also attempts to study the music history of the Chosŏn dynasty from the historical point of view.

Han'guk ŭmak sŏsŏl (韓國音樂序說, 1967) and *Han'guk ŭmak nonch'ong* (韓國音樂論叢, 1976) by Yi Hye-gu, and *Yŏmyŏng ŭi tongsŏ ŭmak* (黎明의 東西音樂, 1974) and *Han'guk chŏnt'ong ŭmak ŭi yŏn'gu* (韓國傳統音樂의 研究, 1975) by Chang Sa-hun were all important essay collections written from the viewpoint of historical musicologists. To make a long statement short, all the writings related to the historical musicology are scholarly works based on careful researches. That is, these books have their analytical and critical bases on painstaking, historical examinations of old materials. It goes without saying that such scholarly and scientific endeavours by musicologists contributed immensely to the transformation of Korean musicology from a more or less unsophisticated early form to a complexly structured discipline with such a high scholarly status as it enjoys now. The kinds of consciencious efforts to reach the historical correct conclusions about Korean musicology which we can detect in the above-mentioned writings were at the very foundation of the two publications I am going to make the major reference point in my further discussion of Korean historical musicology and its problems. These were both published by the most distinguished of the scholars of Korean musicology and are written from the viewpoint of historical musicology. The publications in question are: *Kugaksa* (國樂史, History of Korean Music, Seoul, Korean Musicological Society, 1965) which was jointly published by Yi Hye-gu, Chang Sa-hun and Sŏng Kyŏng-nin in 1965, and *Han'guk ŭmaksa* (韓國音樂史, History of Korean Music, Seoul: Chŏngŭmsa, 1976) by Chang Sa-hun.

The first problem historical musicologists will face in the immediate future in order to broaden the range of interests and achievements of their field further will be to organize and systemize the basic research materials of Korean historical musicology. One item among many that should receive an immediate attention is the fact that to this date there is no accurate and efficient listing of musicological writings so far published. I do not mean by this that there has been actually no attempt to put some system and order to the research materials both in book or other forms up to now. What I am saying is that although there have been efforts put in for this end, they have not been significant enough to bring a new order into the disorganization and confusion of the present state of things. For instance, already in 1943, Song Sŏk-ha[34] tried his hand in giving some order to the existing old musicological materials. Again in 1965, Sŏng Kyŏng-nin presented the result of his effort to reorganize the old materials in his "Interpretation of Korean Musical Scores."[35] Chang Sa-hun too presented the result of a similar effort in his *A Study of Korean Traditional Music* in 1966. During the ten years following this, numerous old scores have been discovered, but I regret to say that they have not yet received a proper historical examination as to their dates of composition, authors, occasions for composition, and so on. Moreover, even the scores that managed to be investigated are not being utilized widely for musicological studies and researches because there is no index made for them. The Asian Music Research Institute at Seoul National University carried out a grand plan of collecting historical source materials on the basis of *Chosŏn wangjo sillok* (朝鮮王朝實錄, Veritable Annals of Yi Kings) and published a source book called *Kugak munhŏn charyo chipsŏng* (國樂文獻資料集成) Vol. I (1978). This was a mean-ingful achievement as far as the gathering of a great sum of loose materials in one place was concerned. But since it did not have an index, its usefulness as musicological research and reference material was not very great. What seems to complicate the study of Korean musicology with a historical approach is that not only the musicological materials but also some materials of other scholarly fields such as archaeology, for instance (in a musicological study of a remoter past time), need to be examined with precision and thoroughness. My belief is that this kind of a thoroughgoing examination of research materials will be helpful not only for the individual studies and activities of musicologists but also for the realization of more ambitious goals such as solidifying the scholarly foundation of Korean historical musicology as a reliable approach to the study of music, broadening its perspective, and finally establishing better methodology for its pursuits. The problems that remain after an analysis of *History of National Music* and *A Study of Korean Traditional Music* are then: 1) the system and organization are lacking in presenting historical and documentary materials, 2) an index which is a vital key to research materials to be found in scholarly publications is not provided. Until the importance and urgency of these factors receive due emphasis in any planning of musicological projects in the field of historical musicology, I am afraid that we cannot hope for the best results for our effort and good intentions.

The second problem Korean historical musicology faces is having to admit the need for it to have a better understanding and firmer sense of history. Because historical musicology is, after all, rooted in the historical reality of our culture, a proper knowledge and sense of history is essential, I think, in grasping the basic situation of Korean historical musicology.

For instance, that kind of knowledge and feeling for history will be a tremendous help when one decides about what are the more important tendencies of historical musicology, or who are most active in forming those tendencies in the field of historical musicology. As far as the present writer knows, there has not been in any scholarly discussions of historical musicologists of Korea, any serious consideration of the specifically historical aspects of historical musicology as it is pursued in Korea. The two representative musicological publications I proposed to use as my reference point are no exceptions in this respect. I regret to point out that there was no significant mentioning or discussion of history in any of these books. The lack of this vital element in the publications of the most outstanding scholars in the field of historical musicology seems to signify in full intensity the need for historical musicologists of Korea to start paying special attention to the historical aspects of their domain. One evidence, at least, of the disadvantageousness of not having a proper and clear historical perspective on the part of historical musicologists is that in giving chronological order to the course of development Korean musicology has followed, the same standard of chronological classifications which are used in the field of Korean history is being used by musicologists. There is little sign of reflection of modification made on the part of musicologists in adopting the principles of historians. We can see this in the two frequently-mentioned books of reference. Now is the time, I believe, the new generation of musicologists should start thinking about how they can make their knowledge of their chosen field most useful so that with the beginning of the new decade, there will be a change in the manner of carrying out musicological research work, in the nature and scale of contribution of musicology to the cultural well-being of Koreans, and also in planning a more useful and creative sphere of work and activity for the future musicologists of Korea. For all of this, I think, a shift in direction, that is, finding a historically-oriented direction for musicological study and activity is urgently needed. Before they begin to take the responsibility of making the new decade worthy of their ambition and others' expectations, the younger scholars engaged in the field should keep it firmly in their mind that without a good understanding and sense of history, half of their endeavours and resources will be lost.

The third problem concerns the interrelatedness of historical musicology with other scholarly disciplines and also other cultural pursuits of our society. To put it more concretely, it seems to me that younger generation historical musicologists have too little knowledge and curiosity about the methodologies and central concerns of other disciplinary spheres, even those whose concerns overlap theirs. Also, they lack a comprehensive understanding of their cultural history and position. One example of how interrelated historical musicology is to other scholarly spheres can be shown in that, researches and studies of ancient music relies for much of their necessary data on the findings and researches of archaeology. As I have mentioned before this situation is unavoidable because of the limitedness of the research materials Korean historical musicology has under its control. We are aware that in recent Western musicology, there have been cross-disciplinary experiments made between musicology and such fields as linguistics, anthropology, and sociology. These interminglings, it seems, are opening up new creative possibilities for the foreign musicologists. My belief is that it would be most profitable for the Korean musicologists, also, to incorporate the theories and methodologies of such fields as the history of Korean folk art, the history of drama, the history of ideas, cultural history, the history of performing arts, and art history. I do not doubt that such an attempt will open a new frontier for the study of historical musicology in Korea. This is the only way, too, by which musicologists can arrive at the right understanding of the history of music itself. It is true that our musicologists have been most diligent in finding our certain historical data and drawing conclusion on that basis, but regrettably enough, they did not try as hard to find out the historical meanings of their findings and think out what they can finally do with them. In order to understand the historical implications of any data correctly, a historical musicologist needs to know how certain data are related to the particular background of the culture and society.

The Ethnomusicological Field

The term ethnomusicology, as I pointed out before, is an appellation the present writer is the first to use as meaning the kind of musicological study which has its emphasis on the researches done through on-the-spot field work by the musicologists. In this context, the ethnomusicologists' main action focuses on finding out and verifying the musicological materials by going to the place where each material orig-inated. His final objective is rediscovering the Korean heritage in music. As a scholarly discipline, this field has a shorter history than the historical musicology, as I pointed out before. Also, it does not have as much bulk of research materials to rely upon. Lately, ethnomusicology has drawn the attentions of younger musicologists who are likely to develop it into a stimulating and sophisticated learning of any high scholarly standing. It is a field of study, however, first opened up by the combined effort of Korean folklorists and the scholars of Korean literature and language during the Japanese Occupation. Among the early works of the ethno-musicological interest, the most outstanding publication is *Chosŏn Fuzoku no kenkyu* (朝鮮巫俗の研究, Tokyo: Osaka Yogo Shoten, 1937-1938) 2 Volumes by Akiba Takashi (秋葉隆) and Akamatsu Chijo (赤松智城). This book presented a competent study of Korean shamanist music related with folk events on the basis of the data collected through field work. Another remarkable publication of the period was Chŏng No-sik's *Chosŏn ch'anggŭk sa* (朝鮮唱劇史, Seoul: Chosŏn Ilbo-sa, 1941) which was written on the basis of interviews with eminent *p'ansori* singers. In 1944 Yi Hye-gu wrote an essay on Korean shamanist music, "*Muak yŏn'gu*" (巫樂研究)[36] through his field work at Ch'ŏngsu village in Kyŏnggi Province. This work may be considered an exemplary achievement of Korean ethnomusicology. Lately, thanks to the scientific facilities available for scholarly research works, ethnomusicology as a discipline is growing faster than ever before. I think, however, that for a fruitful maturation of Korean ethnomusicology, there still need to be an extensive study of *p'ansori*, folk songs, vulgar songs, and farmers' music. What I am going to suggest as special problems in the study of ethnomusicology has some bearing on these.

The first problem I would like to point out is that we do not have a system of organizing the data and materials we have collected through field work. This is indeed a grave problem, and the need to have such a system is very urgent on the part of any level of our academic strata. I would like to emphasize, however, the adequacy of establishing such a system with the facilities of our larger research institutes so that growing young scholars may be able to utilize it to their best capacity. The materials and data that would be included in this reorganization planning would be records, photography, tapes including cassette tapes, movie films, slides, which researchers have collected through direct field work. This kind of comprehensive reorganizing will bring a far more fruitful result if it is taken into the charge of larger institutes such as the Academy of Korean Studies or the Korean Culture and Arts Foundation than when being carried out by individual musicologists on a personal level. It is because such institutes already have most of the modern facilities and equipment needed for that kind of undertaking.[37] The failure on the part of Korea's larger cultural institutions to do something about the ethnomusicological materials to make them easily available and useful for the growing young scholars is really causing a serious loss to the entire ethnomusicological future because younger scholars who have been able to collect valuable materials through painstaking field work are being forced to make their presentations to the ethnomusicological circle without having recourse to the use of their collected materials. To give a more detailed explanation of the situation, let us suppose that here is a scholar named A. He went on field work and collected the material X on his cassette tape and on the basis of it produced theory Y. There is scholar B, on the other hand who has no way of verifying whether or not scholar A's theory is tenable because at the time of A's presentation of the theory, material X was not presented to support his theory. Without finding ways of eliminating this kind of dilemma, the Korean ethnomusicological future cannot be said to be very bright.

The second problem I would like to point out is ethnomusicologists must think out new methods of collecting materials and organizing them, and, moreover, putting them to a maximum use in their studies, presentations, and so on. Beginning from the very elementary questions, they must think carefully about every step they will take in the course of their researches. For instance, what would a researcher need to prepare before setting out on a field trip? What kinds of questionaire forms should he prepare in order to get the best result? What kinds of equipment and tools would he need? All of these things should be his serious and careful concerns before he can begin anything in the nature of research work and before he can expect to do anything spectacular with the result of his field work. The methods by which a musicologist can transfer his materials into record and draw some analyses from them have been studied by a number of scholars. But the problem still remains and we have yet to find out better ways of incorporating the findings, and suggestion of these findings into our presentations and writings, and so on. There is need, therefore, to study methods of getting needful help out of the existing ethnomusicological materials. There is one thing, for instance, Korean ethnomusicologists need to learn from the attitude of Western ethnomusicologists. It is the accuracy and thoroughness with which they make the scores of newly discovered music and analyze them. The importance of making accurate scores and drawing logical conclusions from them has been a concern of Western musicological scholars for a long time. But it has not received enough attention from Korean musicologists so far.

The third problem is that there has been no concern on the part of those engaged in the study of culture of this society about defining the function and role of music. Does music have its own rules to keep, or is it to be considered as following the same rules as those of other cultural domains and share their cultural function and role in the society? These questions have been the object of study and debate among the ethnomusicologists and cultural anthropologists of the West for some time now. Theories about the origin of music, considerations about the factors that decide the different styles of music and about the relations between the different branches of music, may have to relate themselves with the knowledge, methodologies and findings of other scholarly spheres such as the study of human culture or art sociology. As in the case of historical musicology, having a cross-disciplinary interest in these related fields of study will be a great help to them.

The last problem I would like to draw attention to is the need to systematically increase the number of researchers to carry out more active and extensive ethnomusicological research works. I would like to point out that Korean ethnomusicology should find ways of maintaining scholarly exchange programs with the ethnomusicologists of other countries. There is no doubt that the size of a research team in the Korean ethnomusicological field is directly related with what it can achieve. And I think no one would doubt the need and value of such efforts as would incorporate the knowledge and skill of foreign scholars in our search for a better future in Korean ethnomusicology. An exchange project which will enable us to share our knowledge and experience with foreign ethnomusicologists while obtaining valuable information and other assistance from them would be a most desirable thing to consider under the present circumstances.

NOTES

*This article is a slightly revised English version presented on January, 1980 at the First International Conference for Korean Studies at Yŏngnam University.

1. See Han Man-yŏng, "Ŭmak" (音樂), *Munye nyŏngam: 1976 nyŏndo p'an* (1976 年度版 文藝年鑑), (Seoul: Han'guk munhwa yesul chin-hŭngwŏn, 1977), p. 120; and Yi Hye-gu, "Kugakhak e taehayŏ" (國樂學에 對하여), *Kwangjang* (廣場), (Seoul, 1978), pp. 21–22.

2. Song Bang-song, "Han'guk ŭmakhak kwa munhwa yesul kigwan" (韓國音樂學과 文化藝術機關) *Wŏlgan munye chinhŭng* (Seoul: Han'guk munhwa yesul chinhŭngwŏn, 1979), No. 51, pp. 17–18.

3. See Willi Apel, "Musicology," *Harvard Dictionary of Music* (Second Ed. Cambridge, Mass: Harvard University Press, 1969), pp. 558–59. Bruno Nettl, "The Scope of Ethnomusicology," *Theory and Method in Ethnomusicology* (New York: The Free Press of Glencoe, 1964), pp. 5–7. Claude V. Palisca, "The Scope of American Musicology," *Musicology* (Engle-wood Cliffs, N.J.: Prentice Hall Inc., 1963), pp. 116–21.

4. Representative of his work were *Chosŏn aak kaeyo* (朝鮮雅樂槪要, 1915), *Chosŏn akkip'yŏn* (朝鮮樂器編, 1933), *Aakkok haesŏl* (雅樂曲解說, 1936), and *Yijo akche wŏlryu* (李朝樂制流源, 1938).

5. An Hwak, "*Chosŏn ŭmak ŭi yŏn'gu*" (朝鮮音樂의 研究), (I-VII) *Chosen* (Keijo: Chosen sotokufu, 1930), Nos. 149–158; and "Chosŏn ŭmak sa" (朝鮮音樂史), *Chosen* (1931–1932), Nos. 170–171.

6. Song Sŏk-ha, "Genzon Chosen gakufu" 現存朝鮮樂譜, *Tanabe sensei kanreki kinen Tōa ongaku ronsō* (田邊先生還曆記念東亞音樂論叢, Tokyo, 1943), pp. 387–432. This essay has been reprinted in his work, *Han'guk minsokko* (韓國民俗考, Seoul: Ilsin sa, 1960), pp. 441–91.

7. Yi Hye-gu, "Ryokin shimpu no yonbyōshi ni tsuite" (梁琴新譜の 四調子について), *Tanabe sensei kanreki kinen Tōa ongaku ronsō* (Tokyo 1943), pp. 789–822. This article was reprinted in his essay collection, *Han'guk ŭmak yŏn'gu* (韓國音樂研究, Seoul: Kungmin ŭmak yŏn'guhoe, 1957), pp. 26–47.

8. Keh Chung-sik (Kye Chŏng-sik), "Koreanische Musik," Ph.D. Dissertation, University of Strassburg, 1934. Also issued in 1935 by Heitz & Co. without thesis notice as Band 17 in the Sammlung Musikwissenschaftliche Abhandlungen.

9. Maurice Courant, "La musique en Corée," *Encyclopédie de la musiqe et dictionnaire de conservatoire* (Paris: Charles Delagrave, 1913-1931), Vol. I, pp. 211–41.

10. Andreas Eckardt, *Koreanische Musik*. Tokyo: Deutsche Gesellschaft für Natur- und Völkerkunder Ostasiens, 1930.

11. J. L. Boots, "Korean Musical Instruments and an Introduction to Korean Music," *Transactions Korean Branch of the Royal Asiatic Society* (Seoul: Royal Asiatic Society, 1940), Vol. XXX, pp. 1–31.

12. Sara May Anderson, "Korean Folk Songs," M.A. Thesis, Eastman School of Music, University of Rochester, 1940.

13. Shimizu Fumio, "Shiragi-goto ko" (新羅琴考) *Kokokai* (Tokyo, 1908), Vol. VII, No. 6, pp. 251–54.

14. Kishibe Shigeo, "Gakugaku kihan no kaihan ni tsuite" (樂學軌範の開版について) *Tanabe sensei kanraki kinen Tōa ongaku ronsō* (Tokyo, 1943), pp. 213–44.

15. Tanabe Hisao, "Chosen ongaku" (朝鮮音樂), *Nihon chiri fuzoku taikai* (日本地理風俗大系, Tokyo, 1930), Vol. 16, pp. 186–193.

16. Naito Tōrajirō, "Sōgaku to Chōsen gaku to no kankei" (宋樂と朝鮮樂との關係), *Shinagaku* (支那學, Tokyo, 1926), No. 1, pp. 1–26.

17. Takahashi Tōru, "Chōsen minyo," (朝鮮 民謠), *Chosen* (Keijo, 1933), No. 201, pp. 15–33.

18. Taki Ryōichi, "Chōsen gakki genkin no kigen" (朝鮮樂器 玄琴の 起源), *Ikeuchi Hakushi kanreki kinen Tōyōshi ronshō* (池内博士還暦 記念 東洋史論叢, Tokyo, 1940), pp. 491–514.

19. Iwaya Takeichi, "Chōsen gakusei no hensen," (朝鮮樂制의 變遷 1–6), *Chōsen* (Keijo, 1929–1930), Nos. 139–148.

20. Hiraga Ryōzō, "Chōsen gagaku gakki kei shō ni tsuite" (朝鮮雅樂器 磬·鍾に ついて), *Chosen* (Keijo, 1938), No. 280, pp. 108–119.

21. Chang Sa-hun, "*Han'guk kugak hakhoe ūi haksul hwaldong*" (韓國國樂會의 學術活動), *Yōmyōng ūi tongsō ūmak* (黎明의 東西音樂, Seoul: Po-jinje, 1974), pp. 335–352.

22. Song Bang-song, *An Annotated Bibliography of Korean Music* (Providence, R.I.: Asian Music Publications, Brown University, 1971), p. 91.

23. *Ibid.*, pp. 72–77.

24. and 25. see p. 155 in Korean article.

26. Kim Chin-gyun, "*Minyo ūi silch'e*" (民謠의 實體) *Tongsan Sin T'ae-sik paksa songsu kinyōm nonmunjip* (東山 申泰植博士頌壽記念論文集, Taegu: Kyemyōng University Press, 1969), pp. 163–170; and "*Han'guk ūmak minyo ūi yuhyōngjōk koch'al*" (韓國音樂民謠의 類型的 考察) *Tongsō munhwa* (東西文化, Taegu: Kyemyōng University Press, 1970), No. IV, pp. 343–365.

27. Song, "Dissertation" and "Master," *An Annotated Bibliography of*

Korean Music, p. 215.

28–32, see p. 161 in Korean article.

33. Song, *"Han'guk ūmakhak,"* *Wŏlgan munye chinhŭng* (1979), pp. 18–19.

34. See notes 6.

35. Sŏng Kyong-nin, *"Han'guk akpo haeje"* (韓國樂譜解題), *Han'guk yesul ch'ongram: charyo p'yŏn* (韓國藝術總覽資料篇, Seoul: National Academy of Arts, 1965), pp. 126–77. This article was reprinted in his *Han'guk ūmak non'go* (韓國音樂論攷, Seoul: Tonghwa ch'ulp'an kongsa, 1976), pp. 257–369.

36. Yi Hye-gu, *Han'guk ūmak yŏn'gu* (Seoul, 1957), pp. 163–182.

37. Song, *"Han'guk ūmakhak,"* *Wŏlgan munye chinhŭng* (1979), p. 21.

Micro- and Macro-Structure of Melody and Rhythm in Korean Buddhist Chant

YI BYŎNG-WŎN

Korean Buddhism is characterized by a rich variety of ritual performing arts. These ritual arts play a vital role in intensifying religious experience in Buddhist rituals. The use and complexity of *chakpŏb* (Buddhist ritual dance), *chorach'i* (Buddhist instrumental music), and ritual chant prove them to be an embodiment of the characteristics of Mahayana Buddhism in Korea. Some of these traditions are uniquely Korean among East Asian countries.

Of these ritual performing arts, ritual chants assume the most important place in Buddhist rituals. These are three types of ritual chants. Sutras, in Sanskrit or Chinese, are syllabic and are musically the simplest type of chant (Example 1). *Hwach'ŏng* is the only chant style that employs Korean vernacular language and a musical style idiomatic to Korean folksong (Example 2). The secular nature of *hwach'ŏng* probably developed out of a need to make Buddhism more accessible to the laity. *Pŏmp'ae*, the text of which is based on the Chinese language and poetic forms, is not only the most highly developed ritual chant style in Korea, but is also considered the oldest and most sacred form of art music in Korea.

Pŏmp'ae is said to have developed in China during the third-century A.D. (Kim 1961:10), and to have been subsequently

Example 1. *Panyasim-gyŏng*

introduced to Korea and Japan. The term *pŏmp'ae* itself corresponds to the Chinese *fanbei*, and Japanese *bombai* which became *shomyo* around the thirteenth-century. However, the musical style of Korean *pŏmp'ae* had undergone Koreanization by the early part of the ninth-century as noted by the Japanese priest Ennin (793-864) in his diary written during his pilgrimages to T'ang China (Reischauer 1955:152-3).

Traditionally, the performance of *pŏmp'ae* has been limited to five special rituals. These are elaborate and costly. They may last a day or several days. They are undertaken only once

Example 2. *Hwach'ŏng*

a year or in several years. The five special rituals are *Kakpae-je*, a rite in praise of the ten saints of the other world; *Saengjŏn yesu-je*, a rite to purify past life in preparation for nirvana; *Sangju kwŏn'gong-je*, a rite to focus one's whole mind on Buddha; *Yŏngsan-je*, a tribute rite; and *Suryuk-che*, a rite in worship of the river deities. Due to the enormous expense of these rituals, they are usually jointly sponsored by more than one patron. *Pŏmp'ae* plays a major role in the ritual processes, because the content of a ritual is basically fixed, the performance of *pŏmp'ae* is the main factor in varying its length. Understandably, the length of a ritual tends to be proportionate to the amount of the patrons' donation.

Pŏmp'ae is monophonic; it is performed by solo voice or chorus, with or without optional solo interpolations. Its musical style is highly melismatic, and it makes such extensive use of vocable patterns that the original text syllables are difficult to locate during an actual performance. Because the style of *pŏmp'ae*, unlike the sutras and *hwach'ŏng* is extremely difficult, it is performed only by priest-musicians specially trained in its performance.

Pŏmp'ae contains two different musical styles: *hossori* (simple chant) and *chissori* (long chant). A given *pŏmp'ae* text may be performed in either of these two styles, although there are a certain number of *pŏmp'ae* texts which are performed in just one style. Thus a *pŏmp'ae* text may be set in both *hossori* and *chissori* styles, but the music of the two styles will be totally unrelated (Lee 1977:148). The variants of *pŏmp'ae* performance are probably rooted in its non-musical functions. Certain *pŏmp'ae* text can be performed in five different durations by changing the chant style and melodic organization: (1) the text can be recited by "sweeping it through," (2) the text can be performed in *hossori* style with expansive melodic variations, (3) the text can be performed in *hossori* style with the optional interpolations, (4) the text can be performed in *chissori* style and thereby be significantly lengthened, and finally, (5) the text can be performed in *chissori* style with optional solo interpolations; this will be much longer than a performance in regular *chissori* style without solo interpolations. Selection of one of foregoing chanting styles depends on the intended length of the ritual.

Due to its extremely slow tempo, the macro-structure of *pŏmp'ae* music seems, on the surface, to be so irregular and capricious that scholars have defined it as non-metered, or free-rhythmed (Hahn 1969:270; Lee 1977:115). However, analysis of the internal phrase structure of *pŏmp'ae* proves that it is neither irregular nor free-rhythmed. Consequently, the main purpose of this paper is to delineate the structural configuration of *pŏmp'ae* through an analysis of selected examples.

In general the rhythmic structure of world musical systems is either cyclical, with groups of a specific number of beats recurring in regular cycles (e.g. Western measures, Indian *tala*, Indonesian *gongan* and Korean *changdan*); or irregular, with unequal beats or groups of varying numbers of equal beats which are combined in musically unpredictable sequences (e.g. operatic recitative, *Veda* and works by some of the contemporary composers). The prevailing rhythmic structure in *pŏmp'ae*, by contrast, is neither cyclical nor irregular. Not only do the lengths of both individual beats and beat groups vary, but these are organized into sequences that can attain degrees of mathematical complexity, as far as my knowledge permits, only known in *rolmo*, the music of the Tibetan Buddhist temple's instrumental ensemble (Ellingson 1979:225-43). Consequently, the melodic organization of *pŏmp'ae* is influenced by its rhythmic structure.

On a macro-structural level a *pŏmp'ae* piece consists of a number of stock melodies; these appear in more than one *pŏmp'ae* piece (Lee 1977:111-96). Each of these stock melodies are given titles, such as "bugle sound," "double phrase," and "frequent phrase," etc. These stock melodies serve as the main source of the numerous *pŏmp'ae* compositions by their re-shuffling, re-ordering and transposing upon the chanters' discretion. The role of these stock melodies then somewhat parallels the *echoi* of *Znameny* chant of the Russian Orthodox Church, and represents an ancient technique of composition. This compositional technique is not only found in the archaic music of such non-Western cultures as Korea and Africa, but also was commonly practiced by Western medieval composers.

The structure of a typical stock melodic phrase consists of a formula in which the phrase is consecutively repeated or constantly re-appeared throughout the piece. Due to the extremely slow tempo, the macro-structure of *pŏmp'ae* rhythm is difficult to perceive. Indeed, it seems to operate in a free-rhythmic framework.

However, the inner structure of the stock melodies commonly consists of five to eight consecutively repeated short identical melodic cells. These are composed of accelerating, unequal pulses. In other words, the pulses of each repeated melodic cell within the phrase requires a different metronome meter which becomes steadily smaller toward the end of the phrase, increasing steadily in tempo. The general affect can be likened to the quickening rhythm of a bouncing ball.

Because of the conspicuous acceleration of the beats and unequal pulses of the melodic cells the phrase cannot be subdivided into equal temporal units. In this respect, the rhythmic organization of *pŏmp'ae* phrases operates in much

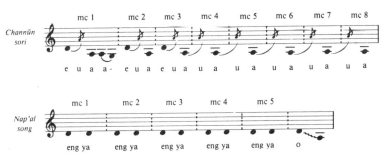

Example 3.
Channŭn sori (frequent phrase) and *nap'al-song* (bugle sound), an excerpt from *chissori* ''Porye.''

the same way as the "logarhythmic" structure of the Tibetan *rolmo* as described by Ellingson (1979:227). The steady decrease in the pulses of the melodic cells inevitably dictates the condensation and reduction of the melodic cells themselves. Thus, the diminishing pulses of the melodic cells within a phrase in *pŏmp'ae* occur not only in time, but also in melodic organization. Both the rhythmic and melodic values of the cells are decreased by steadily reducing the note-values and leaving out certain tones together with their text syllables. The above example (Example 3), an excerpt taken from "Porye," a *chissori*-style *pŏmp'ae*, is representative of the "logarhythmic" structure of *pŏmp'ae*.

The performance of the first phrase, entitled *channŭn sori* (frequent phrase), consists seven repetitions of the melodic cell and takes 26 seconds. Its original vocable pattern of the repeated melodic cell, separated with the dotted bar-lines, consists of *e u a*. It becomes *u a* pattern toward the end of the phrase. The durations of the identical melodic cells in order of appearance are 11 seconds, 6 seconds, 4 seconds, 2 seconds, 1 second, and 2 seconds for the remaining three melodic cells (mc 6-8). In the reduced melodic cell, which appears from the fourth melodic cell (mc 4), the pitch d^1 together with its accompanying syllable *e* is omitted.

Repeated melodic cells

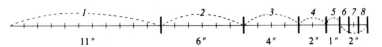

Duration in seconds
Channŭnsori

Repeated melodic cells

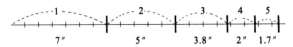

Duration in seconds
Nap'al-song

The stock melody entitled *nap'al-song* (bugle sound) follows immediately after the *channŭn sori* in the piece. Its vocable pattern is *eng ya*. The duration of each melodic cell in order of appearance is 7 seconds, 5 seconds, 3.8 seconds, 2 seconds and 1.7 seconds respectively. A logarithmic graphic representation of the durations of the melodic cells of the two stock melodic phrases would be as follows (one light vertical line corresponds to one second; heavier and longer vertical lines indicate the amount of time the melodic cell took in the actual performance):

In closing, the "logarithmic" structure of the two phrases does not seem to fit into conventional musical form. Rather, it is close to that of Tibetan *rolmo*. It should be mentioned here that the Tibetan version of logarhythmic structure, as described by Ellingson, appears only in Buddhist instrumental ensemble music, whereas it occurs in only Buddhist chanting in Korea. It may be premature to state that there is a relationship between Korean and Tibetan Buddhist music; however it should be noted that Buddhist outdoor band music and Buddhist ritual dances are present in both Tibet and Korea, although they are not common in other East Asian countries. This fact, in addition to their common uses of an unusual musical structure, may contribute to proving a close relation between them.

REFERENCES

Ellingson, Ter, 1979. "The Mathematics of Tibetan *Rolmo*," *Ethnomusicology*, 23(2), pp. 225–43.

Hahn, Man Young (Han Man-yŏng), 1969. "Chit-sori and Hot-sori in Buddhist Chants of Korea," *Essays in Ethnomusicology: A Birthday Offering for Yi Hye-gu*, Seoul: Korean Musicological Society, pp. 267–90. (In Korean with English summary.)

Kim, Tong Uk (Kim Tong-uk), 1961. *Han'guk kayoŭi yŏn'gu* (Studies on Ancient of Korea), Seoul: Ŭllyu munhwa-sa.

Lee, Byong Won (Yi Pyŏng-wŏn), 1971. "A Short History of *Pŏmp'ae:*

Korean Buddhist Ritual Chant," *Journal of Korean Studies,* 1(1), pp. 109–21, 1977. "Structural Formulae of Melodies in the Two Sacred Buddhist Chant Styles of Korea," *Korean Studies,* 1, pp. 111–96.
Reischauer, Edwin O., Tr., 1955. *Ennin's Diary: The Record of a Pilgrimage to China in Search of the Law,* New York: Ronald.

Kaya-go and Other Korean Strings Instruments:

A Contribution in the Form of Questions

MARIA SILVIA CODECASA

From the northern Philippines, in good weather, one can see Taiwan. From northern Taiwan, the most southern Ryukyu islands are visible. And the strait between Japan and Korea is 206km wide. Yet, strangely, only a few scholars have considered the possibility of cultural exchanges between Korean and the chain of islands connecting the peninsula to Indonesia.

Tradition ascribes the origins of the Korean nation to the mythical Tan'gun, who appeared in 2333 B.C. on Kanghwa island, and the whole legend, with the animal symbols it involves, refers to a northern descent of the first inhabitants of the peninsula from Manchuria and Siberia. Yet there is also a southern legend, attributing the origins of the people to three gods, named Ko, Pu and Yang, who materialized in a cave on Mount Halla, on Cheju island, about 700 B.C.: this story should point to some cultural if not ethnic contribution from the south.

The writer of this note, an Italian ethnologist, and no expert in the field of music, while travelling in the Philippines investigating the possibility of such exchanges, happened to find an instrument which might have something to do with the origin of mainland string instruments, and in particular with the Korean *kaya-go*.

The musical instrument in question, called *kullibet* in the local dialect, was collected by Sister Rose Marie Iñigo[1] and comes from the town of Lubuagan, Northern Luzon, Philippines. It belonged to a player of the Kalinga Apayao tribe, but it must be a common item, because other similar instruments, of undetermined origin, are on sale in the touristic Nayon Philipino place, near Manila airport. The *kullibet* is a bamboo zither: it is an internodular tube of bamboo, about 60 cm long, with a diameter of 6 cm (instruments made of bigger bamboo trees are of course a bit larger). It has a lengthwise slit, which is kept open by the insertion of a wooden splint. It has five strings, which are carved out of the very bamboo skin, and stretched with the insertion of two wooden movable bridges under each string. The *kullibet* is held against the shoulder, and plucked by hand.

The area of *kullibet*-like instruments must be very large, since we may find such instruments in Mindanao (the big southern Philippine island) and as far as Java,[2] but its diffusion northwards seems limited to Luzon, since no instrument of the kind is described among Taiwan native ones.[3] Among the most tourist-conscious Ifugao tribes in Banawe (the mountain famous for its rice terraces), the old Ifugao men who play the music for Sheraton-modified Ifugao fertility dances, and who are no longer masters of the technique of *kullibet*-making, have substituted for the original material, bamboo, a little board of wood, and the bamboo strings with three metals bands, about 1 cm wide. It looks like a xylophone, and there is no resonator, but still the metal bands are played by hand, guitar-like. The old man I questioned said that the original instrument was made of bamboo.

Question 1 — Might the replacement of bamboo with wood and metal have been operated elsewhere and with more sophisticated materials, in places where large bamboo was not available, giving origin to the series of string instruments to which the Korean *kaya-go* belongs?

The extant Chinese documents referring to the oldest Chinese zithers seem to prove this derivation from bamboo zithers, which may point to borrowings from the bamboo cultures of the southern chain of islands. There is a legend about the *se*, a very old and large Chinese zither (Korean *"sul"*) with 25 strings, still used only in Korea for Confucian music, and the *cheng* (Korean *chaeng*), also called *Ch'in cheng* because its origin goes back to the Ch'in period (221-206 B.C.). The legend says that a man gave a *se* to his two daughters, who split it in quarrelling for possession of it and got two instruments out, two small zithers with 12 strings each. Of course the story is suggested by a Chinese pun (*cheng* means also "quarrel") but:

Question 2 — Might the element of realism of the legend consist in the splitting of the old bamboo tube zither into two half tubes?

The oldest reference to the *cheng* is to be found in the *Shih-chi* in a quotation of Li Ssu (the minister who ordered the burning of the books), who died in 208 B.C.. The actual object can also be seen among the musical instruments painted on the walls of a tomb near Anak, Hwanghae Province (now in north Korea), in which an inscription is dated 357 A.D..

According to the *Peng-su-tung-i*, a reliable Chinese source of the second century A.D., the *cheng* was created by Meng Tien[4] "with five strings and a body like that of the *chu*, which was an old stringed instrument with a bamboo sound box, held to the shoulder with the left hand and struck with a bamboo stick." The five strings and the reappearance of the bamboo in the making of the zither are certainly remarkable. And, as Van Gulik says,[5] "since the character for *cheng* is composed of two parts, the radical for bamboo and the phonetic element *cheng*, this suggests a musical instrument made of bamboo and called *cheng*."

瑟	chu
筑	se
箏	cheng

The 19th century Chinese scholar Chun Hsimseng, in his commentary to the *Shao wen* (a second century dictionary) says: "the antique *cheng* had five strings, strung over a bamboo body, not unlike that of the *chu*. Meng Tien of the Ch'in period increased the number of the strings to 12, and changed the structure of the instrument after the *se*, using as material wood instead of bamboo. After the T'ang period, the number of strings was increased to 13."

According to Van Gulik, "that the primordial *cheng* had only five strings would seem logical: they would represent the five notes of the antique Chinese scale."

Question 3 — Might it also be that the strings were five because the comparatively slender body of the bamboo zither could hardly hold more than five strings?

Anyway the same author concludes that the name *cheng* was probably borrowed from a crude instrument of bamboo, popular among the people of Ch'in. This seems the simplest explanation of the origin of this instrument.

Question 4 — Might the *kullibet* be the crude zither-like instrument of bamboo? Might the *kullibet*, still in use among the tribes of the southern islands, be the father of the *cheng*, hence of the Korean *Kaya-go* and the Japanese *koto*?

Question 5 — How old may the *kullibet* be? The peoples of the archipelago, of Malay and Indonesian descent, are said to come from Yunnan. Is the *kullibet* a local invention, or is it a survival?

The stringed instruments of Korea, the *kŏmun'go* with six strings, and the *kayagŭm* with 12 strings, are regarded as native inventions. The *kŏmun'go* is an aristocratic instrument, leading chamber ensembles. The *kayagŭm* derives from an older version, the *kaya-go*, meaning "the *go* from Kaya country," which was made of a single piece of paulownia wood, with the insertion of a T-shaped piece, representing the horns of a ram, in the lower end. A tradition ascribes the invention of the *kaya-go* to a King Kasil of Kaya (about 550 A.D.), who would have used the Chinese *cheng* as a model. But this means little; for instance, the above mentioned Meng Tien certainly did not invent the writing brush, which had been in use for a long time before him.

In 1974, there took place the discovery of a pottery jar of the Silla period (57 B.C.-668 A.D.), on which the coarse figure of a pregnant woman is seen playing a six-string *kaya-go*, quite distinguishable because of the two ram's horns. The jar was found near the tomb of King Mich'u (262-283 A.D.). As Ms. Coralie Rockwell points out,[6] the presence of the *kaya-go* in combination with fertility symbols "leaves little doubt that the vase was used as some kind of ritual vessel in fertility ceremonies most probably connected with Shamanism, and that music was an integral part of these ceremonies."

Question 6 — Is the detail that the old *kaya-go* was to be cut out of a single piece of wood significant? Might it refer to its origin from a single bamboo piece? May this be ritualistically significant?

The presence of the horns too may hardly be considered as purely decorative. As Rahmann pointed out[7] "horns are symbols of superhuman power and wisdom" almost everywhere. Astarte was a horned goddess, just as the horned mother of the Gilyak, who live in eastern Siberia near the mouth of the Amur River, and in northwestern Sachalin. Scheftelowitz[8] mentions the horned caps of some Siberian shamans. Among certain ethnic groups, in Siberia, the drum of the shaman was decorated with knobs which symbolized horns[9], and the meaning of this decoration was that these shamans were mediators between man and some gods. The motive is so generalized in the Eurasian world that we cannot infer that the ram's horn piece on the *Kaya-go* has a Siberian origin. Pigafetta[10] describes a sacrificial rite in Cebu Island, Philippines, in which the priestess "puts a kerchief with two horns on her forehead, and another kerchief in her hands, and dancing and blowing upon her trumpet, she calls out the sun." The holy function of horns is not restricted to antiquity, as horn-ridden tourists know all over the Philippines. Therefore, the horn motive is not in contradiction with a southern origin.

Question 7 — Does the presence of the horns point to a ritual use of the *kaya-go*?

Question 8 — Might the details pointing to ritual use entitle us to say that the invention of the *kaya-go* is independent from that of the *cheng*, whether the *kaya-go* be older or as old as the *cheng*, or not?

Conclusion. There is some evidence of a derivation of the oldest Korean zither from a rough bamboo zither still in use in the chain of islands from Java to Luzon. This evidence will be more convincing if further proofs of cultural connections between the southern islands and Korean may be found.

NOTES

1. Of Baguio Holy Family Academy.
2. A sample from Java can be seen in the Taiwan Anthropological Museum. Unfortunately the name of the instrument in the language of Java was not given.
3. Chen Chi-lu, *Material Culture of the Formosan Aborigines*, Taipei, 1968.
4. Meng Tien was a famous general of the Ch'in period, also credited with having invented the writing brush.
5. R.H. Van Gulik, "History of the Cheng and Its Place Chinese Culture," *Dynasty Magazine*, Taipei, February, 1975, Vol. 17, No. 3. To this article I am indebted for most Chinese sources.
6. Coralie J. Rockwell, *Kaya-go: A Study of the Korean Twelve-string Zither, Its Origin and Evolution* (in print) Seoul, 1975, *Transactions*, The Royal Asiatic Society Korean Branch.
7. Rudolph Rahmann, "The horn motif in mythology and folklore" *Philippine Quarterly of Culture Society*, San Carlos University, Sept., 1974, Vol. 2, No. 3.

8. Scheftelowitz, *Das Hornermotif in den Religionen,* 1912, Archiv fur Religionwissenschaft, Vol. 5.
9. Wilhelm Schmitt, *Der Ursprang der Gottesidee,* 1955, Vol. XII.
10. Antonio Pigafetta, *First Voyage Around the World,* Manila, 1969, Filipiiana Book Guild.

The Etymology of the Korean Six-stringed Zither, Kŏmun'go: A Critical Review*

SONG BANG-SONG

The Korean six-stringed zither, *kŏmun'go* (거문고), is one of the oldest stringed instruments in Korea. It belongs to the family of long zithers with movable bridges that is found in several Far Eastern countries. The best known representatives of the family are the *cheng*(箏) in China and the *koto* (琴) in Japan. The most characteristic features of the Korean *kŏmun'go* are probably the following: the zither has sixteen fixed frets and three movable bridges; the instrument has six strings, three of which are stretched over the sixteen frets, and the other three over the movable bridges; and the strings are plucked with a plectrum called *suldae* (술대). These unique properties distinguish the Korean six-stringed zither from the various zither types of China and Japan. The instrument has been frequently called *hyŏn'gŭm* (玄琴) in Sino-Korean, but actually it is more often referred to in Korean as *kŏmun'-go*. The six-stringed zither has long played a significant role in the history of Korean music, and is still used today both in classical court music and folk music. A study of its etymology may yield a better understanding of Korean music. Thus, this study attempts to make a critical review of theories advocated by literary scholars and musicologists, and to shed light on the research of Korean music.

168

The term *kŏmun'go* can be divided into two words, *kŏmun* and *go* (or *ko*). The definition of the first word has been debated mainly from two different standpoints, historical and etymological. The first viewpoint is based on the *Samguk sagi,* in which it is said:

> According to the Old Record of Silla (*Silla kogi* 新羅古記), a Chinese *ch'in* (琴) or seven-stringed zither was brought to Koguryŏ by a man from the Chin dynasty of China.... When the inventor of the instrument, Wang San-ak, played one of his compositions, a black crane [flew into the room and] danced to it. So, the new instrument was called the "Black Crane Zither" (*hyŏnhak-kŭm* 玄鶴琴). Later [the middle syllable *hak* was excluded and finally] it was called the "Black Zither" (*hyŏn'gŭm* 玄琴).[1]

According to the historical source, the term has been defined as a color designation. Thus, the term *kŏmun* has been interpreted as "black," which is referred to in Sino-Korean as *hyŏn.* This definition of the term has been unquestioningly accepted by Koreans. Sŏng Hyŏn (1439-1504), for example, quoted the same statement from the *Samguk sagi* when he compiled the *Akhak kwebŏm*[2] (1493). Another example is the *Yanggŭm sinbo*[3] (1610) by Yang Tŏk-su. The same view has recently been shared by court musicians in the Royal Music Institute of the Yi dynasty (*Yiwangjik aakpu* 李王職雅樂部) and the present National Classical Music Institute (*Kungnip kugakwŏn* (國立國樂院). The head musician of the Royal Music Institute, Ham Hwa-jin (1884-1949), repeats the same story in his publication[4]. The former director of the National Classical Music Institute, Sŏng Kyŏng-nin, also quotes the same statement in his book,[5] and also the present director of the Institute, Kim Ki-su, in his recent work.[6]

An etymological analysis was first attempted by a literary scholar, Yi T'aek:

> Originally the term *kŏmun* could be pronounced as *kŏmu* or

kama (거무 or 가므), which suggests the old Korean term for Koguryŏ and which is identical with the term *kaema*(盖馬). *Kaema* is the name of the place where early Korean tribes established their ancient tribal society. We must remember the term *koma* (高麗) is the Japanese pronunciation of the name of the Koguryŏ kingdom, and the term *kŏmun'go* may be defined as the Koguryŏ zither or Koguryŏ instrument.[7]

He goes on to say that "Just as the twelve-stringed zither was designated as *kayago* (가야고 'Kaya zither'), when the instrument was introduced into the Silla kingdom from Kaya, so the six-stringed zither was called *kŏmun'go* ('Koguryŏ zither') by Silla people when the instrument came from Koguryŏ."[8] Cho Sŏng agrees with Yi T'aek when he cites the latter's etymological interpretation of the term in his essay, "A Study of *Hyŏn'gŭm.*"[9]

Another etymological interpretation has been proposed in a recent work by Chang Sa-hun. After citing an interpretation of the term *kam* or *kŏm*(감 or 검) by Yang Chu-dong, who considers it to be an old designation for "god" or "deity," he suggests a different explanation of the term *kŏmun*, when he explains *kŏmun'go* as a corrupted pronunciation of the word *kamgo* or *kŏmgo*[10] (감고 or 검고). However, Chang Sa-hun does not go on further to discuss whether or not the definition of the term *kamgo* or *kŏmgo* means "god's zither."

There are some problems in accepting the first viewpoint concerning the legend of *kŏmun'go*. The association between the *kŏmun'go* and the black crane, for instance, must be considered in the light of cultural influence from China, for the symbolism in the legend seems to have been a product of ancient Chinese literary culture. Several similar legends relating to the Chinese *ch'in* are found in earlier historical documents of China. An intensive study of the association between Chinese *ch'in* and crane has been presented by Van Gulik in *The Lore of the Chinese Lute:*

The crane is one of the traditional Chinese symbols of longevity.

Just like the tortoise, it is said to live to more than a thousand years.... The *hsüan-ho*, or dark crane, is especially credited with a fabulously long life. The *Ku-chin-chu* says: 'when a crane has reached the age of one thousand years, it turns a dark blue colour; after another thousand years it turns black, and then it is called dark crane.' Since olden times, especially this dark crane has been associated with music. The *Jui-ying-t'u-chi* says: 'A dark crane shall appear at a time when there is a ruler who understands music. When in olden times, Huang Ti executed music on the K'un-lun mountain for all the Spirits to dance, on his right side there flew 16 dark cranes.' Sixteen dark cranes also appear in a story related by the great historian Ssū-ma Ch'ien in his *Shih-chi* ... It is only occasionally, however, that we find faint echoes of the oldest magical character of the association lute [zither] and crane. In later times literary tradition has entirely overgrown these old beliefs; they are replaced by considerations of a purely aesthetical character.... The crane is described as having a great love for lute [zither] music. The *Ch'ing-lien-fang-ch'in-ya* says: 'Lin Pu greatly enjoyed playing the lute [zither]; whenever he played, his two cranes would start dancing.'[11]

The symbolic legend of the *kŏmun'go* seems to reflect close cultural intercourse between Korea and China during the Three Kingdoms period, and also to imply that the author of the legend was much influenced by the classical literary tradition of China. In other words, seen from his historical standpoint, a question is raised as to whether the term *kŏmun* has to be defined as "black." In this respect I agree with the etymological interpretation of Yi T'aek, but his view needs to be supplemented.

It seems very common in Korea and Japan that the name of a certain instrument was designated by its country of origin. The *kayago*, for example, was called the "Kaya zither" by the Silla people when the instrument was introduced to Silla from the Kaya state. When the *kayago* was introduced to Japan during the ancient period, it was referred to in Japanese as the *Shiragi-goto* (新羅琴 "Silla zither") because the instrument was introduced to Japan not from Kaya but from the Silla kingdom. It must be remembered that the Koguryŏ flute was known as the *koma-bue* (高麗笛) and Koguryŏ music as the *koma-gaku* (高麗琴) during the ancient period of Japan. In Korea there is another example of a similar designation of a musical instrument. The conical flute with a brass funnel is still referred to in Sino-Korean as *hojŏk* (胡笛 "Barbarian flute") since the instrument came from the northern barbarian tribe of Mongolia during the Koryŏ period.[12] From our observation, it may be possible to conclude that the term *kŏmun* can not be interpreted as "black" but rather must be defined as the old name of the Koguryŏ kingdom.

Let us now consider the second word *ko* (or *go*). The term *ko* refers to a stringed instrument of the zither family, like the term *koto* in Japanese. One speaks of *kayago* and *kŏmun'go*, for example. An excellent suggestion of the term has been given by Andreas Eckardt who says that the term *ko* may have been the old word for *kŭm* (琴) which was preserved in the Japanese word *koto*.[13] Tanabe Hisao briefiy mentions the problem of interpreting the term *koto* in the course of discussing the Japanese *sō* (箏).[14] Some Korean musicologists have dealt with similar problems through an etymological approach.[15] They suggest the possibility that Korean instruments of the zither family may have been called *ko*, but they do not offer any clear-cut corroboration for their claim. A further discussion of the topic, therefore, will be given here.

Since ancient times music has occupied an important role in Korean cultural life. The old literature of Korea abounds in references to the kinds of musical instruments that were played in the court circle. Among these, several stringed instruments are mentioned. For instance, the *hyŏn'gŭm* (*kŏmun'go*) and the *kayagŭm* (*kayago*) are Korean, whereas the *ch'ilhyŏn'gŭm* (七絃琴 Chinese *ch'in*), the *yanggŭm* (洋琴 Western dulcimer), the *ohyŏn'gŭm* (五絃琴 Five-stringed lute), and the *haegŭm* (奚琴 Two-stringed fiddle) are of foreign origin. In these examples the Chinese character *ch'in*

(琴, read in Sino-Korean *kŭm* or *gŭm*) has been used in order to indicate general stringed instruments of Korean or foreign origin. In other words, the Chinese character *ch'in* does not necessarily mean the seven-stringed Chinese zither.

In the case of the instruments of Korean origin, the *kayago* and the *kŏmun'go*, there is good reason to believe that the term *go* (or *ko*) has been translated into Sino-Korean as *gŭm* (or *kŭm*); thus, the *kayagŭm* for *kayago*, and the *hyŏn'gŭm* for *kŏmun'go*. Concerning the character *kŭm* (or *gŭm*), the old Sino-Korean Dictionary *Hunmong chahoe*[16] (訓蒙字會 , "Teaching the Korean Reading of Chinese Characters") explains that the Chinese character *ch'in* should be read as *ko-kŭm* (고금). The first syllable *ko* indicates old Korean, i.e., the Korean reading of the Chinese character, while the second syllable *kŭm* is the Sino-Korean pronunciation. Thus, there can be no doubt that the Korean word *ko* (or *go*) was used to indicate the zither of Korean origin at least before the early sixteenth century. Another Sino-Korean Dictionary, the *Sinjŭng yuhap* (新增類合 , "Newly Revised Dictionary of Classified Chinese Characters"), reveals that the character *ch'in* should be read as *kŏmun'go kŭm*.[17] The first word *kŏmun'go* indicates Korean, whereas the second word *kŭm*, the Sino-Korean pronunciation. The same reading of the character has been handed down to modern Sino-Korean dictionaries. The *Taejawŏn*[18] (大字源 , "Sources of Chinese Characters") and the *Hanhan taesajŏn*[19] (漢韓大辭典 , "The Great Sino-Korean Dictionary"), for instance, follow the *Sinjŭng yuhap*. It is, then, clear that after the *Hunmong chahoe* (1527), the term *kŏmun'go* for the Korean reading of the character *ch'in* seems to have taken the place of the old word *ko* because the word *kŏmun'go* might have been well known among people rather than the archaic word *ko*. From our investigation we may recognize that the Korean term *ko* was used to indicate Korean zither-family instruments before the early sixteenth century, but since then it has been no longer used in Sino-Korean dictionaries.

It is necessary to take a glance at the Japanese terminology for the instruments of the zither family, for there is an interesting analogy between Korean and Japanese terms. Just as we saw that in Korea the Chinese character *ch'in* has been used in a fairly general sense, so in Japan we find a similar case in the use of the character *ch'in*, as Van Gulik points out:

> One reads about the *wagon* or *yamatogoto* (a six-stringed cither [zither], each string supported by a strut, *ji*), the *sō* (a 13-stringed cither [zither], a Japanese adaption of the Chinese *chêng*, the *Shiragigoto* (a cither [zither], as the name implies, of Korean origin), etc. On the other hand most often we find simply the character 琴 read in Sino-Japanese: *kin*, and in Japanese: *koto*, without further indication of what instrument is meant.[20]

Actually the *kayago* was known in Japanese as the *Shiragigoto* (新羅琴 read in Sino-Korean as *Sillagŭm*, Silla zither), for the instrument might have been introduced into Japan by Silla musicians probably during the ancient period. Although Van Gulik mentions only one example of the instrument of Korean origin in the above, we must call attention to the fact that the *Kudaragoto* (百濟琴 read in Sino-Korean as *Paekchegŭm*, Paekche zither) is another instance of a Korean instrument known in Japan during the ancient period. The *Paekchegŭm* was referred to in Japanese as the *Kudaragoto*, because the instrument might have been introduced to Japan by Paekche musicians probably about the same time as the *kayago*. We must, however, realize that the instrument was not the zither of Korean origin but a type of Assyrian harp of foreign origin.[21] Rather the harp was commonly known as *k'unghou*[22] (箜篌) in China, *konghu* in Korea, and *kugo* in Japan. In order to understand the historical events better, we may glance at the continuous cultural migration from Korea to Japan during the ancient period. It may suffice to cite several statements by Western scholars.

Paikché [Paekche], which had sent in 404 and 405 the learned scholars Achiki [Ajikki] and Wani [Wangin], in 552 sent an image of the Buddha, with a number of volumes of the sutras, and in 554 a number of men learned in, respectively, the Chinese classics, medicine, divination, calendarmaking and music, as well as certain Buddhist monks.[23]

The *Shinsenshōjiroku*, compiled in A.D. 815, contains the genealogies of 1,182 noble families living in Kyoto and the Five Inner Provinces (Go-kinai) at that time. More than thirty percent, or 413, of them were from Foreign Clans (Bambetsu). Of these, 176 were from China, 120 from Paikché [Paekche] (Kudara), 88 from Kōkuli [Koguryō] (Koma), 18 from Silla (Shiragi), and 11 from Imna [Kaya] (Mimana).[24]

There are three great continental traditions that form the beginnings of *gagaku*, the ancient music of India, China, and Korea. The Korean music seems to have been the earliest importation. There are references to it as early as the third century, and further indications of its importation in the fifth century. . . . The various waves of Korean music that entered Japan went under the names of the particular kingdoms in Korea from which they came (*Shiragi-gaku* 453, *Kudara-gaku* in 554, later *Koma-gaku*, etc.). . . . All this complex of music was first classified under the general term *Sankan-gaku* (*Sankan* were three kingdoms in Korea). Later, it was called *Koma-gaku* as the music derived from that of the kingdom of Koma came to predominate.[25]

With a good deal of historical evidence it may be reasonable to believe that Korean musicians might have introduced the old name of a Korean stringed instrument to Japan along with the musical instrument itself. This assumption can be strengthened by etymological evidence. One may already recognize the coincidence of the name for the Korean *kayago* known in Japan as the *Shiragigoto*: *go* (or *ko*) in Korean and *goto* (or *koto*) in Japanese. As shown above, the prefix "*Shiragi*" simply indicates the name of the Silla kingdom. The name of Silla was combined with the word for an instrument of the zither family, the *koto*. Eta Harich-Schneider has already affirmed this, when she states that she inspected:

> The fragment of a musical instrument, probably a *Shiragi-koto*, the zither from the kingdom of Silla in Korea, which was a forerunner of the Japanese *wagon*. The *wagon* is the earliest Japanese stringed instrument of the *koto* type, i.e., hollow oblong zither with movable bridges.... The Japanese claim the *wagon* to be their own invention and unrelated to the various types of continental zithers. Nevertheless, the *wagon* is in fact an import from the mainland; it is developed from the *Shiragi-koto*, from which not only the shape but also the playing technique was adopted.[26]

To further elucidate the etymology of the Korean term *ko*, let us examine several Mongolian terms for stringed instruments. According to the Mongolian-English Dictionary, stringed instruments are referred to as *kho*, [27] so that both a guitar[28] and a lute[29] are called *khoghor*. The word *khoghor-daho*[30] usually means playing on stringed instruments. A similar case of the Mongolian terms can be found in the study by Ernst Emsheimer, when he explains as follows:

> The name given to this type of instrument [fiddle] by the different tribes in Mongolia varies somewhat. Thus, H. Haslund-Christensen notes among the Sunit Mogols the term *khil-khuur* (in the written language: *kili kugur*). In Khalka Mongolia, on the other hand, the instrument is called simply *khil*, while the Buriat Mongols refer to it as *khur*.... As has already been stated above, one finds in Mongolia, besides the type of fiddle just described also another type. Among the Sunit-Mongols it bears, according to H. Haslund-Christensen, the name *dörwen chikhe khuur* (= four-eared *khuur*). The Khorchin-Mongols, on the other hand, have the designation *khorae*, and the Khalkha-Mongols *khuur* or *khuuchir*, the latter term referring to a smaller sub-type. The term *khuuchir* is also current among the Buriat-Mongols for this type of instrument, as is also the term *khor*.[31]

Another Mongolian dictionary gives the fact that the Mongolian term *køg* means "tune" or "music."[32] Thus, tuned musical instruments are referred to as *køgtei*[33] or *køgzim*;[34] and to play music, as *køgle*[35] or *køgzimde*.[36] However, this dictionary does not illustrate further details as to whether a stringed instrument may have been called *køg*-something.

From the viewpoint of etymological probability, it may be said that stringed instruments seem to have been referred to as *ko* in Korean, as *koto* in Japanese, and as *kho* (or *khor*) in Mongolian since olden times. This etymological coincidence could be explained in the light of historical and cultural connections. Historical and etymological considerations, therefore, may suggest the possibilities that the old Korean instrument of the zither family seems to have been referred to in Korean as *ko* from ancient times, and that the Korean zithers might have been introduced into Japan along with their original Korean name, probably *ko*, by Korean musicians in the ancient period.

In short, a close observation of the term *kŏmun'go* leads us to conclude that the etymology of the first word *kŏmun* seems to have nothing to do with a color designation, but is rather concerned with the old name of the Koguryŏ kingdom; and that the second word *go* (or *ko*) not only indicates Korean zither-family instruments, but also shows an interesting aspect of cultural migration in Far Eastern countries. Thus, the original meaning of *kŏmun'go* must be interpreted as "Koguryŏ zither."

NOTES

*This study was originally titled "The Instrument and its Etymology," which is Chapter Two of my doctoral dissertation, *"Kŏmun'go Sanjo :* An Analytical Study of a Style of Korean Folk Instrumental Music." In slightly revising this paper, I have benefited from my doctoral committee members, David P. McAllester (Chairman), Gen'ichi Tsuge, and Mark Slobin. The statements are, however, mine alone, and I am responsible for whatever errors they may contain.

1. Kim Pu-sik, *Samguk sagi* (1145), kwŏn 32, *Chapchi che il: Ak* (雜志第一：樂). For a modern edition of the source see KimChong-gwan (trans.), *Wanyŏk Samguk sagi* (完譯 三國史記 Seoul: Sŏnjin munhwasa, 1960), p. 506 (translation into modern Korean), and p. 512 (original text).

2. Sŏng Hyŏn, *Akhak kwebŏm* (樂學軌範 1493; rpt., Seoul: Yonsei Univ. Press, 1968), *AK* III, p. 19a (kwŏn 7, p. 19a).

3. Yang Tŏk-su, *Yanggŭm sinbo* (梁琴新譜 1610; rpt., Seoul: T'ongmun'gwan, 1950), pp. 2-3.

4. Ham Hwa-jin, *Chosŏn ŭmak t'ongnon* (朝鮮音樂通論 Seoul: Ŭryu munhwasa, 1948), pp. 15-16.

5. Sŏng Kyŏng-nin, *Chosŏn ŭmak tokpon* (朝鮮音樂讀本 Seoul: Ŭryu munhwasa, 1947), p. 68.

6. Kim Ki-su, *Kugak immun* (國樂入門 Seoul: Han'guk kojŏn ŭmak ch'ulp'ansa, 1972), p. 172.

7. Yi T'aek, *Kugŏhak non'go* (國語學論攷 Seoul: Chŏngŭmsa, 1958), p. 99. It must be noted that the English translation is a rough summary of his statement by the present writer. For details of the etymological discussion see the original statement made by the author.

8. *Ibid.*

9. Cho Sŏng, ''Hyŏn'gŭmko,'' *Ko-munhwa* (古文化 Seoul: Association of the Korean University Museums, 1963), No. 2, pp. 33-34.

10. Chang Sa-hun, *Han'guk akki taegwan* (韓國樂器大觀 Seoul: Korean Musicological Society, 1969), p. 68.

11. Robert Hans Van Gulik, *The Lore of the Chinese Lute* (1940; rpt., Tokyo: Charles E. Tuttle Co., 1968), pp. 142-145. As indicated in the title of his work, the Chinese *ch'in* was translated a lute. However, *ch'in* is not a lute but a zither, for which see Chou Wen-Chung's review of the work in the *Musical Quarterly* (April, 1974), Vol. 60, No. 2, p. 302.

12. Chang Sa-hun, *op. cit.,* p. 44. The instrument is often referred to as *t'aep'yŏngso* (太平簫 ''Peace flute'') when it is used in court military music (*ch'wit'a* 吹打). But it is also known as *nallari* (날라리) particularly in farmer's band music (*nongak* 農樂), and also called *soenap* (쇠납).

13. Andreas Eckardt, *Koreanische Musik* (Tokyo: Deutsche Gesellschaft für Natur-und Völker-kunde Ostasiens, 1930), p. 43.

14. Tanabe Hisao, *Nippon no ongaku* (日本の音樂 Tokyo: Bunka kenkyūsha, 1955), p. 245. The study of the term *koto* by Japanese scholars has been well summarised by Willem Adriaansz in his recent work, *The Kumiuta and Danmono Tradition of Japanese Koto Music* (Los Angeles: Univ. of California Press, 1973), p. 22.

15. Yi Hye-gu (Lee Hye-ku), for instance, made a similar interpretation of the term *ko* as that of Andreas Eckardt when he states that "Uncertain zither-type instrument of ancient Korean society might have been called *ko* which seems to be related to the Japanese term *koto*. The Chinese character *kŭm* (read *ch'in* in Chinese) is explained as *ko-gŭm* in Sino-Korean dictionaries." However, he does not provide any example of sources for his claim. For more details see *Kugak-sa* (國樂史 Seoul: Korean Musicological Society, 1965), p. 1.

16. Ch'oe Se-jin, *Hunmong chahoe* (1527; rpt., Seoul: Tan'guk Univ. Press, 1971), p. 94 and p. 283 (*kwŏn* 2, p. 15b and p. 32b).

17. Yu Hŭi-ch'un, *Sinjŭng yuhap* (1574; rpt., Seoul: Tan'guk Univ. Press, 1972), p. 62 (kwŏn 1, p. 24b).

18. Yi Ka-wŏn and Chang Sam-sik, *Taejawŏn* (Seoul: Yugyŏng ch'ulp'an-sa, 1972), p. 979.

19. Yang Chu-dong, *et al.*, *Hanhan taesajŏn* (Seoul: Tonga ch'ulp'ansa 1963), p. 954.

20. Van Gulik, *op. cit.*, p. 217.

21. For more information see Kikkawa Eishi, *Nippon ongaku no rekishi* (日本音樂の歷史 Tokyo: Sōgensha, 1965), pp. 34–35. For illustrations of the instrument see Shōsōin Jimusho ed., *Shōsōin no gakki* (正倉院の樂器 Tokyo: Nihon Keizai Shinbunsha, 1968), Pls. 93–109.

22. For details on the Chinese harp see Kishibe Shigeo, "The Origin of the *K'ung-hou* (Chinese Harp)," *Tōyō ongaku kenkyū* (東洋音樂研究 Tokyo: Society for Research in Asiatic Music, 1958), Nos. 2 & 3, pp. 1–51.

23. G.B. Samson, *Japan: A Short Cultural History* (New York: Appleton-Century-Crofts, Inc., 1962), p. 66.

24. Robert K. Reischauer, *Early Japanese History* (Princeton: Princeton Univ. Press, 1937), p. 19.

25. William P. Malm, *Japanese Music and Musical Instruments* (Tokyo: Charles E. Tuttle Co., 1959), pp. 77–78.

26. Eta Harich-Schneider, *A History of Japanese Music* (London: Oxford Univ. Press, 1973), p. 10. As to ancient Japanese *koto*-type instruments (e.g. *Toro* type of *yamatogoto* in Yayoi period and *koto* appearing in *haniwa*), Japanese musicologists hold different views, for which see "Nihon kodai ongaku wo megutte," (Discussions of Ancient Japanese Music) discussed by Kishibe, Tanabe, Koizumi, Kikkawa, Shinma, Ōba, Nishiyama, and Misumi in *Tōyō ongaku kenkyū* (Tokyo: Tōyō ongaku kakkai, 1965), No. 18, pp. 5–19.

27. F. Boberg, *Mongolian-English Dictionary* (Stockholm: Förlaget Filadelfia, 1954–55), Vol. I, p. 649.

28. *Ibid.*, III, p. 247.

29. *Ibid.*, III, p. 324.

30. *Ibid.*, III, p. 286.
31. Ernst Emsheimer, *The Music of the Mongols* (Stockholm: Tryckeri Aktiebolaget Thule, 1943), pp. 82 and 88. For an essay on Mongolian stringed instruments see Theodore Grame and Gen'ichi Tsuge, ''Steed Symbolism on Eurasian String Instruments,'' *The Musical Quarterly* (New York, 1972), Vol. LVIII, No. 1, pp. 57–66.
32. F. D. Lessing, *Mongolian Dictionary* (Berkeley: Univ. of California Press, 1960), p. 478.
33. *Ibid.*, p. 481.
34. *Ibid.*, p. 482.
35. *Ibid.*, p. 481.
36. *Ibid.*, p. 482.

Brief Introduction to Traditional Korean Folk Music

ROBERT C. PROVINE. JR.

Practically all traditional Korean music, whether from the royal court or from the rice paddy, dates fundamentally from the Yi dynasty (1392-1896): music from earlier times received its final formulation in that five-century period, and recent music written in traditional style harks back to models of the same era.

The most basic social fact of the Yi period was a carefully cultivated distinction between the educated official class and the lower, laboring commoners. This distinction manifested itself in every part of the cultural realm, be it literature, drama, painting, music, or dancing.

Three-quarters of a century and several political changes later, Korean traditional music still exhibits the essential dichotomy of the Yi period: on the one hand, there is *chŏngak* (正樂), which refers to the entire musical tradition of the upper classes, and on the other hand is folk music (*minsok ŭmak* 民俗音樂), referring to music of the lower classes, even if it is performed for entertainment of the aristocracy.

Chŏngak has been described by devotees as elegant, correct, lengthy, profound, and restrained. Lovers of folk music, on the other hand, consider their music straightforward, sentimental, and unrestrained in its expression of feeling. The accuracy of these adjectives is not at issue here, but a basic difference of aesthetic is evident; to this day, musicians tend to be dedicated to one or the other tradition, even though modern musical training invariably involves study of both types.

The *chŏngak* tradition includes incidental music originally used in court rites such as sacrifices, royal audiences, and banquets; refined vocal music such as *kagok* (歌曲) and *kasa* (歌詞); and some instrumental music like the ensemble piece *Yŏngsan hoesang* (靈山會相). It is possible to trace at least the outline of the history of *chŏngak*, as there exist extensive descriptions in the dynastic annals, theoretical treatises, and notation books, all written by educated gentlemen. Folk music has no such written history, and such matters as the relationship between farmers' music and military processions rely entirely upon popular oral history. Much of the information on the history of folk music is necessarily deduced directly from study of the music itself.

If we make a division of Korean folk music into instrumental and vocal types, some of the more important kinds are as follows:

Instrumental:
  Sanjo (散調): virtuoso solo music with percussion accompaniment
  Sinawi (시나위): improvisational ensemble music
  Nongak (農樂): "farmers' music," using primarily percussion instruments
  Muak (巫樂): instrumental music in shaman rites
Vocal:
  P'ansori (판소리): dramatic story-singing
  Chapka (雜歌): "miscellaneous" group songs
  Minyo (民謠): folk songs
  Muga (巫歌): shaman songs
  Tan'ga (短歌): "short" solo songs, usually connected with a *p'ansori*

This sort of arbitrary classification obscures the functional and musical interrelationships: shamanistic music, for example, involves *muak* and *muga* directly, and *sinawi* incidentally, as well as being an important contributing factor in the development of *sanjo* and *p'ansori*. All the above kinds of music share in a common fund of rhythmic patterns distinct from those of *chŏngak*.

Compared to the aristocracy, the low classes in the Yi dynasty were strongly tied to the soil and immobile, leading to certain geographical distinctions in folk musical styles and types. This in turn has led many scholars to propose geographical classifications of Korean folk music. Although this may have been fundamentally true in the early Yi dynasty, geographical differences later became less evident, due to the influence of itinerant musicians who spread the regional styles throughout the country.

This last fact points out that the Korean concept of folk music, as expressed by the term *minsok ŭmak*, is rather broader than the definitions of people like Charles Seeger, since it includes the music of certain professional musicians. Any definition of folk music would naturally include the simple work songs and lullabies of the Korean countryside, but the Korean term also includes highly developed art forms like *p'ansori* and *sanjo* which were created by professional, itinerant troupes of entertainers. The word for folk song, *minyo*, is normally used today for the polished, professional songs developed by these troupes; indeed, if a farmer were asked to sing a "folksong," he would doubtlessly come forth with an imitation of a professional song, not with one of his work songs.

This sort of refined and professional folk music was carried from province to province and came to be the common property of all Koreans, transcending geographical lines. For this reason, geographical classifications of Korean folk music must be taken with a grain of salt, although there is unquestionably still a strong geographical consciousness among Korean musicians themselves.

The professional entertainment troupes performed in the villages at open areas called *nori-p'an* (노리판). The troupes themselves were called *nori-pa'e* (노리牌), and the various games, activities, and performances were known as *p'an-norŭm* (판노름). These *p'an-norŭm* largely originated as activities incidental to shamanistic sacrifices or exorcisms, and later developed an independent existence. The following are a few examples of entertainment troupes common in the Yi period:

Sadang-p'ae (社堂牌): female singers and dancers
Sottaejaengi-p'ae (솟대쟁이牌): masked acrobats who climbed poles to do their tricks
P'unggakchaengi-p'ae (風角쟁이牌): street singers
Kaksori-p'ae (각소리牌): story tellers
Kŏllip-p'ae (乞粒牌): farmers' music bands, employed for shaman rites, fund-raising, and entertainment
Kutchung-p'ae (굿중牌): bands of mendicant priests

Radio, television, movies, and the Koreans' limitless talent and penchant for Western music have spelled the doom of these traveling troupes; the past fifty years have seen their virtually complete demise, with only some occasional so-called "farmers' bands" (農樂隊) remaining. The present handful of traveling bands struggle to survive at all, and typically must be reorganized each year; their function being limited to entertainment, they travel only in the warm seasons at breaks in the agricultural cycle.

The music they perform is almost invariably selected from the *p'an-gut* (판굿), a section of pure entertainment which used to follow the band's participation in religious ceremonies. This kind of farmers' music is still, as an occasional thing, in popular favor today: no rural festival is complete without fifteen to thirty minutes of a farmers' band, typically organized from local talent specially for the occasion.

The great solo art forms of folk music, like *p'ansori*, seem to be regaining popularity, especially among the current college generation. Although its existence is now entirely independent of the itinerant troupes of an earlier day, the music itself still betrays its origins. In a recent performance of *p'ansori*, the singer found it necessary to interrupt his performance in order to coach his (Korean) audience in the matter of how to listen and actively respond to his kind of music. The modern audience, even in a concert hall situation, is well advised to consider the background of folk music and attune its imagination accordingly.

Korean Kwangdae Musicians
and
Their Musical Traditions

SONG BANG-SONG

There is a class of professional folk musicians referred to in
Korean as *kwangdae*,[1] about whose early experience little is
known. From the eighteenth century on, they gradually began
to emerge from the shadows to which the prejudice of the
royal court had confined them, and finally they took their
place in the musical history of Korea. The growth of highly
developed folk music genres such as *p'ansori* and *sanjo*, for
example, are inseparable from the story of *kwangdae*
musicians, particularly in the nineteenth century.

Since *kwangdae* musicians were historically involved not
only in the history of music but also in the history of other
performing arts (drama, masked dance play, etc), they have
been discussed by many Korean scholars. Studies on *kwangdae*
musicians, especially those of Kim Chae-ch'ŏl,[2] Song Sŏk-ha,[3]
and Chŏng No-sik,[4] provide some information. The modern
point of view has been stated by such scholars as Yi Hye-gu,[5]
Kim Tong-uk,[6] and Yi Tu-hyŏn.[7] As far as these literary
scholars and folklorists are concerned, the term *Kwangdae* and
the texts of *kwangdae* musicians seem to be of primary
interest. Thus, only a few of the many publications are
thorough in their treatment of details. The present paper
attempts to present a comprehensive summary of current
knowledge on *kwangdae* musician, and to suggest a possible

direction for future research.

We will try to give the answers to two questions: (1) How did *kwangdae* musicians come to establish their professionalism in the traditional society of Korea? and (2) How and by what means have they contributed to the musical history of Korean? Before turning to discussion of the above questions, we will take up first the historical definition of *kwangdae*, because, though it originally applied to a mask, the word has grown with time, and it has come to mean much more. Far the present purpose it will suffice to outline the available scholarly statements on the subject.

The first known use of the word *kwangdae* is in the *Koryŏ-sa*[8] (History of the Koryŏ Dynasty), where it seems to have been used in the sense of a mask or in the sense of a masked dance player in the later Koryŏ period. In the early sources of the Yi dynasty the word seems to have been used in the same sense as in the later Koryŏ period.[9] When the term came to be employed in the later sources of the Yi dynasty, however, its meaning had so changed that *kwangdae* was a generic term for assorted kinds of folk artists such as *p'ansori* singers, masked dance players, puppet players, drum players, and acrobats.[10] In the society of *p'ansori* singers the term was frequently interchanged with the word *chaein* (lit., "skilled person") in the later Yi period.[11] Since the early period of this century the word *kwangdae* once again has come to have a restricted meaning, now referring to professional folk musicians. Thus, we find that the broadest sense of the word *kwangdae* was its late Yi dynasty use to mean various folk artists,[12] and that since the turn of the century the term has been used in a narrower sense to mean professional folk musicians. But it should be noted that in the middle of the Yi dynasty the word *kwangdae* was applied to the *hwarang,* i.e., the husband of a female shaman.[13]

To trace back the tradition of *kwangdae* musicians, we have to consider the term in its broadest sense, because it has been historically related to other performing arts since ancient times. Perhaps the most remarkable people to compare with the later *kwangdae* musicians are the *hwarang* (lit., "flower boys") and the *chaein* ("skilled persons"). The *hwarang* have been studied by Japanese[14] and Korean[15] scholars, and more recently by an Anglican Church Bishop.[16] We will survey the original *hwarang*, and then examine how they were related with the later *kwangdae* musicians from a socio-historical viewpoint.

The *hwarang* institution appeared when the Silla kingdom was at a crucial juncture of its political, social and cultural history. It was composed of young boys in large numbers, and was an elite group out of which sprang great citizens and soldiers. Music was an important part of their activity.[17] Religious activity was also involved in the institution, as Bishop Rutt points out: "Another point of view seizes on all the religious indications in the sources, and would regard the *hwarang* as a kind of shaman, or at least a shamanistic type of institution."[18] In this religious connection it should be remembered that kings of Silla in the early period were given a shamanistic title, *ch'ach'aung*.[19] Thus we can recognize that the social rank of the *hwarang* belonged to the highest class of the Silla society. After the Silla period and throughout the Koryŏ period, the *hwarang* institution seems to have been continually connected with shamans and travelling musicians.[20] With the advent of the Yi dynasty and their strictly Confucian policies, however, the original image of the *hwarang* institution was corrupted and disappeared. Its religious origins became heavily overlaid with peasant satire, and their stature suffered great change from the highest priest sorcerer to the lowest stratum of the society. From the historical standpoint, then, it is not surprising to find the word *hwarang* used to mean *kwangdae* musicians who were husbands of female shamans[21] and who usually served as assistants for their wives at shamanistic rituals. The fact points out that the descendants of *hwarang* seem to have been socially intermingled with the lowest caste of the Yi society, known as *ch'ŏnin*. The contemporary usage of the word *hwarang* may show how the *hwarang* image was corrupted in the present society of Korea. Murayama Chijun[22] lists *hwarang* as a word for a male shaman. Among the areas in which he notes the word as being in use at the time of his collection of materials (1932) are Masan, Kosŏng, Hadong, Yŏngch'ŏn, and P'ohang.[23] These places are located in Kyŏngsang province, where the original *hwarang* had lived. This point is also brought out clearly in Akamatsu and Akiba's work on Korean shamanism,[24] where they point out that *hwarang* is used to describe a female shaman's husband, especially when he plays, sings, or dances to accompany his wife. They also suggest that the meaning of *hwarang* as shaman's husband is commonest in the provinces of Kyŏngsang and Kángwŏn, and go on to say that it is used to mean a male shaman in South Kyŏngsang and Chŏlla provinces.[25] As Bishop Rutt points out, there are many local or regional variants of the word *hwarang* at the present time: "In colloquial usage there is also *hwallyanggi* (or one of the above forms), or even *hwanyangnom*, meaning a playboy and a lazy good-for-nothing, and also the word *hwanyangnyŏn*, meaning a slut or prostitute."[26]

There existed a low class of society, generally outcast and even feared by the common people, from ancient times. Racially many of them derived from the descendants of Manchurian tribes such as the Khitan and Tartar.[27] These peoples are thought to have appeared in the Three Kingdoms period, and were known as the *yangsuck'ŏk* or *mujari*, the so-called "Korean gypsies" in ancient times. In the Koryŏ period they were called *hwach'ŏk*, *chaein*, or *tartan*, and in the early Yi period, *chaein-paekchŏng*, *chae-paekchŏng*, *paekchŏng*, etc. In the late Yi period these wandering peoples were generally known as *chaein* or *paekchŏng*.[28] The following are some source materials on the early *chaein-paekchŏng*, from the Annals of the Yi dynasty:

Yang Sŏng-ji (1414-1482), the Second Deputy Director of the

Hall of Worthies, reports to the King [Sejo] that the *paekchŏng* are known as *hwach'ŏk*, *chaein* and *tartan* whose origins are varied. They are not of our race.... Their customs handed down to posterity are constant: they assemble together, marry each other, sometimes kill cattle, and live as beggars or thieves.... Those who live lonely in deep mountains, get married to each other, and slaughter animals are bandits, and those who are beggar musicians should be prohibited outside the capital.[29]

To follow the imperial will, the Board of Punishments says that the eight provincial *chaein-paekchŏng* who live as beggars, perform entertainment, and have a peep at houses are robbers, and their life without working should be prohibited from now on.[30]

Chŏng-chaein paekchŏng are originally those who produce nothing and whose profession is acting. They roam from one village to another, and beg for food.[31]

The examples quoted typify the traditional way of life characteristic of all wandering peoples during the early Yi period. They did not have land to cultivate, so that hunting, keeping cattle, and selling meat were their main livelihood. Most of them were not able to stay in one place for long and had to wander from one place to another. They were socially intermingled with other members of the lower *ch'ŏnin* class of the Yi society, such as the descendants of shamans. Singing, dancing and playing were an important part of their life, and sometimes entertainment for common people in the villages was also a way of earning a living. In later days, they are believed to have been regarded as the forerunner of the strolling players and the wandering musicians. We find later Yi dynasty sources which deal with the *chaein*, "skilled persons," who have been related with later *kwangdae* musicians.

The *Wanmun Tŭngjang P'aldo Chaein*[32] (lit., "Petition by the Skilled People of the Eight Provinces") for instance, reveals interesting information about the organization of *kwangdae* musicians. According to this source, *kwangdae* musicians had a well-organized guild system which was officially recognized by the government. The guild was officially referred to as the *Kwangdae-ch'ŏng*[33] ("Office for *Kwangdae*"), and it seems to have been continued to the end of the Yi dynasty. The most famous *p'ansori* singers, such as Song Hŭng-nok[34] and Yŏm Kye-dal,[35] were members of the guild. They were employed at the court when the government had a large scale banquet for the Chinese envoy. Another source is the *Mo Hŭng-gap P'ansori-do*[36] ("Picture of the *P'ansori* Singer, Mo Hŭng-gap"[37]), in which we find that he was hired to perform a *p'ansori* at a feast held for the P'yŏngyang governor around the early nineteenth century.

The majority of *kwangdae* musicians did not seem to have been able to take advantage of the government support. Since these second class *kwangdae* musicians had to find their own way of living, they were often hired to perform at village festivals, or at the *yangban's* parties. In Yi Hye-gu's study on the musical tradition of *kwangdae* musicians,[38] there is an example of how they were invited to a *yangban's* party, and what kinds of music were presented by them. When a *yangban* had passed the civil serivce examination called the *kwagŏ*, his success was celebrated by a festival known as the *hongp'ae kosa*[39] after three or five day's *yuga*.[40] Usually in these festivals, *kwangdae* musicians performed not only *p'ansori* but also acrobatics,[41] and other entertainments. Their reward depended upon both their popularity, and the size of the reward could vary considerably. Thus to earn their living the majority of *kwangdae* musicians seem to have wandered between village festivals and *yangban* parties. However, when *kwangdae* musicians served as assistants for their wives in the performing part of a shamanistic ritual, they tended to settle in a village.[42]

Summing up what has been said, we can conclude that it took the *kwangdae* musicians several centuries to establish themselves as professional musicians. The tradition of *kwangdae* was handed down by the nomadic tribes (Khitan or Tartar) who occupied the northern part of the country, and also their tradition was gradually established in the Korean society by indigenous people (*Hwarang*) who lived in a southern part of the country from ancient times. It was in the late period of the Yi dynasty that the *kwangdae* musicians came to establish their professionalism in the traditional society, in spite of their relegation to the lower strata of the society.

In reply to the question "How and by what means have *kwangdae* musicians contributed to the musical history of Korea?" let us consider first the *p'ansori* tradition that is regarded as part of their musical heritage. Since *kwangdae* musicians have always adapted their music to the requirements of their environment, one must look for characteristic elements in folk song and shamanistic music. Our present incomplete knowledge suggests that *kwangdae* musicians tend to identify with the music of the people among whom they live. The following is a summary of the present knowledge of the *p'ansori* tradition developed by them.

Very little is known about their ancient musical tradition. In the early period of the Yi dynasty they seem to have played relatively simple folk rhythms or folk tunes at village festivals and shamanistic rituals. After the post-war period of the seventeenth and eighteenth century, however, they had to present a higher level of music when they were performed at national events supported by the government. Dance, masked dance play and story telling were essential parts of performance. These stories delivered by *kwangdae* musicians are believed to be the forerunner of the present *p'ansori* tradition. But it is not known today who first invented this vocal genre. What we know about it is that independent *p'ansori* started in the eighteenth century, and that the founding *p'ansori* leader lived in Chŏlla province, in the southern part of Korea. We do not know the exact original form of *p'ansori*. With the help of extant materials, we can only guess about the original situation of *p'ansori*.

Kwangdae musicians usually know more, including some folk tales and folk songs, than the average villager. Not only do they quickly get acquainted with novelties in the course of their travels, but playing to diversified audiences they must also satisfy different tastes. Accordingly in certain portions of a *p'ansori* performance folk songs and other songs of the *kwangdae*'s own creation were frequently inserted into the stories of *p'ansori*, which were mainly derived from traditional folk tales.[44] As Kim Tong-uk points out, a great number of folk songs played a significant role particularly in the formation of early *p'ansori*.[45] With the number of these songs increasing, the rhythms needed for the narration of *p'ansori* became complex and differentiated, so a drummer was naturally employed to set and keep the beat. In the early stage of *p'ansori* development, they sang tales and stories to simple rhythms and melodies which might have been employed in a shamanistic ritual and used by the folk. In his essay on shamanistic melody and rhythm, Yi Po-hyŏng clearly demonstrates that the *ŏnmori* melody and rhythm of *p'ansori* and *sanjo* derived from shamanistic music.[46] The *kwangdae* and his collaborator, the drummer, also had to arrange the rhythms according to content and mood of the narrations; the process of this arrangement was called "weaving" in traditional terminology.

When singing folk tales, *kwangdae* musicians sometimes had to collect linguistic expressions used among the common people and to arrange them in an artistic way. Since audiences ranged from the royal and noble families to the lower class, a great breadth of linguistic expression was inevitably needed. It was, therefore, natural that the *p'ansori* texts embraced all the linguistic expressions existing in the contemporary society, from quotations of classical Chinese literature to folk songs and proverbs.[47] In short, the *kwangdae* musicians had to acquaint the masses with the music and text of the aristocracy and villages.

In order to understand the original nature of the *p'ansori* tradition, however, we should keep in mind that in most cases a *kwangdae* musician inherited and transmitted what his master *kwangdae* musician had done in complete form, because in reality there were no written texts for them to refer to during the early development of *p'ansori*. They had to memorize what they learned from the master *kwangdae* musician. In this sense *p'ansori* was originally an oral tradition in the earlier stage of development.

It was during the second half of the nineteenth century that the oral body of *p'ansori* tradition was written down by the great compiler of *p'ansori*, Sin Chae-hyo (1812-1884). Although it is said that there were twelve pieces[48] of *p'ansori* in the eighteenth century, only six pieces were written down by Sin Chae-hyo, five of which are still performed today. The traditional style of *p'ansori* was the performance by a single *kwangdae* musician with drum accompaniment. But during the early part of this century several *kwangdae* musicians and the successors of Sin Chae-hyo endeavored to devise a dramatized and stage version in the Western operatic style. This new version of *p'ansori* is called *ch'angguk*, literally "sung drama."

Next, let us consider an important musical genre for instruments known as *sanjo* (lit., "scattered melody"), which was developed by *kwangdae* musicians during the late nineteenth century in the Chŏlla province of southern Korea. When a *kwangdae* musician assisted his wife at a shamanistic ritual performance, called *kut* in Korean, he played the shamanistic dance music known as *sinawi* or *simbanggok*.[49] The *sinawi* music was a style of improvization for one or several instruments accompanied by a barrel-shaped drum (*puk*) or by an hour-glass shaped drum (*changgo*).[50] This kind of *sinawi* music is considered to have been the forerunner of *sanjo* developed by *kwangdae* musicians in the course of time. According to Yi Hye-gu's etymological study of *sinawi*,[51] the word means a native or indigenous melody in contrast to an imported foreign melody, and it is also identified with the *saenaenorae*[52] of Silla. If his interpretation is correct, then, we may assume that *sinawi* music includes the most vital musical tradition of Korea.

An outstanding *kayagŭm* (12-stringed zither) player of Chŏlla province, Kim ch'ang-jo, is thought to have synthesized elements of improvization and rhythmic design of *sinawi* with melodic patterns of *p'ansori* in highly developed artistic expression.[53] In fact, a certain melodic pattern of *sanjo* is so expressive and dramatic that *sanjo* is believed to be an instrumental version of *p'ansori*. *Sanjo* was originally played on the *kayagŭm*, but soon began to be played on the *kŏmun'go* (6-stringed zither) and on other instruments as well. The *sanjo* form was naturally adapted to suit the idiom of each instrument. More recently the players of the *haegŭm* (2-stringed fiddle), *ajaeng* (bowed 7-stringed zither), and other instruments have found in the *sanjo* form a perfect vehicle for displaying their musicianship. Today there are several distinctive personal styles of *sanjo*.

To sum up, just as the word *kwangdae* has been greatly changed in the course of time, so Korean traditional music was variously enriched in the late Yi period. In spite of their position as the lowest social stratum of the Yi dynasty, *kwangdae* musicians had to get acquainted quickly with the different tastes of diversified audiences. From the eighteenth century on, they developed their musical tradition into a highly-organized artistic expression, and that is their contribution to the history of Korean music. *P'ansori* and *sanjo* are the most prominent musical genres they developed. When we consider the social and historical connection of *kwangdae* with Korean shamans and the folk, their remarkable musical assets must be understood within the context of such living traditions as Korean shamanistic music and folk music, which have been handed down since ancient times. In other words, *p'ansori* music can hardly be investigated without considering shamanistic dance music and folk songs of Chŏlla province, which might have played a significant role in the melodic and rhythmic formation of the *p'ansori* tradition. On the other hand *sanjo* music should also be studied in relation to the melodic structure of *p'ansori*, and the rhythmic structure of *sinawi* music, which shows the most essential elements of the indigenous musical tradition of Korea.

NOTES

1. The Romanizations used in this essay are McCune-Reischauer system for Korean and Hepburn for Japanese. Korean and Japanese names are given in their original fashion, surname first.
2. Kim Chae-ch'ŏl, *Chosŏn yŏn'gŭk-sa* (1933; rpt. Seoul: Minsok kŭkhoe Namsadang, 1970), pp. 164–72.
3. Song Sŏk-ha, *Han'guk minsok-ko* (Seoul: Ilsinsa, 1960), pp. 224–29 and pp. 249-65.
4. Chŏng No-sik, *Chosŏn ch'anggŭk-sa,* Seoul: Chosŏn ilbo-sa, 1940.
5. Yi Hye-gu (Lee Hye-ku), *Han'guk ŭmak yŏn'gu* (Seoul: Kukmin ŭmak yŏn'gu-hoe, 1957), pp. 164-82.
6. Kim Tong-uk, "Chungsegi ŭi yenŭngin kwangdae," *Sasanggye* (Seoul, 1955), III, No. 3, pp. 37-50.
   _____. *Han'guk kayo ŭi yŏn'gu* (Seoul: Ŭryu munhwa-sa, 1961), pp. 275-551.
   _____. "P'ansori-sa yŏn'gu ŭi che-munje," *Inmun kwahak* (Seoul: Yŏnsei University Press, 1968), No. 20, pp. 1-28.
7. Yi Tu-hyŏn (Lee Duhyon), *Han'guk kamyŏn'-gŭk* (1969; rpt. Seoul: Han'guk kamyŏn yŏn'gŭk-hoe, 1973), pp. 39–44 and pp. 132-35.
   _____. *Han'guk yŏn'gŭk-sa,* (Seoul: Minjung sŏgwan, 1973), pp. 66-71 and pp. 77-82.
8. Chŏng In-ji, *et. al.* (comp.), *Koryŏ-sa* (Seoul: Yŏnsei University Press, 1955), III, p. 693 (*kwŏn* 124, p. 9b.)
9. Kim Tong-uk, *op. cit.* (1961), p. 295.
10. Song Sŏk-ha, *op. cit.,* p. 226.
11. *Ibid.,* p. 256.
12. Besides these meanings, the term *kwangdae* is still used by members of folk culture in the sense of a mask. See Song Sŏk-ha, *op. cit.,* pp. 228–29.
13. For details, see Kim Tong-uk, *op. cit.* (1961), p. 351.

14. Mishina Shōei, *Chōsen kodai kenkyū: Dai ichibu, Shiragi karo no kenkyū*, Tokyo: Sanseidō, 1943.

15. Yi Sŏn-gŭn, *Hwarangdo yŏn'gu*, Seoul: Sŏn'gwang insoe chusik hoesa, 1948.

16. Richard Rutt, "The Flower boys of Silla (*Hwarang*)," *Transactions of the Korea Branch of the Royal Asiatic Society*, 28 (Seoul, 1961), pp. 1–66.

17. Mishina, *op. cit.*, pp. 83–92.

18. Rutt, *op. cit.*, p. 66.

19. For example, "Namhae ch'ach'aung," See Kim Chong-gwŏn, trans., *Wanyŏk Samguk sagi* (Seoul: Sŏngjin munhwa-sa, 1960), p. 18. For an etymological study of the word, see Chi Hŏn-yŏng, "Kōsōgan, ch'achiaung, nisagūme taehayō," *Ōmunhak* (Taegu, 1962), No. 8, pp. 1–18.

20. The dancing of a group called the *sŏllang* was a distinctive feature of the *p'algwanhoe* festival in the Koryŏ court. They presented masked dance plays and the *ch'ŏyong* dance at the festival. The *sŏllang* groups were understood by the people of the time to be the direct descendants of the Silla *hwarang*. For a further discussion, see Mishina, *op. cit.*, pp. 273–87.

21. Ch'oe Se-jin *Hunmong chahoe* (1527; rpt. Seoul: Tan'guk University Press, 1971), p. 68 and p. 226. Kim Tong-uk notes its appearance in Chŏng Yag-yong's *Mongminsimsō, kwŏn* 12, in his work (1961), p. 351.

22. Murayama Chijun, *Chōsen no fūgeki* (keijo (Seoul): Chōsen Sōtokufu, 1932), p. 22.

23. *Ibid.*, pp. 31–33.

24. Akamatsu Chijo and Akiba Takashi, *Chōsen fūzoku no kenkyū* (Tokyo: Osaka yogō shōten, 1937–38), II, pp. 31–32.

25. *Ibid.*, p. 22.

26. Rutt, *op. cit.*, p. 8.

27. Yi Pyŏng-do, *Han'guk-sa* (Seoul: Chindan Hakhoe, 1964), II, pp. 345–46.

28. Kang Man-gil, "Sŏnch'o paekchŏng ko," *Sahak yŏn'gu* (Seoul: Han'guk sahak-hoe, 1964), No. 18, pp. 491–526.

29. Kuksa p'yŏnch'an wiwŏnhoe, *Yijo Sillok* (Seoul: T'amgudang, 1970), VII, p. 124 (*Sejo taewang sillok, kwŏn* 3, p. 30b., March, the 2nd year of the King Sejo's reign).

集賢殿直提學 梁誠之 上疏曰…(中略)…盖白丁或 稱釋或 才人 或稱韃粗 其
種類非一…(中略)…本非我類 遺俗不變 自相屯聚 自相婚嫁 或殺牛 或訴
乞 或行盜賊…(中略)…其獨處山谷 或自相婚 或行宰殺 或行寇賊 或作樂丐
乞者 京外痛禁.

30. *Ibid.*, VIII, p. 628 (*Sŏngjong taewang sillok, kwŏn* 14, p. 15b., January,

the 3rd year of King Sŏngjong's reign).

傳旨刑曹曰 諸道諸邑才人行乞者 群行作戲 窺覘人家 因行盜劫 遊手而食 今
後成群行乞者 一禁.

31. *Ibid.*, XVIII, p. 465 (*Chungjong taewang sillok, kwŏn* 95, p. 28a.,
Ma., the 36th year of the King Chungjong's reign).

呈才人白丁等 本是無恒產之人 專業優戲 橫行閭里 稱爲乞糧.

32. For the original text, see Pak Hŏn-bong, *Ch'angak taegang* (Seoul:
Kukak yesul hakkyo ch'ulp'anbu, 1966), pp. 53–54, Kim Tong-uk, *op.
cit.* (1961), pp. 301–302; and Yi Hye-gu, *op. cit.*, pp. 356–57.

33. It was also called the *Hwarang-ch'ŏng* (lit., "Office for *Hwarang*"), and
the *Chaein-ch'ŏng* ("Office for Skilled People"). For a further discussion, see Kim Tong-uk, *op. cit.* (1961), p. 302.

34. For his short biography, see Chong No-sik, *op. cit.*, pp. 20–25.

35. *Ibid.*, pp. 25–28.

36. For the illustration, see Pak Hŏn-bong, *op. cit.*, p. 35.

37. For his short biography, see Chŏng No-sik, *op. cit.*, pp. 28–30.

38. Yi Hye-gu, *op. cit.*, pp. 318–64.

39. *Hongp'ae* (lit., "red stick") was a red sheet in which a certification of
passing the civil service examination issued by a king is indicated. *Kosa*
was a kind of festival usually performed by *kwangdae* musicians. For
a further discussion, see Ch'oe Nam-sŏn, *Chosŏn sangsik mundap:
Chedo-p'yŏn* (Seoul: Tongmyŏng-sa, 1948), p. 126. See also Yi Sang-
baek, *Han'guk-sa* (Seoul: Chindan Hakhoe, 1962), III, p. 284.

40. *Yuga* (lit., "strolling street") indicated a kind of parade showing his
success in the civil service examination. In this parade *kwangdae* musicians were always hired to perform music and other plays. For a further
discussion, see Ch'oe Nam-sŏn, *op. cit.*, p. 140, and Yi Sang-baek, *op.
cit.*, p. 285 (his footnote 4). For an illustration of the *yuga*, see the
P'yŏngsaeng-do (lit., "Picture of One's Whole Life") in *Space Architec-
ture Urban Design & Art* (Seoul: Konggan-sa, 1974), Vol. 81, pp. 56–57.

41. Yi Hye-gu, *op. cit.*, p. 355.

42. According to a recent study of Korean shamans, Korean shamans are
financially supported by their clients organized by the guild system of
their society called *tan'gol*. For details, see Kim T'ae-gon, "Components
of Korean Shamanism," *Korea Journal* (Seoul, 1972), XII, No. 12, p. 18.

43. Kim Tong-uk, "On P'ansori," *Korea Journal*, XIII (1973), No. 3, p, 11.

44. *Ibid.*

45. Kim Tong-uk, *op. cit.* (1961), pp. 332–37.

46. Yi Po-hyŏng, "Muga wa p'ansori wa sanjo esŏ ŏnmori karak pigyo,"
Yi Hye-gu Paksa songsu kinyŏm ŭmakhak nonch'ong (Seoul: Han'guk
kukak hakhoe, 1969), pp. 81–115.

47. For example, see the text of the first chapter in Kim Yŏn-su, *Ch'angbon*

Ch'unhyang-ga (Seoul: Kugak yesul hakkyo ch'ulp'anbu, 1967), pp. 41–42. For a facsimile edition of original *p'ansori* texts, see Sin Chae-hyo, ed., *Sin Chae-hyo P'ansori chōnjip,* Seoul: Yōnsei University Press, 1969.

48. Yi Hye-gu, "Kugak-sa: Yijo hugi ūi ūmak, *Kugak-sa* (Seoul: Han'guk kugak hakhoe, 1965) pp. 56–56. For an English survey, see Yi Po-hyōng, "P'ansori," *Survey of Korean Arts: Traditional Music* (Seoul: National Academy of Arts, 1973), pp. 214–15.

49. Yi Hye-gu, *op. cit.* (1957), p. 246. For a report on *sinawi,* see Yi Po-hyōng and Yu Ki-ryong, *Sinawi* (Seoul: Munhwajae gwalliguk, 1971, Muhyōng munhwajae chosa pogosō No. 85 pp. 21–31.)

50. For an illustration of *kwangdae* musicians performing shamanistic dance music, see Kim Wōl-yong, *Han'guk misul-sa* (1968: rev. ed., Seoul: Pōmmun-sa, 1973), p. 352, color figure 31. According to the picture, *Munyō-do* (lit., "Picture of Female Shaman") by Sin Yun-bok (1758–?), two *kwangdae* musicians are playing shamanistic dance music with a *changgo* (hour-glass shaped drum) and *p'iri* (slender bamboo oboe).

51. Yi Hye-gu, *op. cit.* (1957), p. 249.

52. For an etymological study, see Yang Chudong, *Koga yōn'gu* (Seoul: Pangmun ch'ulp'ansa, 1943), pp. 33–65. For the same subject in English, see Yi Peter H. (Peter H. Lee), *Studies in the Saenaenorae: Old Korean Poetry* (Roma: Instituto Italiano per il Medio Estremo Orients, 1959), pp. 99–100.

53. To my knowledge, it is the *Choson ūmak t'ongnon* (Seoul: Ūryu munhwa-sa, 1948, p. 210) by Ham Hwa-jin which mentions, for the first time, the founder of *Kayagūm sanjo,* Kim Ch'ang-jo. For an English survey of the instrumental solo music, see Yi Chae-suk (Lee Chae-suk), 'Sanjo,' *Survey of Korean Arts: Traditional Music* (Seoul, 1973), pp. 202–11. See also Barbara B. Smith, "Kayagūm sanjo: A Korean music," in the booklet, *Notes to Music from Korea, Vol. I: The Kayagūm* (Honolulu, East-West Centre Press, 1965), pp. 3–5.

Korean Music Culture:
Genuine and Quasi-Korean Music[1]

For hundreds of years Korean musical culture was influenced by China. However, with increasing influence from other foreign sources particularly from the West since the beginning of the twentieth century, Korean culture and music began to take on a more heterogeneous flavor. Because of this continued pressure from outside sources the majority of Korean people presently appear to have lost their musical identity. What has clearly emerged in Korea over the last few decades is a music culture that may be described as one having both genuine and quasi-Korean music, the greatest emphasis being given to the quasi-Korean music. It is the author's goal in this study to make a distinction between the genuine and quasi-Korean music currently practiced in Korean culture.

Although the Korean people had experienced some sporadic contact with the West prior to 1884, Western music had made almost no inroads into the country before that date. However, with the appearance of the first publication of the Christian hymnal *Ch'ansongga* in 1893 and with the political Reform Movement of 1894 and its resultant social changes, Western musical ideas began to permeate Korean musical cultures.[2]

The influence of the West was further demonstrated in 1900 with the establishment of the royal military band, based on the Western model. This military band was one more link in the chain of the Korean governmental program of

Westernization. More specifically, it served in Seoul as Western styled diplomatic etiquette to honor visiting dignitaries. Franz von Eckert is credited with introducing this specific band type to Korea, which he patterned after the form be developed in Japan.[3]

After the introduction of Western music around the turn of the century, a conflict arose between pro-Western and pro-Korean musical viewpoints. A sharp disagreement prevailed between proponents of the alien Western style and those who defended the traditional Korean style which had a history of at least a thousand years. In these musical debates the Western style usually received stronger support. This was an apparent result of the government-sponsored policy of Westernization that affected certain key social and educational circles, rather than from any inherent superiority of Western music.

The official inclusion of Western music in the schools occurred for the first time in 1904,[4] and it rapidly permeated Korean urban and intellectual society. Although a study group of Korean traditional music called *Choyang Kurakpu* (調査倶樂部) was organized in 1909 for the purpose of combating the encroaching influence of Western music, no power seemed able to block the onward march of Westernization. Even the *Choyang Kurakpu* itself could not resist including courses in the new form in its curriculum.

In 1919 Hong Nan-p'a composed *"Pongsŏnhwa."* The latter is one of the earliest art songs in Korean history to be done in Western style. This song, and others like it, became very popular throughout the country, gaining almost as great an acceptance as the traditional Korean folk song.

With the appearance of this new art song, Korean musical culture leaned more and more away from traditional influences. Consider, for instance the adoption of the English melody "Auld lang syne" as one of Korea's first national anthems, a step which had been taken before, in 1902,[5] but which gained renewed interest at this time. Somewhat later, in 1936, the present anthem was composed by a Korean, again using a Western melodic type with Korean text.

While European composers were abandoning their traditional forms during the first half of the century in search of new musical innovations, Western-influenced Korean composers were only beginning to accept the practices that their European contemporaries had already given up. From this time to the present day there has been a continuing trend on the part of Korean composers and music educators to almost worship Classical and Romantic European music.

Today, Korean musical life is dominated by three basic categories: 1) Western-oriented music, 2) Korean indigenous music, and 3) an experimental combination which attempts to reconcile Western with Eastern.

The Western-oriented style can be roughly broken down into three sub-categories with songs similar to "*Pongsŏnhwa*," using the Western melodic type and Korean text, the most popular in urban society. Also included in this category would be "Korean pop" and the Westernized version of the Korean folk song. The second sub-category consists of various musical pieces from classic to pop which are written by Western composers and performed by Korean musicians in their original form. The next sub-category is comprised of instrumental compositions by Koreans, done in strictly Western style.

Among these three sub-categories the music written by Western composers and performed by Koreans, and the music written by Koreans in Western style retain an identity that is uniquely their own, distinct from the traditional Korean style. The pieces are purely Western in nature and contain no elements of genuine Korean musical character. However, compositions of the "*Pongsŏnhwa*" type may be referred to here as "quasi-Korean" as they use a Korean text with strictly Western melodic types. In this discussion the author will attempt to differentiate between this so-called quasi-Korean and genuine Korean music by analyzing in detail representative examples of each. By genuine is meant that type of music which is uniquely Korean, that which can only be understood and explained in terms of traditional Korean culture. In other words, music in this category is the second basic group: Korean indigenous music. The Korean indigenous form can also be broken down into several sub-categories which will be fully discussed at some other time.

The experimental combination form, the third major group to be considered, has a perspective so vast that it can be limited only by the imagination of each individual composer. Moreover, it can become a topic of such breadth that critical analysis is almost impossible in a study of this scope.

Thus there remains for this discussion the two significant types, the genuine Korean form and quasi-Korean, examples of which will now be considered in detail to show their basic differences.

Quasi-Korean Music

There is a children's song in Korea called "*Hakkyo*" (학교) ("School"). The author deliberately chose this song for analysis because it is first of all comparatively simple and easily understood by anyone and, secondly, because it is popular in Korea and provides valuable insight into the nature of the "quasi" form. It is a song similar to "*Pongsŏnhwa*," in a Western scale with Korean text.

At the present time, however, this song is erroneously considered by a majority of Korean people to be a Korean song

Example 1. *Hakkyo*

in terms of its musical structure. Many non-Korean music specialists also share this view due only to the fact that it is widely accepted by the native populace.

Example 1 is not merely a Westernized transcription of a traditional Korean folk song but one written by a Western-influenced Korean composer who meant it to be sung as it is written. A Westernized transcription of a traditional Korean folk song is not normally meant to be sung as transcribed, but in terms of traditional intervals unique to that culture.

Even without analyzing the piece, one can immediately notice, if he ignores the text, that this song is not Korean in nature. To belong to Korean musical culture, it should be related to Korean musical language, should it not? One might examine the song in terms of its rhythm, form, melody, harmony, and text to see if it really has something of this relationship.

Rhythm: Korean rhythm can be characterized as either "elastic" or trochaic, as Yi Hye-gu observes:

> There are several concepts of rhythm in the music played in Korea.... Korean classical styles,... are based on unequal duration of syllables and melodic tones. In court and aristocratic music, tempo may be as slow as MM. 30. If unaccompanied, it would be almost impossible to communicate a rhythmic feeling to the duration of several of these beats tied together....
> Folk songs are seldom as slow as the classical songs; and *kut-kŏri*, a rhythmic pattern in triple meter, 6/8, is a characteristic of Korean folk music....
> The Korean language has neither article nor preposition, but does have postposition. For this reason, the Korean song is trochaic rather than iambic....

The rhythm of Example 1 obviously has nothing to do with the characteristic Korean rhythm since its rhythm is clearly in duple meter.

Form: The form of Example 1 is clearly a period in parallel construction, i.e., the same material is employed for the antecedent and consequent phrases. Example 1 meets, of course, the essential characteristic of a parallel period in that the antecedent phrase ends with a weaker cadence (the dominant) than the consequent (the tonic). Korean form in music has again nothing to do with this type of common cadence practice, which serves in Western music to punctuate a given piece. This does not mean, however, that there is no sense of punctuation and no feeling of a tension-release relationship in traditional Korean music. The idea implied here is that the technique used to punctuate a continuum of sounds and to connect the isolated sounds or groups of sounds into a musical shape is substantially different. At this point, it can be concluded that Example 1 is unlike the Korean musical form in that it is related to the common cadence practice.

1: C, D, E, G, and A. In other words, the melody of "School" might be said to be made up of a scale typical to an Oriental song, namely, a five-note (pentatonic scale). Indeed, much Oriental music is based on a pentatonic scale. However, it is extremely important not to confuse an equal tempered pentatonic scale with an unequal tempered one. A five note scale means nothing in Korean music unless the appropriate relationship between each note in terms of its intervals is held constant. To belong to the Korean pentatonic scale, *p'yŏng-jo* for example, the interval relationships should be uniquely Korean. Further, although Example 1 consists of only five notes, the melody is actually based on the Western major scale. In the melody itself, there is neither an F nor a B. However, the last note of the antecedent phrase of this melody strongly implies the dominant harmony which obviously includes B, a leading tone. In short, the melody has nothing to do with *p'yŏng-jo* or *kyemyŏn-jo* which comprise the basic musical vocabulary of genuine Korean music.

It may be noted that there is a theory regarding Korean modes which claims that *p'yŏng-jo* is similar to the Western major mode while *kyemyŏn-jo* is similar to the minor mode. To a certain extent this may be acceptable. However, the author will conclude in the course of this study that the above theory could be highly misleading to the serious student of multicultural music.

Harmony: It can be simply said that there is no concept of harmony as such in Korean music with regard to the tertian type. The concept can occur, however, if the term is used to literally designate the meaning of the word harmony, that is, a pleasing arrangement of things, parts, colors, or musical agreement in ideas, feelings, etc, or the sounding together of tones in a way that is pleasing to the ear.[7] Since the Korean concept of the blending of tones in a way that is pleasing to the ear is totally different from the Western concept, when one deals with Korean harmony one should use the term with a highly comprehensive definition. In the example song, "School," the concept of tonic and dominant is obviously used. Thus, the piece is quite unrelated to the Korean form of harmony.

Up to this point, it has been shown that none of the musical characteristics of "School" is related to genuine Korean music. In this song, the text is the only truly native element. Due to the functionality of the language, this type of song must be characterized as "Korean" along with the added prefix, "quasi."

The question now arises, why do the majority of Korean people think that this song is purely Korean? The reason is simple; they have been educated to look upon this and similar songs as "Korean" since 1900 when Western music was first introduced, and officially included in the school music curriculum. In other words, the majority of Korean people have not had the opportunity to hear and experience traditional music in the school environment due to government policy in this regard. Fortunately, however, after about seventy years of public neglect, genuine Korean music has now been given some systematic attention by the government in its effort to establish a new sense of Korean identity among the general populace. Thus, school music texts are now required to include material which deals at least fifty percent of the time with various aspects of Korean culture. This includes traditional music. The author is not saying that it is wrong to include Western music in the Korean music curriculum; Western music as an art form is perfectly acceptable in any part of the world. But it is imperative that the distinction be made between Western music, Western influenced Korean music, and the genuine Korean form in order to develop a solid base on which to build a strong multicultural music education system in any part of the world. Without this crucial distinction such a system would be impossible, because students might continue to learn quasi-Korean music under the guise of genuine Korean music. In short, when Korean music is taught as an integral part of a multicultural music education program, a song similar to Example 1 should not be chosen as being representative of genuine or truly indigenous music. Instead, music similar to Example 2 (cited on the following page) might be selected as a representative of genuine Korean music.

Genuine Korean Music

Example 2 is a musical excerpt from *"P'yŏllak,"* one of the Korean lyric songs of the *kagok* genre. This excerpt consists of the first two sections of *"P'yŏllak."* It might (at least initially) be beyond the immediate comprehension of students at any level. However, at the end of a required period of classroom activity, they should be able to read, sing, and accompany the song with enthusiastic involvement. The following discussion of Example 2 will provide the general characteristics that allow it to be included under the heading of genuine Korean music.

Rhythm: Example 2 is by no means dominated by commonly

Example 2a. Excerpt from *P'yŏllak*

Example 2b. Excerpt from *P'yŏllak* (Transcription)

used Western meters such as duple or triple. Repeated, attentive listening might lead one to discover an underlying rhythmic pattern which consists of ten pulses. These ten pulses are grouped by accents of varying intensities into two parts on the one level and six parts on the other. See Example 3. This pattern, called *yŏlbak changdan*, is played by an hour glass-shaped drum called the *changgo* and repeated throughout the piece.

The whole feeling of movement in the temporal organization of this piece is quite different from that of the past two hundred years in the Western classical tradition. One might try to put a time signature in an analysis as follows: 2-2-1-2-2-1/4. However, these notated meters are not perceptually established well enough to become aurally relevant. Even if they become so, it might merely be a rhythm of, say, twentieth century Western music and not Korean rhythmic feeling. Just as it is very difficult to appreciate the genuine beauty of poetry which is translated into a foreign language, it is also difficult to feel Korean rhythm in Western oriented meters. In order to learn the genuine rhythm of this piece, one must learn *yŏlbak changdan* in its own terms.

Form: In the literature of Korean traditional music very little is mentioned about Korean musical form. If any, the discussions are always centered on form *of* music rather than form *in* music. According to the *Harvard Dictionary of Music*, form *in* music depends upon certain basic inner principles and relationships that are arranged in a cohesive manner to produce an orderly, animated whole. It goes on to say that form *of* music is more of an external feature which governs the overall structure of a piece, such as the term sonata or rondo.[8] When musical forms are considered by Korean scholars, the following terms are usually discussed in brief and emphasized: strophic, Dal segno-like form, *hwandu* and *hwanip*.[9] However, this author contends that these should not be considered unique to Korean music. The crucial point is to specifically determine the form *in* Korean music. The form *of* the entire

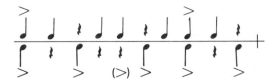

Example 3.   Yōlbak changdan

"P'yŏllak" is not unusual, as it consists of five sections with a prelude, interlude, and postlude. However, the form *in* "P'yŏllak" is unique to Korean music, particularly the sections exemplified and discussed in this study.

One might say, at the first hearing, that the piece has no thematic material, no motivic development, no sharp contrast between similar and dissimilar items. In Western terms the result is ostensible (and easily avoided) musical chaos. But does this mean that the piece lacks musical cohesiveness, even in its own terms? Or does this simply mean that there is no place to apply these Western musical terms to the composition? Does this also mean that here one must recognize a vastly different aesthetic phenomenon? If one approaches the piece in truly comprehensive terms without assuming inevitable application of Western art musical tools and grammar, one might very easily find a logical cohesion present. (This kind of open-minded musical attitude probably accounts for the success that youngsters have when learning to function properly with various music cultures.) As mentioned earlier, Western classical music of the past two hundred years has employed the common cadence form as a means of punctuating a continuum of sounds into various levels. As a means of punctuating, Korean music employs quite different but equally logical techniques. There is always a means to produce stronger or weaker punctuation at various levels throughout a piece. Even in a small musical shape, there can be a weaker punctuation in the middle and a stronger at the end.

"P'yŏllak" is successfully punctuated throughout by pauses instead of the common cadence form of Western classical music. In addition whenever comma-like punctuation is needed, an ascending second, neither major nor minor in interval, is employed, immediately followed by a brief pause as evidenced in the excerpt. These are used to reinforce the feeling of the closure of the antecedent phrase. In twentieth century Western music, the pause is sometimes used as a means of punctuation, but seldom this ascending motion or intervallic sound. Whenever the stronger, period-like punctuation is needed, the descending second, neither major nor minor in interval, is used, immediately followed by notes of increased length. These reinforce the feeling of a closure of the consequent phrase. In short, although the techniques are different in Korean music, there is obviously a principle to form musical cohesion in its own terms.

Melody: Of primary importance, as far as the author is concerned in discussing genuine Korean music, is a demonstration of the nature of the melody or the idea of melody in Korean music. It must be understood and explained in terms of Korean modes which have intervals differing from Western modes. Perhaps the most unfortunate situation that exists in the total study of Korean music is, however, the scholar's attempt to interpret genuine Korean music in terms of Western sound relationships. Western terminology can only be used to describe Korean music with the greatest reservation, requiring detailed explanation as to the variations in the two systems. For instance, to differentiate middle "C" from the "c" an octave higher in the Western system, large and small letters are sometimes used. However, in the Korean system (for *kayagŭm*, for instance,) the two pitches have completely different names, *ching* and *tchong* respectively.[10] The properties of the lower Korean pitch are considered to be substantially different from those of the higher even though they are an octave apart, and would not be readily apparent to the unconditioned listener. Thus, whenever Western terms are used to describe Korean traditional music extreme care should be taken so as not to distort the essence of Korean aesthetic principles. Besides its rhythm and form discussed earlier, the melody of *"P'yŏllak"* is uniquely Korean in that it is based on the modes *u-jo* and *kyemyŏn-jo*. Although the author feels reluctant to use Western notation in Example 4 to explain *u-jo* and *kyemyŏn-jo*, he has done so at this time because it would be impossible to communicate with readers and students who are as yet unfamiliar with the Korean system of symbols.

Korean melody in American musical publications is neither based on *u-jo* nor *kyemyŏn-jo*. In other words, a quasi-Korean melody is used and based on an equal-tempered pentatonic scale. It would not be an exaggeration to say that Example 4 has nothing to do with the pitch concept on the piano. Playing a Korean melody on the piano often seriously devaluates the essence of the music. Anyone who wishes to become familiar with genuine Korean music should first experience it on a native instrument. He must also realize the crucial differences between the genuine and quasi-Korean intervals, shown in Example 5. To follow Example 5 the word "cent" ought to be explained. The word was first introduced by A. J. Ellis (1814-90), an English philologist, to designate a unit of an exact scientific method for measuring musical intervals. The

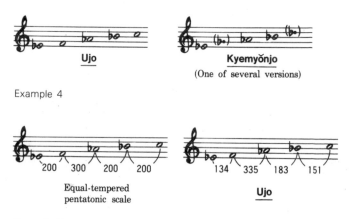

Ujo

Kyemyŏnjo
(One of several versions)

Example 4

200   300   200   200

Equal-tempered
pentatonic scale

134   335   183   151

Ujo

Example 5

word has been widely adopted in acoustics as well as in ethnomusicology. The cent is equal to 1/100 of the semitone on the equal-tempered scale. Thus, the semitone equals 100 cents and the octave contains 1200 cents. For example, the interval of a minor third contains 300 cents while that of the perfect fourth contains 500 cents.

One might say that the difference between intervals of Example 5(a) and Example 5(b) does not seem to be great in terms of aural perception. In a sense this could be correct because the aural distinction between them is difficult to make for those who are still unfamiliar with the music. However, it is extremely important to note that the uniqueness of the Korean melody in terms of its pitch lies in this minute difference. If one ignores this little subtlety, saying that it is actually irrelevant, one misses the depth and richness of Korean music. Love, for example, is substantially different from love-like. Korea is substantially different from Korea-like. 0.99 is substantially different from 1. What makes a particular melody a Korean melody may depend wholly on the subtle difference between, say, 0.99 and 1.

Harmony: The concept of harmony in Korean music can only be considered in comprehensive terms, disregarding once again any preconceived ideas of Western tertian harmony. To appreciate the essence of Korean harmony (the term harmony, henceforth, will be used only in a comprehensive sense,) one should be culturally conditioned first. No one would enjoy the ruins of Rome without some prior conditioning as to their nature and historic significance. Take, for instance, the story of a man who travelled to a foreign country and was shown a particular rock that held great cultural significance for the native people. Upon being told that this was an article of great beauty, the traveller laughed because all he could see was an ordinary rock that could be found anywhere in the world. He was unhappy that he had wasted so much money only to see this plain rock. However, when he was told that a noted artist of the time had been killed by falling from a cliff while attempting to grasp this rock for use as a subject for his painting, the traveller's perception of its beauty began to change. He now began to accept the symbolic meaning of the rock, and consequently it was no longer plain to him. This attitude could be compared to a Catholic's attitude toward holy water which actually has the same chemical composition as ordinary tap water.

Even individuals with similar cultural conditioning will react to concepts of beauty and harmony in different ways. Consider, for instance two different gardens. The first is very orderly in appearance; the trees, bushes and step-stones are thoughtfully placed with regard to their relation to the whole, and all shrubbery is well trimmed. The second is like a forest, totally unplanned and left in a natural state. However, here one can also see a mysterious beauty. In the first garden there is an ordered harmony while in the second the harmony is unregimented, left to discover its own order in its own terms. One often thinks that an equal tempered scale is more sophisticated tonal material than an unequal tempered scale. To say this, however, is as unjustifiable as to say that the first garden is more sophisticated than the second.

In "*P'yŏllak*" there is a pleasing blend of instruments and voice. While the melody is vocal, several instruments maintain a slightly varied form in a pleasing arrangement of rhythms, tones, and timbres. Whether this harmonious blending of tones can be a musical stimulus to one or not, entirely depends upon one's cultural background. If one is properly conditioned, one might respond aesthetically and successfully to the musical stimulus of "*P'yŏllak*."

Text: Needless to say, the text is genuine Korean poetry. It is impossible for the author to translate Korean poetry into English without distorting the original poetic meaning. This is particularly true with the text of "*P'yŏllak*." Therefore, he simply avoids discussing the text except to say that it is about love: the grief of one who loses his lover cannot compare with any other. Such generality captures the literal meaning without jeopardizing the poetic essence.

Thus far, the author has tried to make a distinction between genuine and quasi-Korean music. However, the problem still remains: what is the proper method to use in teaching the genuine form? How this can be done is the central thesis of the author's dissertation. (Refer to Note 1.)

NOTES

1. This article is taken from the author's doctoral dissertation, *The Development and Trial of Korean-based Musical Activities for the Classroom*, Ann Arbor, Michigan: The University of Michigan. 1975.
2. Sŏ Ch'ang-ŏp (Sur Chang-up), ed. in chief, *Ŭmak Taesajŏn* (Encyclopedia of World Music) (Seoul: Sinjin Press, 1972). p. 1431.
3. *Ibid.*
4. *Ibid.* p. 1432.
5. Ŭryu munhwasa, *Han'gukhak Taebaekgwasajŏn* (Encyclopedia of Korean Studies) Vol. III (Seoul: Ŭryu munhwasa, 1972). p. 518.
6. Yi Hye-gu (Lee Hye-ku), "Introduction to Korean Music," *Mandang Munch'aeknok* (A Collection of Hye-gu Yi's Essays) (Seoul: Korean Musicological Society, 1970), pp. 64–5 of the index.
7. David B. Guralnik, ed. in chief, *Webster's New World Dictionary: Elementary Edition* (New York: The World Publishing Co., 1966), p. 322.
8. Willi Apel, *Harvard Dictionary of Music*, 2nd ed, Revised and Enlarged (Cambridge, Mass.: The Belknap Press of Harvard University Press, 1969). p 327.
9. Yi Hye-gu (Lee Hye-ku), *Han'guk Ŭmak Yŏn'gu* (Studies in Korean Music) (Seoul: National Music Research Society, 1957). p. 82.
10. Yi Chae-suk (Lee Chae-suk), "Kayagŭm Sanjo ŭi T'ŭl e Taehan Sogo," ("Diverse Styles of Kayago Sanjo (Solo Music for Kayago)," *Yi Hye-gu Paksa Songsu Kinyŏm Ŭmakhak Nonch'ong* ("Essays in Ethnomusicology: A Birthday Offering for Lee Hye-ku") (Seoul: Seoul National University Press, 1969). p. 136.
11. Coralie Rockwell, *Kagok: a traditional Korean vocal form* (Providence: Asian Music Publication, 1972). p. 81.

Asian Influence on Western Music

Influence or Confluence ?

Chou Wen-chung

More than a decade ago, in a speech given at the 1966 International Music Symposium in Manila, I stated that I believed the traditions of Eastern and Western music after a thousand years of divergence were now merging to form the mainstream of a new musical tradition. It is my present opinion that this is indeed what has been happening, although the progress is still at a very slow pace and the process a very subtle one — as is to be expected. Indeed, at the conclusion of that speech, I cited the Chinese philosopher Chuang Tzu's exhortation, "using things as things, but not being used by things as things" (*wu wu erh pu wu yö wu*), and warned: "There is always the danger of superficially acquiring new concepts and techniques purely as a matter of extrinsic procedure and calculation. The greatness in Eastern music is indeed in its wisdom of 'using things as things' and in its avoidance of any kind of extraneousness. Without an understanding of Chuang Tzu's teaching, the purely materialistic adoption of Eastern practices will only bring forth more 'Turkish marches', twentieth-century style." (The speech has since been published in the first issue of *Asian Music*, the journal of The Society for Asian Music.)

Today, a decade later, this warning remains pertinent, in my opinion. This is why I do not attach much significance to which particular Asian concept or performance practice is currently in vogue in the West, or which Western composer has lately succeeded in creating a new cult on his adoption of something Asian. On the contrary, I am more concerned in watching how fundamental Asian concepts and practices in music are gradually and unobtrusively being integrated into the mainstream of Western contemporary music, and how they are revitalized and transformed by the Eastern composers in evolving their own contemporary styles. What I am saying is that by now there should be less talk about influence than confluence, which prescribes the inevitable mutual or reciprocal actions and influences. Consequently, it is my belief that there is a timely need to examine the question of interaction in music between the East and the West. In doing so, we must first understand the role of both the Eastern and the Western composer and the role of both traditions in contributing to the confluence of musical cultures.

Let us first discuss the role of musical traditions. The tradition of Western music and its role in the development of twentieth century music in the West are on-going topics that have been continually discussed and debated on a broad scale as well as in depth. Therefore, a cursory discourse on these topics is hardly a necessary or even appropriate task at this time in the context of our discussions today. Suffice it to say that it has been evolving and broadening continuously over the past several centuries, has interacted with other cultures — though on a limited scale — from time to time, and has remained a force in the development of a new Western music in the face of technological advances and inter-cultural exposure. Moreover, in the East there has been in recent decades a general emergence of Western-influenced contemporary music; some Asian countries have in fact already produced a substantial number of notable composers who fundamentally write in a Western-oriented style, though with a growing awareness of their own tradition.

What is paramount in speaking of the musical tradition of the East is that we must recognize it as a living tradition in the same manner as we just spoke of the Western tradition. We must not regard Eastern music as an artistic achievement of the past to be kept within the confines of an archives or museum, to be preserved as a historical treasure, to be used for educational purposes, or to be dissected by ethnomusicologists and anthropologists. As a matter of fact, concurrent to the development of an Eastern contemporary music referred to above, there has been, as we all know, a slow but noteworthy movement towards a revival, reform and reconstitution of the traditional music in the East. Equally significant is the interest it has stimulated in the West. This, however, is not the appropriate occasion to investigate the causes for its renaissance, if that should indeed be the case, nor to examine its relations with certain new developments in the West in our century as I have already done in my essay, "Asian Concepts and Twentieth century Western Composers", in the April 1971 issue of *The Musical Quarterly*. Instead, and in light of our discussions today, let us first discover what the aspects are in the Eastern tradition — aside from the literature itself — that have stimulated the Western and the Eastern composer alike and will contribute to the confluence in the foreseeable future.

These aspects obviously fall into two broad categories: (1) Instrumental techniques and performance practices: and (2) esthetic and philosophical foundations of the tradition. Concerning instrumental techniques and performance practices, I have already made some preliminary and generalized observations in a paper given at the Second Summer Institute in Compositional Studies in 1968, sponsored by the American Society of University Composers. The paper is entitled "Single Tones as Musical Entities: An Approach to Structured Deviations in Tonal Characteristics." In discussing the growing awareness on the part of Western composers of "a supposedly new dimension in compositional resources — the so-called 'deviations' in tonal characteristics" — I cited certain Eastern techniques and practices to illustrate how these so-called 'deviations' are often an integral part in the music of the East. Let me quote:

"One of the earliest sources on the Confucianist concept of music, *Yüeh Chi*, states that 'one must investigate sound to know tones, investigate tones to know music' (*shen sheng i chin yin, shen yin i chih yüeh*) and that 'without the knowledge of sound... one cannot speak of music' (*pu chih sheng che pu k'o yü yen yin, pu chih yin che pu k'o yü yen yüeh*). It is therefore believed that single tones, rendered meaningful by their acoustic attributes, are musical entities by themselves as well as musical events within the context of a composition. This concept, the true meaning of which is often made ambiguous by frequent poetic and mystic references, is at the root of the means of musical expression in the East.

"For example, (in Indian music)... each tone in a *raga* is in fact treated as having its own specific expression within the expressive context of the *raga*. This is why I find what is even more interesting than the use of the *raga*... and the *tala* is the use of *gamakas*, which are often translated as ornaments. But the use of *gamakas* is far more than embellishing an existing melody with certain simple devices as in Western music. The *gamakas* have their own expressive values and are the blood that brings life to the tones of a *raga*. They are assigned to specific tones according to the tones' structural relationship within a *raga*. The execution of a *gamaka* can be highly intricate and can involve subtle inflections in pitch, timbre, and loudness.

"In the case of the music for *ch'in*, the Chinese zither, we find the use of the so-called 'ornamentation' even more integrated into the musical structure, being totally absorbed in the finger technique and its notation. Ch'in notation is a unique type of tablature, meticulously indicating not only the string, the finger, the stopping position, the mode of articulation, but also subsequent changes in pitch and timbre. Symbols for the right hand specify single, successive, simultaneous attacks, and their combinations. They also specify the choice of finger or fingers, the direction of movement, and the use of nail or flesh. Symbols for the left hand specify portamentos from one position to another, slides representing pitch deviations, vibratos of various combinations of width, speed and duration, and vibratos with slides. They may also specify certain types of left hand excitation which provide additional modes of articulation to supplement the vocabulary of the right hand.

"The result of this finger technique and its notation is that each single excitation in *ch'in* music is a sound event of varying significance: a single tone, a two-tone chord, a figure of two or more tones, a complete phrase—the last two being accomplished by means of shifting the finger after the attack and during the decay. The meaning of such an event is generally even more precisely defined by the inclusion of factors in the notation which may well be called modifiers and which control pitch deviations and timbral modifications, such as the slide, the vibrato, changing the fingering, varying the speed of slide, and altering the type of vibrato.

"Emphasis on the production and control of single tone is equally notable in the music for wind instruments. This is so even in ensemble music, particularly those with a long tradition, such as *togaku*..., *hyang-ak*..., and *nohgaku*.... For example, in *togaku* the linear material is entrusted to a *ryuteki*...,and a *hichiriki*.... The attack and the release of a tone on these instruments are frequently accomplished in conjunction with a sliding pitch adjustment, which is accompanied by modifications in timbre and loudness. Even during the course of a so-called 'sustained' tone, the embouchure may be altered, thereby causing deviation in timber as well as in pitch.... In solo music Japanese and Korean wind players seem to be particularly aware of almost every potential on their instruments, and often display a dazzling agility in varying the lip aperture and air pressure to control various types of vibrato and tremolo in addition to fluctuations in pitch and loudness....

"Technical vocabularies exploiting all manners of articulation and varieties of timbre are applied to some percussion instruments as well. For example, the technique for such drums as the Indian *tabla* and *mridanga*, and the Indonesian *kendang*, takes into account such factors as the specific finger or fingers, whether the fingers are closed or spread, with the fingertips, the joints or the palm, at or near the rim or the center of the drum head, and the degree of damping. Moreover, the apparently infinite possible permutations of these strokes are used as much for their structural as for their timbral value. The subtle control of timbre and fluctuation in pitch on the Japanese *ko-tsuzumi*..., is another noteworthy case.

"As for the voice, the use of *gamaka* is not only a vital part of but actually originated from the art of singing. Indian vocal music is of course only one example. More remarkable from our point of view is the fact that in certain types of vocal music there is an ingenious exploration of the musical values derived from the speech sounds. As examples, we find in the Japanese *gidayu* and the Korean (*p'ansori*) nasals, fricatives, glottals and other speech sounds isolated and transformed into musical events by themselves, each with its own specific dramatic expression.

"The fundamental concepts cited and the examples given, pertaining to diverse performance practices from singing to drumming, should clearly bear out my contention that in the East the so-called 'deviations' are as much an integral part of music as the tonal characteristics, and are assigned as much a structural function as an expressive one." (The paper is published in *Proceedings of the American Society of University Composers*, vol. 3, 1968.)

To the above, one could of course add a long list of others, such as the temporal and rhythmic procedures in the various types of ensemble music in Southeast Asia, or the use of specialized improvisational technique in the Korean *sanjo* and other types of music elsewhere, or the evocation of imagery and symbolism for attaining the state of mind necessary for the production of the proper tone quality in the music for *ch'in* in China and other instruments elsewhere. Fundamentally, those examples cited in the article do go a long way to illustrate that the exploration of the articulatory and vibratory characteristics of the instruments and the control of inflections in pitch, timbre and intensity are two prominent aspects in the tradition of Eastern music that differ vastly from the basic concerns in the tradition of Western music. An understanding of these practices and the concepts behind them seems to me to be crucial to both Western and Eastern composers who are concerned about the East-West interaction in music.

The esthetic and philosophical foundations of Eastern music is a harder question to deal with. First of all its influence on Western composers as is manifest so far tends to be more a Western interpretation of or response to the original in the Eastern tradition. I have discussed this at length in the *Musical Quarterly* article cited above, in which particular attention is given to certain prominent and recent Western responses to various Asian practices and schools of thought. Suffice it to say that such responses, as significant and consequential as they may have been in the West, remind me of Ezra Pound's translation of the Chinese Book of Poetry *(Shih Ching)*. Pound's poetic imagination and cultural conditioning clearly made his so-called translation a new creation that is inspired by but otherwise scantily related to the original. Should this kind of modern *chinoiserie* still be encouraged or tolerated in the twentieth century and, in turn, applauded and imitated in the East? To answer this question, we must bear in mind that Western fascination with Indian concepts, Zen and *I Ching* (Book of Changes) — as applied in music — was epoch-making in the middle of the century, and only a beginning. Newer trends have continued to be developed and perpetuated by both Western and Eastern musicians with the claim of having been based on some Eastern thinking. While every attempt and experiment deserves a place in the East-West interaction, we must nonetheless determinedly separate the kernel from the chaff, ascertaining in each case whether it is a genuine contribution to the confluence or part of what I called "neo-exoticism" in the *Musical Quarterly* article.

This brings up another factor that plays an important role in any true interaction between the music of the two worlds, namely, the level of performance that is heard in the West and the quality of scholarly writing on Eastern music that is known in the West. After all, the performance, including instrumental teaching that has by now become available in the West, and the scholarly writing, particularly those written in Western languages or available in translation, is basically responsible for the West's exposure to Eastern music. In this respect, the role of the Eastern performer, scholar — and one must include in this category the ethnomusicologist in the West as well — and the composer is paramount in the process of interaction. Of the three, we are concerned about the role of the performer as the interpreter of the traditional literature, of the scholar as the keeper of knowledge in the tradition's theory and esthetics, and of the composer as the heir-apparent of the tradition, who alone is responsible for transforming a tradition of the past into a living one.

If the West's understanding of certain aspects of Eastern music has not been beyond reproach, it may well be that these roles have not always been successfully fulfilled by those who have the responsibility to do so. The performer's role, which appears to be simple and direct on the surface, is in truth an uncertain one since tradition has experienced a prolonged period of decline in most parts of Asia. Moreover, tradition in literally every part of Asia is a complicated matter in view of the long history and involved cultural cross-fertilization in the past. Additionally, since traditional teaching in music in the East is mostly by rote, the Eastern performer is not necessarily always in possession of reliable knowledge in theory and history. Consequently, in the modern atmosphere of intellectuality and scientific methodology, the performer has perhaps been unjustifiably cast in the role of the principal transmitter of information in the quest of learning the Eastern tradition. It is, therefore, not surprising that more than a few performers of our time have contributed towards a general state of misconception in the West.

By contrast, the significance of scholarly studies — whether of the past or today — has not always been appreciated. In a recent article, entitled "Chinese Historiography and Music: Some Observations", which appeared in the April 1976 issue of *The Musical Quarterly*, I pointed out that much is still to be desired in the field of Chinese musicology, which is as good an example as any for the purpose of our present discussion. For example, to fully understand *ch'in* music, which is perhaps the most important type of music in China whose tradition is still intact, one would have to depend on modern researches on the early treatises on this music. And yet, such researches remain a task that has been barely begun in China and a task that has not been at all recognized in the West. Furthermore, to know this music really, one cannot rely only on performances available today but would have to have a knowledge of the various early editions of its music. Yet, once again, the task that will eventually supply this knowledge still remains to be undertaken. Few Westerners even realize that *ch'in* music is so intricately notated, and that knowledge of its notation alone holds the key to a true appreciation of the unique features of this music. If we recognize the above examples as fairly representative of the situation, it is hard to imagine how a true interaction can take place in the face of such a dearth of real knowledge — or even the awareness of the need of such knowledge. Thus, the role of the scholar, who is neither an interpreter nor a creator, is a challenging one that must be responsible for providing the missing links in East-West interaction.

The role of the composer is a most difficult one. While he is fundamentally a creative artist who is expected to write the new music of his time and his world, he is at the same time the vehicle by means of which the tradition of his music survives as a living culture. In this context, whether he likes it or not, neither writing strictly in a traditional style nor in a purely Western style will make it possible for him to fulfill his role or to contribute to the East-West interaction. Much then depends on his understanding of the music of his own tradition and on his ability to communicate through a musical language of his own society and his own time that speaks also to willing and cultivated ears elsewhere. Ultimately, his language is the touchstone not only for his own music, but also the music of his culture and, above all, the music of the world in the future. Surely traditional Balkan music was never as widely appreciated as since the time of Bartok and his lesser known colleagues. Surely the music of the world would have been poorer if he failed to forge a language of his own through his knowledge of more than one musical culture. What the composer has to face in order to achieve bi-cultural or multi-cultural competence and to evolve a language thereof is certainly the crucial ingredient in the East-West interaction. Thus, the key role in this interaction is that of the composer, be he Eastern or Western. Today, the Western composer is at the crossroads — indeed, one might say at a complex interchange of an international superhighway. He is still recovering from a rebellion against his tradition, still under the shadow of the innovative giants of the century such as Schoenberg, Varese and Webern, while experiencing an ever-accelerating influx of non-Western ideas, and confronted with a maze of revolutionary possibilities proffered by electronic devices and computer science, and by acoustic and psychological studies, all of these at a time when he has to cope with a new social, economic and demographical order that no composer ever faced before. This is the time then when a true understanding of some refreshing concepts from another culture can be as revelatory as a miracle or a Zen enlightenment — not so much that these concepts provide the answer to his quest than that they serve as the catalyst that brings about a new order in his own world of art. This hopefully is what a true East-West interaction will bring to the Eastern composer and his quest, which will in turn be his contribution to the confluence of musical cultures.

For the Asian composer, the situation is quite a different one. By and large, to him the influence of the West is by now a kind of modern tradition. Yet, there is of late a revivified awareness of his own tradition, the dawn of a desire to create a new music that is neither Western nor traditional, but embodying the best of both cultures. His task is perhaps unlike that of his Western brethren, which is ever to conquer new horizons, but to build on the crumbled glories of the past something that is neither a replica of what it replaces nor a copy of a blueprint borrowed from a foreign land. Perhaps out of his task the phoenix will finally rise out of its own ashes. Such poetic imagery will remain a metaphor until the Asian composer has truly mastered his own tradition and learned from the Western tradition. This pressing need for bi-cultural or multi-cultural competence is indeed his advantage over his Western colleagues. His ultimate goal however will not be different from that of the Western composer, and his quest for which will also in turn bring about his contribution to the confluence of musical cultures.

It is for this common goal in music that we all strive, whether seeing it from the East or West. Let us not speak of influence but *confluence*. Let the different traditions intermingle to bring forth a new mainstream that will integrate all musical concepts and practices into a vast expanse of musical currents. But let us also make sure that each individual culture will preserve its own uniqueness, its own poetry. The haunting beauty of such music as *hyang-ak* and *p'ansori* must never be lost. Indeed, let it rise again in transfiguration.

Contributors in This volume

Yi Hye-gu

Professor Emertitus of Korean Classical Music, Seoul National University

Han Man-yŏng

Professor of Korean Classical Music, Seoul National University

Robert C. Provine, Jr.

Professor of Music, University of Durham, England

Chang Sa-hun

Professor of Korean Classical Music, Seoul National University

Yi Po-hyŏng

Advisor, Cultural Property Preservation Bureau, Ministry of Culture and Information

Coralie J. Rockwell

Master of Arts in Ethnomusicology, University of California

Song Bang-song

the former Director of the National Classical Music Institute and Professor at Yongnam University at Present

Yi Byŏng-wŏn

Professor of Music, University of Hawaii, Manoa

Yi Kang-suk   Professor of Music, Seoul National
                     University

Chou Wen-chung   Assistant Dean, School of Arts, Co-
                     lumbia University, USA